THEODORE PARKER'S WRITINGS.

A Discourse of Matters Pertaining to Religion. Fourth Edition. 1 vol. 12mo. Cloth, $1.25.

Sermons of Theism, Atheism, and the Popular Theology. Second Edition. 1 vol. 12mo. Cloth, $1.25.

Ten Sermons of Religion. 1 vol. 12mo. Cloth, $1.00.

Critical and Miscellaneous Writings. 1 vol. 12mo. Cloth, $1.25.

Speeches, Addresses, and Occasional Sermons. Second Edition. 3 vols. 12mo. Cloth, $3.00.

Additional Speeches, Addresses, and Occasional Sermons. 2 vols. 12mo. Cloth, $2.50.

A Critical and Historical Introduction to the Canonical Scriptures of the Old Testament. From the German of De Wette. Translated and enlarged by Theodore Parker. Third Edition. 2 vols. 8vo. Cloth, $5.00.

The Trial of Theodore Parker for the "Misdemeanor" of a Speech in Faneuil Hall against Kidnapping, before the Circuit Court of the United States, at Boston, April 3, 1855. With the Defence. 1 vol. 8vo. Cloth, $1.00.

The Two Christmas Celebrations, A. D. I. and MDCCCLV. A Christmas Story. 1 vol. Cloth, 50 cents.

IN PREPARATION, AND NEARLY READY.

Historic Americans. Containing Sketches of Washington, Adams, Jefferson, Franklin, Webster, and other eminent Americans. By Theodore Parker. Uniform with his other writings as above.

SERMONS

OF

THEISM, ATHEISM,

AND

THE POPULAR THEOLOGY.

BY

THEODORE PARKER,

MINISTER OF THE TWENTY-EIGHTH CONGREGATIONAL SOCIETY IN BOSTON.

THIRD EDITION.

BOSTON:
TICKNOR AND FIELDS.
M DCCC LXI.

University Press, Cambridge:
Printed by Welch, Bigelow, and Company.

TO THE

REV. WILLIAM H. WHITE,

AND THE

REV. GEORGE FISKE,

WITH GRATITUDE FOR EARLY INSTRUCTION RECEIVED AT THEIR HANDS,

THIS VOLUME IS DEDICATED

BY

THE AUTHOR

PREFACE.

The present volume forms part of a long series of Sermons, but has a certain completeness in itself, and is, perhaps, intelligible without reference to what preceded or followed. Almost the whole of the volume is printed from the notes of Mr. Leighton, an accomplished phonographer; only the three latter sermons were written out by myself. I have often been asked to repeat this portion of the series, but prefer to lay it before a larger public than a merely spoken word can reach.

Boston, July 16th, 1853.

A*

CONTENTS.

VI.

VII.

VIII.

IX.

X.

INTRODUCTION.

SOME THOUGHTS ON THE CONDITION OF CHRISTENDOM.

At Rome, eighteen centuries ago this very year, Nero was married to a maiden called Octavia. He was the son of Ahenobarbus and Agrippina; the son of a father so abandoned and a mother so profligate that when congratulated by his friends on the birth of his first child, and that child a son, the father said, what is born of such a father as I, and such a mother as my wife, can only be for the ruin of the State. Octavia was yet worse born. She was the daughter of Claudius and Messalina. Claudius was the Emperor of Rome, stupid by nature, licentious and drunken by long habit, and infamous for cruelty in that age never surpassed for its oppressiveness, before or since. Messalina, his third wife, was a monster of wickedness, who had every vice that can disgrace the human kind, except avarice and hypocrisy: her boundless prodigality saved her from avarice, and her matchless impudence kept her clean from hypocrisy. Too incontinent even of money to hoard it, she was so careless of the opinions of others that she made no secret of any vice. Her name is still the catchword for the most loathsome acts that can be conceived of. She was put to death for attempting to destroy her husband's life; he was drunk when he signed the warrant, and when he heard that his wife had been assassinated at his command he went to drinking again.

Agrippina, the mother of Nero, and the bitterest enemy of Messalina, took her place in a short time and became the fourth wife of her uncle Claudius, who succeeded to the last and deceased husband of Agrippina only as he succeeded to the first Roman king — a whole commonwealth of predecessors intervening. Octavia, aged eleven, was already espoused to another, who took his life when his bride's father married the mother of Nero, well knowing the fate that else awaited him. Claudius, repudiating his own son, adopted Nero as his child and imperial heir. In less than two years Agrippina poisoned her husband, and by a *coup d' état* put Nero on the throne, who, erelong, procured the murder of his own mother, Seneca the philosopher helping him in the plot, but also in due time to fall by the hand of the tyrant.

Eighteen centuries ago this very year, Nero, expecting to be emperor, married Octavia, — he sixteen years old, yet debauched already by premature licentiousness, — she but eleven, espoused to another who had already fallen by his own hand, bringing calculated odium on the imperial family; a yet sadder fate awaited the miserable maid thus bartered away in infancy.

This marriage of the Emperor's adopted son with his only daughter was doubtless thought a great event. Every body knew of it: among the millions that swarmed in Rome, probably there was not a female slave but knew the deed. Historians in their gravity paused to record it; poets, doubtless, with the customary flattery of that inconstant tribe, wrote odes on the occasion of this shameless marriage of a dissolute boy and an unfortunate girl.

The same year, fifty-three after the birth of Christ, according to the most ancient chronological canon which has come down to us, there came to Rome an obscure man Saul by name which he had altered to Paul; a sail-maker, as it seems, from the little city of Tarsus in Cilicia. Nobody took much notice of it. Nay, the time of his coming is quite uncertain and hard to ascertain; and it appears that the writer of this most ancient chronicle, though he lived sixteen or seventeen hundred years nearer the fact than we do, was mistaken, and that in the year fifty-three Paul went to Corinth for the first time and dwelt there; and eight years after, in the spring of the year, was brought a prisoner to Rome. These curiosities of chronology show how unimportant Paul's coming was thought at that time. The marriage of a dissolute boy, with an unfortunate girl, was set down as a great thing, while the coming of Paul was too slight a circumstance to deserve notice.

He came from a hated nation, — the Jews were thought the enemies of mankind, — he was a poor plebeian, a mechanic, and lived in an age when military power and riches had such an influence as never before, or since. He was apparently an unlettered man, or had only the rough, narrow culture which a Hebrew scholar got at Tarsus and Jerusalem. He had little eloquence; "his bodily presence was weak, and his speech contemptible." He came to the most populous city in the world, the richest and the wickedest. Nero and Agrippina were types of wealthy and patrician Rome; for that reason it is that I began by telling their story, and, though aware of the true chronology, have connected this atrocious wedlock with the coming of the Apostle.

The city was full of soldiers; men from Parthia and Britain, who had fought terrible battles, bared their scars in the Forum and the Palace of the Cæsars. Learned men were there. Political Greece had died; but Grecian genius long outlived the shock which overturned the state. Of science Greece was full, and her learned men and men well-born with genius fled to Rome. The noble minds from that classic land went there, full of thought, full of eloquence and song, running over with beauty. Rough, mountainous streams of young talent from Spain and Africa flowed thither, finding their home in that great oceanic city. The

Syrian Orontes had emptied itself into the Tiber. There were temples of wondrous splendor and richness, priests celebrated for their culture and famed for their long descent. All these were hostile to the new form of religion taught by Paul.

But the popular theology was only mythology. It was separate from science, alienated from the life of the people. The temple did not represent philosophy, nor morality, nor piety. The priests of the popular religion had no belief in the truth of its doctrines, no faith in the efficacy of its forms. Religion was tradition with the priest; it was police with the magistrate. The Roman augurs did not dare look each other in the face on solemn days, lest they should laugh outright and betray to the people what was the open secret of the priest.

Everywhere, as a man turned his eye in Rome, there was riches, everywhere power, everywhere vice. Did I say everywhere? No; — the shadow of riches is poverty, and there was such poverty as only St. Giles's Parish in London can now equal. The shadow of power is slavery; and there was such slavery in Rome as American New Orleans and Charleston cannot boast. Did I say there was vice everywhere? No: in the shadow of vice there always burns the still, calm flame of piety, justice, philanthropy; that is the light which goeth not out by day, which is never wholly quenched. But slavery and poverty and sin were at home in that city, — such slavery, such poverty, and such sin as savage lands know nothing of. If we put together the crime, the gluttony, the licentiousness of New Orleans, New York, Paris, London, Vienna, and add the military power of St. Petersburg, we may have an approximate idea of the condition of ancient Rome in the year fifty-three after Christ. Let none deny the manly virtue, the womanly nobleness, which also found a home therein; still it was a city going to destruction, and the causes of its ruin were swiftly at work.

Christianity came to Rome with Paul of Tarsus. The tidings thereof went before him. Nobody knows who brought them first. It was a new "superstition," not much known as yet. It was the religion of a "blasphemer" who had got crucified between "two others, malefactors." Christianity was then "the latest form of infidelity." Paul himself came there a prisoner, but so obscure that nobody knows what year he came, how long he remained, or what his fate was. "He lived two years in his own hired house," — that is the last historic word which comes down to us of the great apostle. Catholic traditions tell us of missions to various places, and then round it off with martyrdom. The martyrdom only is probable, the missions obviously fictitious. Probably he was in jail to the end of his days, when the headsmen ferried that great soul into heaven; — and very seldom was it, so it seems, that he took over so weighty a freight as Paul made for that bark.

The sail-maker brought the new religion. It was an idea, and action also; belief in men and life out of them. It had nothing to recommend it, only itself and himself. Paul offered no worldly riches, no honor, no respectability. A man who "joined the church" then, did not have his name trumpeted in the newspapers; did not get introduced to reputable society; did not find his honor and respectability everywhere enhanced by that fact.

Christianity had these things to offer, — scorn, loathing, contempt, hatred from father and mother, from the husband of the wife's bosom, — for probably it was the wife who went first, it is commonly so, — and at last it offered a cruel death. But it told of a to-morrow after to-day; of a law higher than the statutes of Nero; of one God, the Father of all men; of a kingdom of Heaven, where all is sunlight and peace and beauty and triumph. Paul himself had got turned out of the whole Eastern world, and the founder of this scheme of religion had just been hanged as a blasphemer. Christianity was treason to the Hebrew State; to the Roman Church the latest form of infidelity.

Doubtless there were great errors connected with the Christian doctrine. One need only read the epistles of Paul to know that. But there were great truths. The oneness of God, the brotherhood of men, the soul's immortality, the need of a virtuous, blameless, brave life on earth, — these were the great truths of Christianity; and they were set off by a life as great as the truths, a life of brave work and manly self-denial and self-sacrifice.

The early, nay, the earliest Christians had many an error. How does wheat grow? With manifold straw; and there are whole cart-loads of straw for a single sack of wheat corn. The straw is needful; not a grain of corn could grow without it; by and by, it litters the horses, and presently rots and fertilizes the ground whence it came. But the grain lives on; and is seed-corn for future generations, or bread-corn to feed the living.

Christianity as an idea was far in advance of Judaism and Hebraism. As a life it transcended every thing which the highest man had dreamed of in days before. Men tried to put it down, crucified Jesus, stoned his disciples, put them in jail, scourged them, slew them with all manner of torture. But the more they blew the fire, the more swiftly it burned. Water the ground with valiant blood, the young blade of heroism springs up and blossoms red: the maiden blooms white out of the martyr blood which her mother had shed on the ground; and there is a great crop of hairy men full of valor. Christians smiled when they looked the rack in the face; laughed at martyrdom, and said to the tormentors, "Do you want necks for your block? Here are ours. Betwixt us and Heaven there is only a red sea, and any axe makes a bridge wide enough for a soul to go over. Exodus out of Egypt is entrance to the promised land. Fire is a good chariot for a Christian Elias."

In a few hundred years that sail-maker had swept Rome of Heathenism: not a temple remained Pagan. Even the statues got converted to Christianity, and Minerva became the Virgin Mary; Venus took the vow and was a Magdalene; Olympian Jove was christened Simon Peter: everybody sees at Rome a bronze statue of Jupiter, older than Paul's time, which is now put in the great cathedral and baptized Simon Peter; and thousands of Catholics kiss the foot of what was once "Heathen Jove." The gods of Rome gave way to the carpenter of Nazareth; he was called God. The Christian ideas and great Christian life of Paul of Tarsus put all Olympus to rout.

Then in thirteen or fourteen hundred years more there slowly got builded up the most remarkable scheme of theology that the world ever saw. Hebraism went slowly down; Heathenism went slowly down. Barbarism, a great storm from the North, beat on the roof of the Christian house, and it fell not;— No, barbarism ran off from the eaves of the Christian church to water the garden of Italy, Spain, France, Germany, England; they were blessed by that river of God which fell from the eaves.

But Hebraism, Heathenism, Barbarism — as forms of religion — did not die all at once, they are not yet wholly dead. No one of them was altogether a mistake. Each of them had some truth, some beauty, which mankind needed, and there they must stand face to face with Christianity till it has absorbed all of their excellence into itself: then they will perish. Individual freedom was the contribution which German Barbarism brought, and we have got much of that enshrined in our trial by jury, representative democracy, and a hundred other forms. Deep faith in God and fidelity to one's own conscience, — these are the great things which Moses and Samuel and David and Esaias and Ezra taught; and accordingly the Old Testament lies on every pulpit lid in all Christendom to this day, and will not sink because it has those excellences. Heathenism had science, beauty, law, power of organization; they also must be added to the Christian civilization before Heathenism goes to its rest. We have not got all the good from Heathenism yet; and accordingly the superior culture of Christendom is based on Greek and Roman classics: Fathers send their boys to superior schools that they may learn from the Heathen; that they may acquire strength of reasoning from Aristotle and Plato, the bravery of eloquence from Cicero and Demosthenes, and the beauty of literary art from Homer and Horace and Sophocles and Æschylus, and that mighty army of genius whose trumpets stir the world. From many a clime, for many an age, do "pilgrims pensive, but unwearied, throng" to Athens and Rome, to study the remains of ancient art; remnants of temples are brought over the sea to every Christian land, to bless the Christian heart with Pagan beauty. Patient mankind never loses a useful truth.

It is curious to look and see how little notice was taken of Christianity coming to Rome. The men of pleasure knew nothing of the strife betwixt the old and new in Paul's time; the political economists of that day, as it seems, foresaw no productive power in Christianity; the politicians took little notice thereof, till Nero sought to cut off the neck of Christendom at one blow. A historian — Roman all through, in his hard powerful nature, but furnished with masterly Greek culture, — spoke of Christianity as "that detestable superstition," which, with other mischiefs, had flowed down into Rome, the common sink of all abominations. Sour Juvenal gave the new religion a wipe with his swift lash, dipping it first in bitter ink. Pliny the younger wrote a line to the emperor, asking how he should treat these pestilent fellows, the Christians, who are not afraid to die. This is all the notice literary Rome took of Christianity for a century or so. Men knew not the force which was going to baptize Pagan Rome with the Christian name. Yet in their time, while the voluptuous were seeking for a new pleasure, while the Stoics and Epicureans were doubting which was the chief good, while politicians were busy with troops and battles, — there came silently into Rome a power which shook Heathenism down to the dust; and the great battle betwixt new and old took place, and they knew it not. So an old story tells that when Rome and Africa crossed swords in great battle on Italian soil, they fought with such violence and ardor, that while an earthquake came and shook down a neighboring city they kept fighting on, and knew only their own convulsion. So in the fray of pain and pleasure, the great earthquake which threw down the Hebrew and Pagan Theology "reeled unheededly away."

Now old Rome is buried twenty feet thick with modern Rome; the civilization of Europe is Christian, — all but a corner of it where the Crescent eclipses the Cross. Nay, in London and Boston and New York is a society of "unsocial Britons divided from all the world," which spreads abroad the words of Paul and of Jesus, and in twenty years has translated the gospel of Christ and the epistles of Paul into one hundred and forty-seven different tongues, and spread them amongst men from the Thames to the "fabulous Hydaspes;" yea, from one end of the world to the other. In countries alike unknown to the science of Strabo and Plato's dream, the words of these two Hebrews have found a home: and now two hundred and sixty millions of men worship the Crucified as God. Not a great city all Europe through, but has a great church dedicated to that sail-maker of Tarsus, whose journey to Rome was so significant and so unchronicled.

What power there must have been in the ideas and the life of those men, to effect such a conquest in such a time! It is no wonder that many ordinary men, who know Christianity by rote and heroism by hearsay, and who think that to join a fashionable church is "to renounce the world,"—it is no wonder that they think Christianity spread miraculously, that God wrote a truth and sowed Christianity broadcast and, if men would not take it without, He harrowed it into them by miracle. Judging from their consciousness, what is there that they know which could explain the spread of Christianity, and the heroism of a man laying his head, and his wife's and children's heads, on the block for a conscientious conviction? Doubtless they are just and true to what is actual in themselves in believing that Christianity spread by miracle; and if a man has not soul enough to trust that soul, it is easy to see how he may think that every great truth came by miracle. An Esquimaux would suppose that a railroad car went miraculously.

Eighteen hundred years, with threescore generations of men, have passed by since Paul first went to Rome. What a change since then! It is worth while to look at the ecclesiastical condition of Christendom at this day. The Christian Church has very great truths, which will last for ever. But as a whole it seems to me that at this day the Christian Church is in a state of decay. I do not mean to say that Religion decays,—piety and morality: the sun will fade out of the heavens before they perish out of man's heart. But the power of that institution which is called the Christian Church the power of its priesthood,—that is assuredly in a state of decay. It has separated itself from new Science, the fresh thought of mankind; from new Morality, the fresh practical life of mankind; from new Justice; from new Philanthropy; from new Piety. It looks back for its inspiration. Its God is a dead God; its Christ is a crucified Christ; all its saints are dead men: its theology is a dead science, its vaunted miracles only of old time, not new. Paul asked for these three things,—liberty, equality, brotherhood. Does the Christian Church ask for any one of the three? It does not trust Human Nature in its normal action; does not look to the human Mind for truth, nor the human Conscience for justice, nor the human Heart and Soul for love and faith. It does not trust the living God, now revealing himself in the fresh flowers of to-day and the fresh consciousness of man. It looks back to some alleged action in the history of mankind, counting the History of man better than man's Nature. It looks back to some alleged facts in the history of God, counting those fictitious miracles as greater than the nature of God; He has done his best, spoken for the last time!

In all this the whole Christian Church agrees, and is unitary, and there is no discord betwixt Catholic and Protestant. But they differ in respect to the things to which they pay supreme and sovereign homage. The Catholic worships the Church: that is infallible, with its biblical and extra-biblical tradition, and its inspiration. The Roman Church is the religion of the Catholic. He must necessarily be intolerant. Two writers prominent in the Catholic Church of America within the last few months have declared that the Catholic Church is just as intolerant as she always was, and as soon as she gets power there shall be no more freedom of thought and speech in the new continent; she only waits for a hand to clutch the sword and put Protestantism to death. This comes unavoidably from her position. She must be sure that everybody else is wrong.

The Protestants worship the Bible, with its Old Testament and New; that is infallible. The Bible is the religion of the Protestants, as the Church is the religion of the Catholics, and the Koran of the Mahometans. This is the ultimate source of religious doctrine, the ultimate standard of religious practice. Here the Protestant sects are unitary; even the Universalists and Unitarians agree in this same thing, or profess to do so.

Then the Protestants differ about the doctrines of that infallible word; and so while one hand of Protestantism is clenched on the Bible, the other is divided into a great many fingers, each pointing to its own creed as the infallible interpretation of the infallible word: the one pencil of white Protestant sunshine, drawn from the Bible, is broken by the historic prism into manifold rays of antithetic color.

It is a great mistake for the Christians as a whole to maintain that they have nothing to learn from the Hebrews, the Heathen, the Buddhists and the Mahometans;—though the Christians are in many respects superior to these other sects of the world, yet they have much to teach us. It is a mistake for the Protestant to say he has nothing to learn from the Catholic: the Catholic — though far behind the Protestant — has many things to impart to us. And it is a mistake for the Unitarian, or Universalist, to declare that he has nothing to learn from the Trinitarian and Partialist. As yet no one of these great world sects, Christian, Heathen, Hebrew, Budhist, Mahometan, has the whole Human truth; and in Christianity no one sect has the whole of Christian truth.

But the Christian churches have broken with Science, and are afraid of new thought. This is somewhat less true of the Protestant than of the Catholic priesthood. They have broken also with fresh Morality, and are afraid of that. And so the Christian Church to-day is very much in the same condition that Heathenism and Judaism were at the time when Paul first went to Rome.

Nearly twelve centuries ago the subtle Grecian intellect separated from the practical sense of the western world, and for more than eight hundred years there were two Christian churches, the Greek and the Latin. Three hundred years ago a deadly blow was struck at the unity of the Latin Church. Since then there have been three Christian churches, the Greek, the Catholic, and the Protestant; the two former only conservative, the latter also progressive, but not progressive in orthodoxy, progressive only by heresy, — for the Church carefully cuts off the top of its own tree as soon as it is found to have new and independent life therein; it falls to the ground, and grows up a new tree. The Catholic Church cut off the Protestants; in the Protestant Church the Trinitarians cut off the Unitarians; and now the Unitarians seek to cut off those who have newer life than theirs, newer blossoms.

In the Christian Church there are many churches. But there is not one that bears the same relation to the civilization of the world which Paul bore eighteen hundred years ago. He looked forward; they look back. He asked liberty of thought and speech; they are afraid of both. There is not a Christian government which has not some statute forbidding freedom of thought and speech. Even on the statute-books of Massachusetts there slumbers a law prohibiting a man to speak lightly of any of the doctrines in this blessed bible; and it is not twenty years since a magistrate of this State asked the grand-jury of a county to find a true bill against a learned Doctor of Divinity, who had written an article proving there was no prophecy in the Old Testament which pointed a plain finger to the person of Jesus of Nazareth.

All over Europe religion is supported by the State, by the arm of the law. The clergy wish it to be so, and they say Christianity would fail if it were not. Hence come the costly national churches of Europe, wherein the priest sits on the cartridge-box, supported by bayonets, a drum for his sounding-board, and preaches in the name of the Prince of Peace, having cannon balls to enforce his argument. What a contrast, between the national churches of Russia, Austria, Prussia, England, and the first church which Paul gathered in his prisonhouse, where he preached with his left hand chained to a soldier's right hand, "his bodily presence weak and his speech contemptible."

But there has been a great and rapid development of humanity since Paul first came to Italy. What a change in agriculture, mechanic art, commerce, war, in education, politics! What new science, new art, new literature has sprung up! How the world's geography has changed, from Eratosthenes to Ritter! But the interior geography of man has altered yet more. The ancient poles are now in the modern equator. Compare the governments then and now; the wars of that period; the condition of the people. The Peasant was everywhere a slave at that time. Now slavery has fled to America — she alone of all Christendom fosters in her bosom that odious snake which has stung and poisoned so many a departed State. Compare the condition of Woman. The change has been immense. The compass gave mankind America; gunpowder made a republic possible; — it could not have been without that; — the printing-press made education accessible to everybody. Steam makes it easy for a nation to secure the material riches which are indispensable to civilization, and yet leave time for culture in the great mass of men. How have the humanities gone forward, — freedom, education, temperance, chastity; concern for the poor, the weak, the abandoned, the blind, the deaf, the dumb! Once the Christian Church fostered the actual humanities of the times. There was not a temperance society in the world; the Church was the temperance society. There was not a peace society, the Church was the peace society: not an education society; the Church opened her motherly arms to many a poor man's son who had talent, and gave him culture; and he walked through the cathedral door into the college, thence to the great mountain of the world and climbed as high as he could get. Now as the Church is in the process of decay we need special missionary societies, societies for preventing drunkenness and every vice. The function of the ancient Church has passed to other hands. She teaches only from memory of times long past. The national churches apologize for the national sins and defend them. In Europe the established clergy are seldom friendly to any movement for the benefit of mankind. In America it is they who are eminent supporters of every public enormity which the nation loves, willing to send their mother into slavery, pressing the Bible into the ranks of American sin.

The Christian Church early departed from the piety and morality of Jesus of Nazareth. Taken as a whole it has made some great errors and is now suffering the penalty thereof. It has taught that God was finite, and not infinite; that man's nature was a mistake, a nature which could not be trusted; it has put fictitious miracles before real law, and forced the heretic philosopher to confess that the Church was right, though the earth did still move; it has taught that religion was chiefly to save mankind from the wrath of God in the next world, not to bless us here on earth.

The Christian churches neglect the evils of their own time. To judge from the publications that have been sent forth by the American churches in the last twenty years, — the tracts of the Orthodox, Baptists, Methodists, Unitarians, — what would a stranger suppose was the great sin of America at this day? He might read them all through and scarcely conjecture that there was a drunkard in the land; he would never think there was any political corruption in the country; he would suppose we had most of all to fear from "doubt of theological doctrines;" he would not ever dream that there were as many slaves in America to-day as there are church-members. Why is this? Because the churches have concluded that it is the function of religion to save the soul from the wrath of God; not to put down great sins here on earth, and make mankind better and men better off. These mistakes are the reason why the Christian Church is in this process of decay.

It does not appear that Jesus of Nazareth separated his thought from the new Science of the age, and said "Do not think;" or that he separated his religion from the new Morality of the age, and said, "Never reform a vice, oh! ye children of the Kingdom!" He laid his axe at the root of the sinful tree and sought to hew it down. With him the problem was to separate religious ideas and life from organizations that would not admit of a new growth; to put his new wine into new bottles. With Luther there was the same problem. He endeavored to make new ecclesiastical raiment for mankind, tired of attempts to mend and wear the old and ill-fitting clothes of the Church which became only worse for the botching. In the present time there is the same problem: to gather from the past, from the Bible, from the Catholic and Protestant churches, from Jew and Gentile, Buddhist, Brahman, and Mahometan, every old truth which they have got embalmed in their precious treasuries; and then to reach out and upwards towards God, and get every new truth that we can, and join all these together into a whole of theological truth — then to deepen the consciousness of God in our own soul, and make the Absolute Religion the daily life of men.

Let the word Philosophy stand for the whole sum of human knowledge, and be divided into five great departments, or sciences, namely: Mathematics, treating of quantity and the relations thereof; Physics, including a knowledge of the statical, dynamical, and vital forces of matter, — mechanics, chemistry, and physiology in its various departments, as it relates to the structure and action of the material world as a whole, or to any of its several parts, mineral, vegetable, or animal;

History, embracing the actions of man in all his internal complexity of nature and in all his external complications of movement, individual or collective; Psychology, which includes all that belongs to human consciousness, instinctive, reflective, and volitive — intellectual, moral, affectional, and religious; and Theology, which treats of God and his relations to matter and man.

The progressive welfare of man demands a free development in all these five departments of activity. All these sciences are equally the productions of the human spirit and equally amenable to the mind of man, which collects, classifies, and studies both facts of observation and of consciousness.

To make a special application of this doctrine — the religious welfare of man requires, as its condition, freedom to study the facts of observation and consciousness, and to form such a scheme of Mathematics and Physics, of History, Psychology, and Theology, as will correspond to his general spiritual development and his special religious development. If a man, a nation, or mankind, lacks this freedom and accepts such a scheme of these sciences as does not fit his spiritual, or religious condition, then there is a contradiction in his consciousness; and there is no peace until he has cast out the discordant element and so established unity.

At the present day in Protestant Christendom, philosophers study the first four disciplines with entire freedom. No mathematician feels bound to stop where Archimedes, Newton, or La Place, finished his career;

no naturalist checks his steeds at the goal set up by Von Buch, or Hippocrates; the historians and metaphysicians voyage beyond the Hercules' Pillars of Thucydides and Aristotle, not fearing to sail the seas with God. It is universally admitted by the students of truth that all these sciences are progressive, amenable to perpetual revision; and that in all of them the human mind is the final umpire. The inquirer looks for the facts, their law, their meaning, and their use. There is no artificial norm established beforehand to which the mathematician, naturalist, historian, or metaphysician must make all things agree. There is no Procrustes' bed in any of these four sciences whereon to torture ideas.

In Catholic countries the case is often different; the Roman Church hinders the progress of each of these sciences — even the Mathematics so far as that treats of the relation of quantities, as the Earth and Sun for example — by prohibiting freedom of thought and speech; this Church has established its own artificial norm, the standard measure of all science.

In Protestant countries, it is commonly thought, or at least alleged, that Theology is an exception to the general rule which controls the other sciences; that it is not progressive, not amenable to perpetual revision; therein the human mind is not the final umpire; that it is a divine science, the facts not derived from human observation and consciousness, but miraculously communicated to man. Accordingly, the men who control the Popular Theology and occupy most of the pulpits of these countries, accept an old system of opinions which does not correspond to the general consciousness of enlightened men at this day. This obsolete Theology is set up either as religion itself, or else as the indispensable condition of religion. Thus the religious, the moral, and indeed the general spiritual development of mankind, is much retarded. Nay the theologians often claim eminent domain over the other sciences, insisting that the naturalist, the historian, and the metaphysician shall conform to their artificial standard and interpret facts of observation and of consciousness so as to correspond with their whimsical dreams; so that now the greatest obstacle which lies in the way of human progress is the Popular Theology.

In the time of Jesus and Paul the spiritual progress of mankind was hindered by the theological conclusions and ritual forms of previous generations. What was the result of hard thinking and manifold effort on the father's part was accepted by the sons as a foregone conclusion, as a Finality in religion. So the sons inherited their father's thought, but not his thinking, and made his religious form the substitute for religious life on their own part. If we sum up the theologies and rituals of ante-Christian antiquity in two words, we may say that at the time of Jesus and Paul Heathenism and Hebraism hindered the spiritual development of mankind. The wheels of the human chariot, deep in a rut, had reached the spot where the road ended;

the wheels must be lifted out, and a new highway made ready, reaching further on. The religious problem of the human race then was to separate the human spirit from the Mistakes and Errors and Sins of the past, and furnishing itself with all the good of old times, to press forward to new triumph. The old bottles were empty, there must be new wine, and that put in new bottles. The attempt to solve this problem was the greatest revolution which the world ever saw. What destruction was there of the old! The flame of old mythologies, burning to ashes, licked at the stars of heaven. What construction was there also! The "Christian Theology" and the "Christian Church" are the most remarkable organization of thoughts and men which the world has ever seen.

At this day the civilized world is divided into five great world-sects having each a special Form of Religion, all of Caucasian origin, coming either from the Sanscrit or the Hebrew stock, — the Brahmans, the Buddhists, the Jews, the Mahometans, and the Christians. They are now in a state of territorial equilibrium, neither gains much upon the other by means of theological conversion. Soon after the death of Buddha, Jesus, and Mahomet, their respective Forms of Religion spread with great rapidity. For many centuries there has been no national conversion. In three hundred years Christendom probably has not converted as many thousand Heathens to its own mode of belief. The Christians conquer, they do not convert, the barbarians in either hemisphere.

These five great world-sects embrace perhaps eight hundred million men; and with them Theology, where studied at all, is commonly studied in fetters. Just now the spiritual progress of the world is most promoted by the Christians. This comes partly from the superiority of their Form of Religion; but partly also from the youth and superior vigor of the leading nations of Christendom. But here also the progressive power is quite unequally distributed. Christendom is broken into three great sects, namely, the Greek, the Latin, and the Teutonic churches.

I. The Greek Church finds most of its followers in the Greek and Sclavonic nations, and thus serves to unite the oldest and the newest families of Christendom.

The Greeks, the sad remnants of a nation long since decayed, have now little influence on the religious development of the world. For a thousand years past the descendants of the Basils and Cyrils, of Chrysostom and Athanasius, of Origen and the Clements, have done nothing for the religious, or intellectual, advance of Christendom. Genius flees from nations in their dotage and decay. At present the Greeks seem to find no contradiction in their consciousness between the theological doctrines of their church and the religious instincts, or intellectual convictions, of the individual Christian. They are unproductive, generating no new religious sentiments, no new theological ideas. Too far gone to be conservative, they do not even reproduce the works of the ancient masters of Christian thought or Christian feeling. Athanasius would be more a stranger in his own Alexandria than in any city of the west. Chrysostom is better known at Berlin than Byzantium. The churches which once boasted that they had "the chairs of the Apostles" are now indebted to the charity of London and Boston for the Epistles of Paul and James, even for common benches to sit on. Even the manuscripts of the Bible and of the Fathers have followed the Star of Empire which stands still in the west. Superstition takes the place of genius; and doting Greece seems as incapable of intellectual and religious originality as of political freedom. There is an old age of nations as of men. Most intellectual of nations, the golden mouths of Homer and Chrysostom were fed at her bosom; Socrates and Aristotle, Origen and Athanasius are her children. She has rocked the classic and Christian civilization in her cradle. Let the world's benediction fall on that aged head.

The Slavonic population is not yet far enough advanced in civilization to have any influence on the Theology of Christendom. Some of this stock are members of the Latin church; the vast majority are of the Greek communion. To these sixty, or eighty million men the Czar is an incarnate God. He is their living Law, their living Gospel too, superior to all constitutions of the state; to all traditions, written, or only remembered, of the church; to all aspirations and intuitions of the individual man; amenable only to the dagger of the assassin. In theological and military affairs he commands with equal audacity; and with the same submissiveness his slaves obey. His will is alike the standard for the length of the priest's beard, the fusee of the canon, and the doctrines of the catechism. He is the universal norm of faith and practice, the great fugleman of the Sclavonic family, sixty or eighty millions strong. Oriental fatalism preponderates in the immovable Russian church. There is a mechanical adherence to the Byzantine forms of worship. The old ritual is retained, the old symbol respected. But the nation has not philosophical curiosity enough to study and comprehend the old, nor historical interest sufficient to republish, or read, the ancient masters of its own church; still less instinctive religious life enough to produce new sentiments in the form of mysticism, new ideas in the shape of dissentient Theology, or new actions in the guise of fresh, original morality. With the people, the ceremonies of the church and obedience to the Czar, pass for religion; with the small class of educated men the cold negations of the French mind in the eighteenth century, are taken for philosophy. The nation is still sunk in semi-barbarism. Here and there a few great minds, like the rivers of the empire, emerge from this swamp and sweep on in grand majestic course. There is probably but little contradiction between the religious instinct of the people and the ecclesiastical forms imposed thereon. There is no new, normal Russian Science — Mathematics, Physics, History, Psychology, — to conflict with the abnormal Theology inherited from Byzantium. The chief characteristics of the Russian church are Czarism and Immobility — it is so steadfast that it never seems to stir. But let no man mistake — there is no stillness to a young nation's mind, the root grows underground before the blade appears. In time of peace Russia controls Europe by her diplomacy, in time of war by her bayonets. When she cannot win a battle she can buy the result of victory. Doubtless these expectant conquerors of Europe, — nay, its present masters, — will one day have a religious consciousness of their own, with sentiments, ideas, and actions new and original. When Cæsar and Tacitus wrote of the Germans, who foresaw the Luthers and Schleiermachers that were to come? Nay, in the time of Henry the Eighth, subtle Erasmus knew nothing of the religious America soon to be born of that English mother.

II. The Latin Church includes a small part of the Sclavonic tribes in the north of Europe; the Celtic in Ireland and Scotland; a portion of the Teutonic in Germany, Switzerland, and the Low Countries; and the Romanic tribes in the south and west of Europe — the Italo-Romans, the Hispano-Romans, and the Gallo-Romans — with their descendants in America and other quarters of the globe. A few other disciples of the Latin church are scattered up and down the world, but they may be neglected in a sketch so brief as this.

The Sclavonic, Celtic, and Hispano-Romanic members of the Latin church, at present, exercise no considerable spiritual influence on the world. They affect Christendom chiefly by their brute numbers and brute work. The Celtic and Spanish populations are plainly in a state of decay; they can only look back with pride to the days when Ireland and Spain were the intellectual gardens of Europe; or forward to the time when the remnants of those once famous tribes shall mingle their blood with the fresh life of other families still vigorous with new fire, and so shall add their tribute to the great stream of humanity now spreading so rapidly over the western continent and the islands of the sea. The impotence of the Hispano-Romanic population has been demonstrated by the experience of the last three hundred years. Both Europe and America are witnesses to the sad fact. When Germany invented the printing-press, Spain set up the inquisition. Dr. Faustus and Torquemada are types of the two nations. Spain has not added a thought to the world's consciousness since Ferdinand and Isabella, by the butchery of their subjects, won from the Pope the title of "Catholic." In America the Spanish families have spread only as the simoon in Africa, bringing storm and desolation. The Theology of the Latin church is a curse in South America and Mexico. Loving the Inquisition it hates the printer and the schoolmaster: but like the ruins of Persepolis it retains the great sculpture of ancient times.

Italy is Catholic in name and form. But the Italians and the Greeks present us the same spectacle, with a difference only in the degree of national decay; a Tartar troop has subjugated Greece; Romanic Turks rule Italy in her decline, the dissolution not so complete as yet. Four great Italian navigators made America known to the world. But the continent slipped through the fingers of Italy. Genoa, Florence, Venice own not an inch of American Soil. The tongue of Columbus and Cabot is not the language of a town in the new world. There is no Italian church in the western hemisphere: yet New York has better Italian newspapers than Rome or Naples, Florence or Venice. Italy has added little to the world's thought since a Roman Pope forced Galileo to crouch and deny the movement of the world; "and yet it moves," leaving Pope and Rome and Italy behind. Martin Luther fled out of the "Christian Capital," disgusted with the heathenism he saw. Italy affects the world by her past history, by her ancient art, and her literature of beauty. The prestige of the proud city has still a charm for Christian and for cultured men. The works of Leonardo, Angelo, Raphael, Domenichino, Titian,—when will they die? The laurels of Dante, Petrarch, and Tasso lose not a leaf; what thunder shall scorch the crown on the brows of Lucretius and Virgil, or blast the beauty of the Horatian muse? Rome, the widow of two civilizations, sits there on the shore of the Tiber, sad, yet magnificently beautiful; she bears in her bosom the relics of heathen and Christian martyrs, but with atheistic feet tramples the ashes of her own victims, martyrs not less noble. The dust of Arnaldo da Brescia, and of many a noble soul, yet cries out of the Tiber against her. Ignoble sons, a populace of priests, at her feet consume their bread. Austria and France court and insult her by turns. The Queen-Mother, she has lost her power.

Yet piety still treads the aisles of the Italian church: but alas, it is the mediæval piety which tolls bells, fasts, sings antique psalms with a half manly voice, prays, and gives alms, but dares not think, nor work, nor do justly and walk manly with its God. Popeism is to Italy what Czarism is to Russia—only the Italian more thoughtful hates the hand that rules.

In the educated classes scepticism seems chiefly to prevail; the negations of the French and English Philosophers of the last century. Able men reproduce the thoughts of Aristotle and Aquinas. The bold voice of German philosophy is echoed from the Sorbonne at Paris, and a feeble note of the echo reaches the domos of Italy. Little new philosophy gets spoken there. Who supposes the educated clergy believe the Theology they profess, or trust the ritual and sacrament which they administer? It is plain there is a contradiction in the consciousness of the Italian church. There seems a negation of the substance of religion, and an affirmation of only its form. Italy does nothing to advance the Theological Science of the world, or to diffuse a fairer form of religion amongst mankind; the Roman Church, the mediæval Nightmare of the Caucasian race, presses her in her sleep. Shall the Teutonic race spread over Italy, as the Sclavonic over Greece; the "Barbarian" possess those crops of ancient art? Who can say what shall succeed an effete race of men?

In the ecclesiastical condition of France there is the same wavering to and fro, which has long distinguished all the action of this Gallo-Romanic people. Since the Reformation, her course has been fearfully inconsistent; the Protestant Theology came to France in the form of Calvinism. The political character of that form of religion, so inimical to royalty and all centralization of power, made it hateful to the monarchic politicians, even Francis the First regarding it as hostile "to all monarchy, divine or human;" its severe morality, its devout earnestness and simplicity, were detestable to the wealthy nobles. But it was welcomed by the manufacturing and mercantile classes, and gained for a time such privileges as even Catholicism did not possess.

But the Protestant star set in a sea of blood. Now France is more ultramontane in its character than ever since the days of Chancellor Gerson. In all things the nation fluctuates: now with loud acclaim the public declare the unalienable Rights of Man and seek to build thereon a Human State; then, with acclamations yet louder, they welcome a despotism. One day they deify a courtezan as Goddess of Reason, then turn and worship the Pope, and enthrone Louis Napoleon as Emperor.

At this day France seems to reproduce the phenomena of the Lower Empire. Paris is a modern Byzantium — the period of decadence appears to have begun. But there is intellectual activity, profound, various, and versatile; no nation had ever such talent for clearness of sight, accuracy of discrimination, and attractive nicety of statement. Not bewildered as the Germans by the refinement of subtlety, the French mind sees and reports the real distinctions however nice. But no nation has a more divided consciousness. Catholicism is the religion of the State; with the wealthy and educated classes of men it seems to be only a state-religion, a mere spectacle, as remote from their convictions as the heathenism of Rome from the mind of Cicero and Cæsar. The priests forget the lessons of Bossuet and are Roman rather than Gallic, so mediæval in their tendencies. But the philosophers — the historians, naturalists, metaphysicians, economists, — what is their religion? The two extremes of speculation are united in the consciousness of the nation, which accepts alike Helvetius and Thomas à Kempis. France does nothing to remove the contradiction from the mind of Christendom; nay, she increases the trouble by developing each extreme. The "Eclectic Philosophy" of modern France does not appear as yet in the Theology of this most elastic nation.

Yet at this time France has a great influence on the mind of Christendom. The powerful Catholic party reprints the old masters of thought, expounds the history of times gone by, not forgetful that scholasticism — which sought to reconcile the history of the Church with the nature of man — was borne in her bosom. Catholic France has more intellectual life than all the other Romanic races, and does great service to mankind. Abelard and Descartes were her children. But alas, her theological function is only conservative, not creative, not even critical. The clean and the unclean are equally taken into her ark, and equally honored while there.

The philosophical party influence the world by their science, history, and letters; the rich wine of Germany is here clarified, decanted, and made ready for popular use. But enlightened France does not study Theology. Few important works in that science have got printed there since the "Great Encyclopedia" made its appearance and smote theology to the ground. The Bible is printed in France as in England; it is studied in Germany. The philosophers do little to mediate between

Scepticism — which stops with d'Holbach, or Voltaire — and Superstition which seeks to believe what is impossible and because it is impossible. It is a strange phenomenon that there should be a "new advent of the Virgin Mary" in France at the same time M. Comte publishes his "System of Positive Philosophy," making "a new Supreme Being" out of the mass of men, all of them deemed merely mortal! The old defences of the Popular Theology are republished; but of what avail are they to men who have read Bayle and the Encyclopédie? At one extreme of society, the Jesuits revive the theology of Thomas Aquinas; at the other extreme there is the foremost Science of the age. Religion never fails from the heart of a nation — but when the Theology which is taught in the name of religion, and as the indispensable condition thereof, is at variance with the convictions of every enlightened man; when it is not believed by the priests who teach it more than by the philosophers who will not smile at it, — why, the religious development of the nation is attended with the greatest difficulties.

The Latin church has disciples in the Teutonic family — among Scandinavians, Germans, and Anglo-Saxons. But they are chiefly found in those countries where the government is most despotic, or where the intellectual activity of the people, even of the learned, is the feeblest. The cruel persecution of the Irish Catholics, so long and so systematically carried on by the

British government, converted men and women of Protestant families to the faith of the patient and heroic sufferers. Of late years some of the most pious and most learned men of England — so it seems to one at this distance — have gone back to the bosom of the Latin Church. Doubtless there is much in that church which the English Establishment has unwisely left behind. The relapse of English Churchmen to Catholicism shows at least that there is some life and a real desire for piety and religious tranquillity in that least Protestant of the new churches. Within twenty years past the Catholic Theology has had considerable influence on the English mind.

The Scandinavian, Dutch, and Belgic Catholics have little appreciable influence on the mind of Europe at this day. The intellectual activity of these nations does not appear in a Catholic form. Perhaps it would not be possible to mention a Catholic book published in these countries during the present century, which has had any appreciable influence on the thought or feeling of Europe. Yet in Belgium there is considerable religious life; at this distance it appears the most religiously Catholic country of Europe.

Amongst other Catholics of the Teutonic family there is more intellectual activity. Valuable books relating to Catholic Theology are published in the German tongue. Hebrew and Christian antiquity is carefully studied; much thought goes to the exposition of the Scriptures, to the study of ecclesiastical history. An attempt is made by able and learned men to reconcile the Catholic Theology of the middle ages with the most advanced speculations of Kant and Hegel. Among the German Catholics of the present century there are the honorable names of Jahn, Hug, Wessenberg, Möhler, Movers, Staudenmaier, and others of perhaps equal merit, who would be an honor to any nation. Books full of religious life also come up from the fresh consciousness of men, — both mystical and practical. The Latin Church seems to have more intellectual and religious life in the country of Martin Luther than elsewhere in the world. But still the new thought, the new feeling which controls the Teutonic population is far from Catholic. The new religious life — mystical or practical — is not Roman. The German Catholic movement of Ronge only weakens the Latin Church. Of the six eminent Catholics just named, half are obviously heretical; two of them have been put in the Index. Intellectual activity is the deadliest foe of the Roman church and its mediæval divinity. Any attempt to reconcile her Theology with the Science of the nineteenth century must needs end, as the Scholasticism of the Middle Ages, in the conviction that the two are natural opposites.

It is idle to suppose the Latin Church can accept any thing new and good from the science of these times. Her only strength is to stand still; if she moves she must perish: "infallible," Immobility and Intolerance are the indispensable conditions of her existence. The

Protestants may learn from the Catholics as the Christians from the Jews and the Heathens; but it is not possible for the Catholics to learn from the Protestants — more than for the Heathen, or the Hebrew, to take any new truth from the Christians.

Celtic and other disciples of the Latin Church appear in the portion of America settled by the Teutonic population. They have influence only by their numbers and gregarious action. The laity are subordinate to the clergy, who are the lowest, the most ignorant, filthy, and oppressive ministers on the continent, and as elsewhere, studiously keep the people in darkness and the most slavish subjection. The Latin Church has lost none of her intolerance and despotism by removing to America; learning nothing and forgetting nothing, she still claims the right to cut off the head of heresy with the sword. She only wants the power. The toothless old lion of the mediæval wilderness, his claws pared off, roams abroad in the new world; he journeys in "clippers," in steamboats, in railway cars; looks at the ballot-box, the free school, the newspaper, and the Bible, hating them all. Now and then he roars after the old fashion; but no Inquisition echoes his voice. He has no teeth, no claws; is not a dangerous beast. He loved European Slavery; he loves also American Slavery; and equally hates a negro and a scholar.

A great tide of immigration sets continually to America. It is chiefly Catholics who come, many pious and holy men among them with whom their Theology is the result of conviction, at least of satisfied experience; many are ignorant, low, and unfortunate men, who are Catholics from position, they cannot yet go alone in religion, and wish a priest with assumed authority to guide, or push, or drive them. Fear of the priest and of hell is the hangman's knot to hold them in order. But many are Catholics in Europe from indifference or from fear. In America they cease to be Catholics. If the immigrants from Catholic countries in the present century, with their descendants, amount to four millions — a moderate estimate — then it appears that out of thirteen persons who were reputed Catholics in Europe, or are actually born of such, not four remain in the communion of the Catholic Church of America.

In the Latin Church as a whole, little is done to reconcile the actual consciousness of men with the traditional Theology. Scotus Erigena taught that "all authority which is not confirmed by right reason seems to be weak;" "accordingly we must resort to reason first and authority afterwards." The Scholastic movement may be dated from these words, whereon Erigena stood wellnigh alone in his time. Now the aim of the Latin Church, — nay, it always has been, — is to subordinate Man to the Church, reason to the tradition of the past, or the caprice of the present: accordingly she does not allow her disciples to study any one of the sciences in the normal manner, with perfectly free individuality of spirit. Hence she aims to control the intellectual convictions of mankind, making her mediæval catechism the norm of all science. To this end she endeavors to keep the mass of her people uneducated, for "ignorance is the mother of devotion" such as she requires; so she hates the free school and the free pulpit and the free press. She hampers the learned class of men and prohibits them from publishing their individual opinions; and hinders them from reading the books which contain the new sentiments and ideas of the times. The bosom of this church feeds the most odious tyrannies of the age. Her clergy — with honorable exceptions — are the allies, the advisers, and the tools of the tormentor; and deserve the scorn and loathing of the people whom they deceive, beguile, and oppress. The name of Jesuit in all countries has won a reputation which no class of men ever had before. In America, the managers of the Catholic pulpits, with their subordinates, favor the most iniquitous measures of Spanish cruelty, or of our own Anglo-Saxon hardheartedness. It is sad to see the well-meaning, but ignorant, disciples of this church in America exploitered by a twofold jesuitry — Romish priests unfeignedly despotic, and American politicians pretending to democracy. But I doubt not there are in the United States individual priests of sound learning, of true and beautiful philanthropy, of natural piety. Some have been born here, others have found in republican and protestant America the asylum which the old world could not offer. In Europe there are many such scattered abroad in the humble offices of the Church. Nay, sometimes they find their way to a lofty place. Such men in a Church which suits their consciousness break the bread of humanity from house to house. Long after Christianity became one of the religions of the world there were truly religious men and women who found rest for their souls in Hebraism or Heathenism, in the faith of their fathers.

The last great sect may be called the Teutonic Church, distinguished by its Protest against some of the doctrines of both its predecessors. Catholicism is the religion of the Romanic families of Christendom; Protestantism of the Teutonic families. The love of free individuality, which has always distinguished this great family of men, began its opposition to the Latin Church more than six hundred years ago. From Dutch Peter of Bruis, in the twelfth century, to Swabian Dr. Strauss in the nineteenth, the most powerful religious opponents of the ancestral Theology of Christendom have been of the Teutonic stock. Even the French anti-Catholicism of the last century was of English origin and went over the channel to make its fortune.

Protestants there are of other families scattered about in all corners of Christendom. But those of the Sclavonic and Ugrian families in the East of Europe, of the various Romanic tribes in the South and West, have now little influence on the mind of Christendom, and may be neglected in this brief sketch. But the services of those tribes, in the cause of religious freedom, should not be forgot. The world ought to remember that, spite of ethnological diversities, human nature is still the same, loving the true, the beautiful, the just, the holy, and the good; that Jesus and Paul were Jews; that Origen was an Alexandrian Greek; that Pelagius was a Celt; that Spain bore Servetus in her bosom; that France was the mother of John Calvin; that Italy gave birth to Occhino, the Socini, and many of their kin; that John Huss and Jerome of Prague, though lighting their lamps at a Teutonic spark, were yet of another family; that Sclavonians in Poland, and Mongol Ugrians in Transylvania afforded sympathy and shelter to men who fled thither, centuries ago, with the Ark of the Covenant of religious freedom in their hands. Still the territorial home of religious freedom in modern times, and the eminent love of free individuality in religion belong distinctively to the various tribes of the Teutonic family. They may be divided as before into Scandinavians, Germans, and Anglo-Saxons.

The religious sentiments and theological doctrines of the Scandinavians have little influence on the spiritual development of the other nations of Christendom at present; and so in this sketch they may be passed by, not without gratitude for the obstinate heroism which went from the North with Gustavus Adolphus and secured existence to Protestantism in the centre of Europe when Jesuitism and royalty clutched at its life. The Germans and Anglo-Saxons require further and extended notice: for one of them is the most speculative and scientific, and the other is the most practical people that can be found anywhere in the history of mankind; and both have a deep and wide influence on the affairs of Christendom at this day.

In Germany the natural religiousness of the people has been much hindered by the political circumstances of the several States. The frequent wars that since the days of John Huss have disturbed the land, which is the battle field in the long contest between ancient bondage and modern freedom; the oppressive character of the local governments; the ecclesiastical routine, established by the State and enforced with the bayonet; the restrictions of industry in many forms — all tend to hinder the development of religion in the people, and still more in the most enlightened classes of the nation. But serious and most profound and most varied attempts have been made by this people to reconcile human consciousness with the traditional Theology of the Christian Church. In some Universities Theology is studied with the same freedom as the other sciences. Germany is the only country of Christendom where this Queen-mother of Science is treated with such respect. Paul and Jesus are regarded as men, not as babies. The mind of the Germans has some qualities well fitted to solve the theological problems of the age. Intuitive to a great degree, as their originality in many departments abundantly proves; deeply religious by nature as the ante-Christian modes of worship made plain to Roman Tacitus, and as the mysticism of the nation has shown ever since the days of Saint Bonifacius; creative and imaginative as no other nation has ever been, — a fact proven by the wide spread and characteristic national music, by the rich and various literature of the educated, and still more by the legends and songs, the wild flowers of imagination, which have sprung up from the bosom of the people, as the Forget-me-not, the Violet, the Daisy, and manifold Heaths from their meadows and mountains, for the creative imagination seems as universal in the people as the plastic forms of vegetation in Nature; laborious and patient, so that their scholars are the most numerous and learned that the human race ever bore; cosmopolitan and universal to a degree not deemed possible to the ancient Greeks, counting nothing unclean because it is common, nothing inaccessible because lofty and hard to come by, and nought barbarian however foreign; subtle in discrimination; nice in analysis of facts of observation and still more of facts of consciousness; of great power to generalize, often running to excess; with a natural or acquired tendency to the world of thoughts and feeling rather than to the details of commerce and art; with a language so pliant that it takes any form which the human mind needs for its most various purposes of intellectual advancement, inferior only to the ancient Greek, — it seems that the Germans are singularly fitted to solve the theological problems of the world. All the new theological thought of Christendom for the last three hundred years has come from some tribe of this great Teutonic family. The Roman State was broken by Saxon Herman; the Roman Church by Saxon Luther on the same "red earth" of Germany. In vain Rome cried "Give me back Varus and his legions;" in vain "Give me back my infallible Pope and his Indulgences." Germany broke with Rome. The nation which invented Gunpowder and the Printing-Press demanded free individuality of spirit in matters of religion.

Since Luther's time, and long before it, the German mind has studied Theology devoutly and manfully. The interference of government has indeed checked both religious feeling and theological speculation; it has prevented neither. Free thought, however, has not found any general expression in the pulpit, but in the colleges; it speaks by the iron lips of the press, not the living tongue of the preacher; it is addressed to the learned, not the people. So while the Shepherd has revelled in intellectual plenty with all the corn of whole Egypts at his command, the flock has grazed in scanty parish-commons, waterless and brown, or browsed on Theology, on dry and leafless catechisms. The learned philosopher must preach what the unlearned kings command; he may think, and print for the army of scholars, what heresy he will. The result has been a sad one for the shepherd and the flock, the philosopher and the kings.

The great army of theological scholars in Germany may be divided into two grand divisions, namely: the Biblicists who make the Scriptures the norm and standard measure of Religion, Theology and all which pertains thereto; and the Philosophers, who make the human Spirit the standard measure in Theology as in all science, in religious, as in æsthetic, ethical, or affectional affairs.

Each of these parties, the Biblicists and the Philosophers, may be again divided into two brigades: namely, the Supernaturalists who believe in miracles, and the Naturalists who reject miracles; and each brigade into its Right Wing and its Left Wing; each of these into an Extreme Right and Extreme Left. So in this theological host there are the Biblicists and Philosophers, made up of biblical Naturalists and biblical Supernaturalists, and of philosophical Naturalists and philosophical Supernaturalists; with their Extreme Right and Extreme Left. In the line of Christians, for mastery of the world battling face to face against the great antagonistic sects — Brahmans and Buddhists, Jews, Mahometans, and Heathens,— the Biblicists stand next to the Catholics, the Extreme Right of the Biblical Supernaturalists touching the Left Wing of the Latin Church. The Philosophical Naturalists are at the opposite end of this German army, their Extreme Left bordering, not distinguishably, upon Atheists and others of like sort.

All phases of Christian speculation and Christian feeling are reproduced, examined, and judged by this army of students. The air rings with the thunder of the captains and the shouting. The ground is cumbered with the missiles — historical, exegetical, philological, philosophical, mystical — which are cast at the other sects, at the Catholics, and still more at each other. But to drop the military metaphor — a serious attempt is making in Germany to study Theology as a Science, with freedom and impartiality. Mistakes and Errors must needs be made. Many Sins also will be and are, doubtless, committed, but much truth comes to light. Some writers affirm the absolute truth of every word in the Bible; others deny the immortality of the soul and the existence of God, and demand the "Rehabilitation of the Flesh in its aboriginal supremacy over the spirit of man."

Not to dwell on the monstrous tyranny now exercised by the government in some parts of Germany, to one at this distance there appear three difficulties in the way of the German Protestant churches; namely, the great mass of the people are not even spectators to the controversy, for the difference of culture between the scholar and the practical man is so great that the two are incomprehensible to each other. Then the scholars, in consequence partly of their seclusion from the people and of their unpractical character, use such vague terms that it is often difficult to apprehend their meaning; subtler than Athenian and Alexandrian Greeks, nice as the quibbling schoolmen of the Middle Ages, they seem often entangled in their own intricate phraseology. Again, they are intellectual and speculative more than ethical and practical.

But spite of these faults Christendom owes a great obligation to the German Scholars of the last seventy years, not to mention the noble men who preceded them, for the services they have rendered mankind by exploring the depths of human consciousness and expounding the past history of the race. The immoral and atheistical philosophers are but exceptions to the general rule. In the breaking up of old dogmas there is always much abnormal action; a revolution is a turning over and over.

The Anglo-Saxons are a burly-minded race of men; more ethical than imaginative, artistic, or philosophical, they are the most practical people at this day in all Christendom. With consummate skill to organize things into machines, and men into industrial States, they have now the same controlling force in the practical affairs of the Teutonic nations, — yes, of Christendom, — which the Germans have in the world of pure thinking. The Anglo-Saxon loves things; the German thoughts. The one symbolizes his individuality by a visible hedge about his field, distinguishing it from his neighbor's property; the other by some peculiar Idea of his own; one conquers new lands, accumulates material riches, and founds States; the other conquers ideas, accumulates vast intellectual treasures and founds Systems of Philosophy and Theology. The Anglo-Saxon is singularly direct, simple, and devoid of subtlety; his mind, his language, and his government, are distinguished for plainness and simplicity — for absence of complication. He seizes things by their great relations, and seldom understands the nicer complications which are so attractive to the Germans. This simplicity appears also in the metaphysical systems of the Anglo-Saxons, and in their Theology. There are numerous sects in their churches; but they depend on obvious and palpable differences, not on nice and abstruse distinctions. The sects differ in the form of church-government — by Bishops, by Elders, or the People; in the form of the ritual — baptizing in babyhood, or in manhood, from a porringer or a pond; in the arithmetic of deity — considering the Godhead as one person, or as more than one; in the damnation, or salvation of mankind. These and similar differences, easily comprehended by any one who can count his fingers, are the matters on which the Anglo-Saxons divide into sects. The subtle questions which vexed the Greeks in the Patristic age, the Italians and Celts in the Scholastic age, or the modern Germans in the Critical age, seldom disturb the sturdy and straightforward intellect of the English and Americans, intent on the ultimatum of practice, not the process of speculation.

This great tribe of the Teutonic family — distributed into English and Americans — is just now in a quite interesting period of spiritual development. It has accepted the traditional Theology of the Christian Church with various superficial modifications; has taken pains not to improve this Theology, deeming it not susceptible of improvement, not amenable to the mind of man. And it has now come to such a pass that there is a plain and painful contradiction between the Popular Theology and the consciousness of enlightened men.

In England the majority of the people are doubtless open dissenters from the Established Church. It is not easy to estimate the amount of secret dissent in that Church itself, or of private disgust at the Popular Theology in the ranks of professing dissenters. But to judge from the scientific, the historical, and the æsthetic literature of England for the past twenty years, and from the avidity with which profound treatises that show the insufficiency of this Theology have been received, it is plain that the mind of that country no longer accepts the Theology of the churches. The negations of both the biblical and philosophical Naturalists of Germany, have had a rather silent, but apparently a profound influence on the theological opinions of the nation. Eminent talent seldom appears in her churches — established, or dissenting. They are not the centres of religious life. Valuable institutions, as a whole, to keep the average men from falling back; valuable to urge some of the hindmost men forward, they yet do not lead the nation in philanthropic and religious feeling, in theological thought, or in moral action; and accordingly fail of the threefold function of a Church.

In America no form of religion is established by law; all the world-sects, as well as all the Christian sects, are theoretically free and equal, subject to the same economical and ethical supervision of the civil power. This circumstance has been eminently advantageous to the spiritual growth of the people. No clergyman can appeal to the bayonet to enforce his feeble argument, or to bring hearers to his meeting-house. A few laws depriving men of certain civil rights if they lack the legal minimum of religious belief, or punishing them for the utterance of antichristian opinions, still live on the statute-book, but they are eminently exceptional in this country, and fast becoming obsolete. All is left to the voluntary activity of the people. The immediate practical consequence has been a multiplication of churches, of preachers, and of hearers. No Christian country of large extent is so well furnished with meeting-houses and with clergymen; in no country is so large a proportion of the population found in the churches on Sunday; nowhere is the Bible, with religious books and periodicals, so common, and universally diffused. Theological Seminaries are erected by each denomination, and the means provided for educating, up to the level of the nation, such talent as moves towards the pulpit. Each denomination takes great pains with the ecclesiastical training of the children. Competition has the same effect in the churches as the market.

The Americans have applied the first principles of the Cartesian method in philosophy to every thing except what concerns Theology and Religion. There they have mainly consented to walk by the old traditions. But the difference between the old and the new, between the intellectual principles of the accomplished and philosophic lyceum-lecturer, and those of the theological preacher holding forth on the same theme, from the same desk, to the same audience, springs in the eyes of all. The contradiction between Theology and the other Sciences is seen and understood by a large class of intelligent men; it is felt, but not understood, by a much larger class, men of genuine piety who reproach themselves because they doubt the miracles of the Bible and fail to relish the eternal damnation of men, or because they take so little interest in the dull routine of what in the churches is called religion. With the wide spread of a very superficial intellectual culture, and with the immense intellectual activity brought out by the political institutions and the industrial movements of the country, a great amount of doubt on theological matters has also been developed. Sometimes it is public, oftener it is secret. But it is plain that the contradiction between the Theology of the churches and the Science, the Literature, the Philanthropy, and the Piety of the age, is very widely felt and pretty widely understood.

Clergymen endeavor to solve this contradiction in two ways. Men of one party attempt to put man down and bring him back to the old Theology. They deride new Piety; they rail at new Philanthropy; they decry Science; and at each new-comer in Theology who puts his yeasty wine into the old bottles of the Church, or, still worse, into others of a newer make and pattern, they call out "Infidel! Atheist! Away with him!" But they have no physical force at their command as in continental Europe. It is almost three hundred years since Calvin burnt Unitarian Servetus alive at the stake, where now a Unitarian college teaches the obnoxious opinion. Quakers and Baptists are never disturbed in Boston which once shed the blood of the founders of these earnest and important sects.

The other party, scanty in numbers, endeavors to bring Theology up to the level of the science of the times, and to engage the churches in new piety and new philanthropy.

The retrogressive and the progressive party are both needed; and have valuable functions to perform. There is always danger that some good things should be left behind; and not only feeble and timid persons, but warworn veterans also, are therefore properly put in the rear of the human army marching to the promised land; else baggage might be abandoned, and even stragglers lost. The Christians left good things behind in the Hebrew and Heathen cities they marched out of, or passed through; they must send back and bring away all those things. The Protestants rejected much that was excellent, perhaps indispensable to the welfare of mankind; so pious men and women must go over to the Latin Church and reclaim it.

How is the Anglo-Saxon Church, with its many denominations, performing its theological and religious function? Certainly not very well. As a whole it rebukes no great popular Sins; it corrects no great popular Mistakes and Errors. The Churches of England and America do not rebuke the actual evils of these two nations; they preach mainly against small vices which the controlling classes of the people have little temptation to commit. In England and America, the strong often exploiter the weak, consciously, or ignorantly. The Anglo-Saxon,—whether Briton or American,—has a most inordinate lust for land: he wishes to annex the universe to his estate. How has England pillaged India; how has America plundered Mexico, and now goes "fillibustering" towards Cuba! The commercial policy of Christian England is quite as selfish, and almost as cruel, as the military policy of Heathen Rome—abroad it aims to impoverish other countries, ruin their manufactures, and cripple their commerce, in order to heap up enormous riches in England; at home it aims to concentrate great wealth, and its consequent power, in the hands of a few strong men who shall exploiter the mass of the people. The policy of America is to keep one seventh part of the population in such slavery as exists nowhere else in Christendom; nay, more, the Christian "Barbary States of America" cherish the slavery which the Mahometan Barbary States of Africa have cast off with scorn and loathing. The English and American churches do not oppose the Sins, but encourage them.

In the ante-Christian governments the State and the Church were identical, the national religion was prescribed by the national law and enforced by the sword of the magistrate. The function of official priests was to appease the wrath of God, or purchase his favor; it was not to develop the spirit of the people. In Rome, such was the eclectic spirit of the nation, all forms of devotion were allowed to exist along with the national religion, so long as they did not disturb the peace of the city. But when Christianity came, affirming the unity of God and the falseness of all antecedent, or other, forms of religion, the Roman State, in preserving its own form of worship, must of necessity attempt to suppress the Christian religion. Christianity grew up in opposition to the magistrate. So there were at the beginning two powers in the nation — the State, the carnal temporal power; and the Church, — the spiritual power whose kingdom was "not of this world." When Christianity became a "lawful religion," and when it became the national religion, there still continued this division between the State and Church; two distinct organizations were established, the "carnal" and the "spiritual." This separation of the civil and religious authorities has been of great value to the world. In the Middle Ages, the Church was one established power, and the State another, each independent. The Church was a critic and check upon the State, the State upon the Church. Ecclesiastical conformity was often political dissent. The government of Christendom was monarchic; but the monarchy was two-headed. The practical effect of this was important, in many respects, to mankind. But in the Roman States, and in all countries which owed exclusive civil obedience to the Pope the Church swallowed up the State; the "spiritual" became also the "carnal" power, and the people were ruled with terrible oppression. The same result took place when the "carnal" became the "religious" power, as it sometimes did. In both of these cases the monarchy became single-headed; the State and the Church were merged into one; there was no city of refuge for the victim of the magistrate, or of the priest, to fly to. If he ran from the king's axe, he fell over the Pope's fagot. Thus was he overtaken by one or the other horn of the tyrannical dilemma, and if he escaped beheading he was sure to be burned. In countries where this division of powers was recognized, the man fled from the court house to the temple, or from the temple to the court house, and humanity had a fairer opportunity to obtain justice.

But when the scholastic philosophers, after struggling for centuries, had failed to reconcile the consciousness of mankind with the dogmas of the Church; when the Church itself became corrupt in head and members, and the Priests of Christendom were more tyrannical and shameless than the magistrates of Heathendom, then human consciousness broke with the Roman Church. But the people, long accustomed to passive submission under the State and Church, gained apparently little by the change. The kings, or other civil magistrates, took possession of the spiritual power which in Protestant countries had been wrested from the hands of the Pope. Thus as the Church grew weak the State again grew strong, and assumed the same authority in matters of religion which had formerly been claimed by the Pope in Christian, or by the king in Heathen countries. This was not effected without a struggle. In some countries the spiritual power, in carnal hands, became absolute; in others it was conditioned by a constitution; but in all the countries of Protestant Europe the State still claims eminent domain over the Church, prescribes the ritual, and establishes the creed. Thus in Prussia the king demands that every man shall be a soldier and a church-member; he is drilled in the manual exercise and the catechism. Even England has her national religion, and rejects with scorn from her two wealthy universities all who cannot subscribe to the contradictory formularies of belief: though she allows dissent, she by no means admits the dissenters to an equality with the disciples of her own Church, in which the aristocratic element preponderates over the popular — for the congregation is only of "dead-heads," which have no voice in making the doctrines of the Church, or even in electing its minister.

In this way the Protestant Church of Europe has lost one of its most valuable functions — it is no longer a critic on the State, it is the servant and creature of the State. If the magistrates are corrupt, the laws unjust and oppressive, the clergy dare not say a word against the iniquity. The Bench of Bishops is seldom found to be more humane than the House of Lords where it sits; and the Protestant Pulpit, in these countries, takes special care not to rebuke any popular Error or Sin. So the established Church in Protestant countries is commonly found siding with Government and not with the People: it attends to the Form — the ritual and the creed — not to the Substance of Religion. It does not demand a free mind, free conscience, free affection, and a free soul, all in their normal mode of activity.

In America there is no State-religion and no national Church. Each denomination determines its creed for itself, and manages its own affairs. But such is the dependence of the preacher on his parish for pecuniary support, and so much is that thought to depend on servility to the controlling and wealthy classes of society, that any popular wickedness is pretty sure of the support of the greater part of the American clergy. This is eminently the case in the great towns — the seat of riches, of commercial and political power.

The minister may forget his God, his Conscience, his Self-respect; he must not attempt to correct "the hand that feeds him." Slavery, the great sin of America, has long found its most effectual support in the American Church. The powerful denominations are on its side, the Tract Society says nothing against it; the leaders of the sects, with the rarest exception, are in favor of this wickedness. When prominent political men deny that there is any law of God to overrule the most wicked enactment of corrupt politicians, the wealthy churches say "Amen!"

In England the churches seem no better; they can rebuke American, but not British Sins, as the American British and not their own. In the military age the spiritual and carnal powers were independent of each other, and mutual checks; in the commercial age the Spiritual depends on the carnal power for daily bread, and dares not offend the hand that feeds it; forgetting the Eye which "seeth not as man seeth." The great theological movement of the Anglo-Saxons, the great religious movement, is not carried on by the churches but in spite of them.

To sum up the theological and religious condition of the Protestant countries as a whole, it must be confessed that there is a great contradiction in the consciousness of the people; that the Popular Theology is at variance with the other sciences, and is fading from the respect of the people. A great intellectual movement goes on, a great moral, philanthropic, and religious movement, but the preachers in the churches do little directly either to diffuse new truths, or to kindle a deeper sentiment of piety, or philanthropy. The Protestant Church, counts this its chief function — to appease the wrath of God and to admininister the Scriptures to men, not to promote piety and morality.

Take the whole Christian Church at this day — where is the vigor, the energy, the faith in God, the love for man, which marked the lives of those persons who built churches with their lives? Taken as a whole, the clergy of Christendom oppose the foremost science, justice, philanthropy, and piety of the age. The ecclesiastical institutions seem to bear the same relation to mankind now, as the ecclesiastical institutions of the Hebrews and Heathens two thousand years ago. Every year the Science of the scholar separates him further and further from the Theology of the churches. The once united Church is rent into three. The infallibility of the Roman Church — who believes it? the Pope, the superior Catholic clergy? The Infallibility of the Bible, — its divine origin, its miraculous inspiration — do the Scholars of Christendom believe that in defiance of Mathematics, Physics, History, and Psychology? They leave it to the clergy. The Trinity is shaken; men lose their faith in the efficacy of water-baptism, and other artificial sacraments, to save the souls of men; miracles disappear from the belief of all but the clergy. Do they believe them? The Catholic doubts the mediæval miracles of his own Church; it is in vain that the Virgin Mary reappears in Switzerland and France; that Saint Januarius annually liquifies his blood; that statues weep: the stomachs of reapers refuse such bread. It avails nothing to threaten scientific doubters with eternal hell. Superior talent forsakes the Church, — even in Catholic countries, there are few clergymen of genius, or even great talent. In Protestant Germany theological genius teaches in the college, not in the pulpit; and with new science destroys the mediæval opinions it was once set to defend. Will the spirit of the human race come back and reanimate the dry bones of dead Theology? When the mummies of Ægypt shall worship again their half-forgotten gods — Osiris, Orus, Apis, Isis; when mankind goes back to the other sciences of half-savage life the Theology of that period may be welcomed again. Not till then.

Is Religion to die out of the consciousness of man! Believe it not. Even the protests against "Christianity" are oftenest made by men full of the religious spirit. Many of the "Unbelievers" of this age are eminent for their religion; atheists are often made such by circumstances. Even M. Comte must have a New Supreme — *Nouveau Grand Etre*, — and recommends daily prayer to his composite and progressive deity! There was never a time when Christendom was so pious — in love of God; so philanthropic — in love of man; so moral — in obedience to the law of God; so intellectual — knowing it so well; so rich — possessing such power over the material world. Yet through lack of a true Idea of God, from want of institutions to teach and apply the Absolute Religion — there is not that conscious and total religious activity which is indispensable for the healthy and harmonious development of mankind.

What need there is of a new religious life! The three great public forces of the leading nations of Christendom, — Business, Politics, and the Press, excite a great intellectual activity. Christendom was never so thoughtful as now. Shall this great movement of mind be unreligious, without consciousness of God? It will not be controlled by the Theology of the Christian Church. But it is not a wicked age. What philanthropies are there new born in our time? Catholic France is rich in the literature of charity, shaming the haughtiness of the Anglo-Saxon Church. Yet within not many years at what great cost has England set free almost a million men "owned" as slaves! Nay, Russian Nicholas emancipates his serfs. Socialists seek to abolish poverty, and all the curses it brings on the body and the spirit of man. Wise men begin to see that the majority of criminals are the victims of society more than its foes, and seek to abolish the causes of crime; what pains are taken with the poor, the crazy, the lame, the blind, the deaf, the dumb; nay, with the fool! Great men look at the condition of woman — and generous hearted women rise up to emancipate their sex. The churches are busy with their Theology and their ritual, and cannot attend much to these great humane movements; they must appease the "wrath of God," or baptize men's bodies with water and their minds with wind. Still the work goes on, but without a corresponding consciousness of God, and connection with the religious emotions. No wonder Christendom seems tending to anarchy. But it is only the anarchy which comes of the breaking up of darkness.

There must be a better form of Religion. It must be free, and welcome the highest, the proudest, and the widest thought. Its organization must not depend on the State; it must ask no force to bring men to meeting, to control a man's opinions, to tell him on what day he shall worship, when he shall pray, what he shall believe, what he shall disbelieve, or what he shall denounce.

The Christian world has something to learn, at this day, even from the Atheist; for he asks entire Freedom for human nature, — freedom to think, freedom to will, freedom to love, freedom to worship if he may, not to worship if he will not. And if the Christian Church had granted this freedom there would have been no atheism. If Theology had not severed itself from Science, Science would have adorned the Church with its magnificent beauty. If the Christian Church had not separated itself from the world's life there would be no need of anti-slavery societies, temperance societies, education societies, and all the thousand other forms of philanthropic action. A new religious life can beautify all these movements into one. There is one great truth which can do it: that God is not finite, as all previous forms of religion have taught, but is Infinite in his Power, in his Wisdom, in his Justice, in his Holiness, and in his Love.

It is for earnest men of this age to protest against the evils of the Christian Church, as Luther against the Catholic Church, as Paul against the Heathen, as Jesus against the Hebrew Church. This can be done only by a Piety deeper, a Philanthropy wider, and a Theology profounder than the Church has ever known; by a life which, like that of Luther, Paul, Jesus, puts the vulgar life of the churches all to shame. The new Church must gather to its bosom all the truth, the righteousness and beauty of the old world, and add other excellence new got from God. Piety must be applied to all daily life, to politics, to literature, to all business: it must be the creed which a man repeats as he delivers goods over his counter, repeats with his hands, which he works into every thing that he manufactures. That is a Piety already on its way to success, and sure to triumph.

There are evils which demand a religious hand to redress them. The slave is to be freed, the State and Society to be reorganized; woman is to be elevated to her natural place; political corruption to be buried in its grave. Pauperism is to end, war to cease, and the insane lust of our times for gold and pleasure is to be tamed and corrected. This can be done only by a deep religious life in the heart of the people. All great civilizations begin with God.

It is a sad thing to look at the noble and large-minded men who in this century have become disgusted with the Popular Theology, and so have turned off from all Conscious Religion. In a better age they would have been leaders of the world's piety. It is for men who have sought to cut loose from every false tradition, to worship the Infinite Father and Infinite Mother! They may scold, and are then the Church termagant, worth nothing but their criticism. They may toil to remove these evils, their life making a new Church, and then they are the Church beneficent; their influence will go into the world's life, and hasten the development of mankind.

How much does all Christendom need a new Form of Religion, to reconcile the understanding, to bring the conscience, and the heart, and the soul, to the great work of life! Then if men are faithful, when eighteen hundred other years have passed by, they will have produced an influence in the world's history like that of the great Christian apostle, who went to the Gentiles so poor and so obscure that no man knows of his whereabouts, or his whence, or his whither. Now, as of old, "God hath chosen the weak things of the world to confound the mighty," and the true to confound the false. There is no reason to fear. The Infinite God is perfect Cause and perfect Providence; He made the universe from a perfect motive, of perfect materials, for a perfect purpose, and as a perfect means thereto. Shall He fail of his intentions? Man marches forth to fresh triumphs in Religion as in Philosophy and Art. What is gained once is gained for all time, and for eternity. Hebraism, Heathenism, Christianism are places where Man halted in his march towards the Promised Land, encampments on his pilgrimage. He rests awhile; then God says to him, "long enough hast thou compassed this Mountain; turn and take thy journey forward. Lo! the Land of Promise is still before thee." In the anarchy of this age are we taught to feel,

> "That man's heart is a holy thing,
> And Nature, through a world of death,
> Breathes into him a second breath,
> More searching than the breath of spring."

SERMON I.

OF ATHEISM AS THEORY.

PSALM XIV. 1.

THE FOOL HATH SAID IN HIS HEART, THERE IS NO GOD.

I.

OF SPECULATIVE ATHEISM REGARDED AS A THEORY OF THE UNIVERSE.

On this and several following Sundays I propose to speak of Atheism, of the Popular Theology, and of pure Theism: of each first as a Theory of the Universe, and then as a Principle of practical life; first as speculative Philosophy, then as practical Ethics

The Idea which a man forms of God is always the most important element in his speculative theory of the universe, and in his particular, practical plan of action for the church, the state, the community, the family, and his own individual life. You see to-day the vast influence of the popular idea of God. All the great historical civilizations of the race have grown out of the national idea which was formed of God, or have been intimately connected with it. The popular Theology, which at first is only an abstract idea in the heads of the philosophers, by and by shows itself in the laws, the navies, the forts, and the jails; in the churches, the ceremonies, and the sacraments, the weddings, the baptisms, and the funerals; in the hospitals, the colleges, the schools, in all the social charities; in the relation of a husband and wife, parent and child; in the daily work and the daily prayer of each man. Thus, what at first is the abstractest of thoughts, by and by becomes the concretest of things. If a man concludes there is no God at all, that conclusion, negative though it is, will have an immense influence; subjectively on his feelings and opinions, objectively on his outward conduct; subjectively as the theory of the universe; objectively as the principle of practical life.

Speculative Theism is the belief in the existence of God, in one form or another; and I call him a Theist who believes in any God. By Atheism I mean absolute denial of the existence of any God. A man may deny actuality to the Hebrew idea of God, to the Christian idea of God, or to the Mahometan idea of God, and yet be no atheist.

The Hebrews formed a certain conception of a being with many good qualities, and some extraordinarily bad qualities, and called it Jehovah, and said, "That is God: it is the only God." The majority of Christians form a certain conception of a being with more good qualities than are ascribed to Jehovah, but with some most atrociously evil qualities, and call it Trinity, or Unity, and say, — "That is God: it is the only God."

Now a man may deny the actuality of either or both these ideas of God, and yet be no atheist. He may do so because he is more of a theist than the majority of Hebrews or Christians; because he has a higher development of the religious faculty, and has thereby obtained a better idea of God. Thus the Old Testament prophets, with a religious development often far in advance of their Gentile neighbors, declared, that Baal was no God. Of course, the worshipper of Baal called the Hebrew prophets atheists, for they denied all the God that Gentile knew. Paul, in the New Testament, more of a theist than the Greeks and Asiatics about him, with a larger religious development than they dreamed of, said, — "an Idol is nothing." That is, there is no divine being which corresponds exactly to the qualities ascribed to any material idol. Their idea of God, said Paul, lacked actuality; it was a personal or national whimsey; not a perfect subjective representation of the objective fact of the universe; but only a mistaken notion of that fact.

If a man has outgrown the Hebrew, or common Christian idea of God, he may say what Paul said of the Idol, — "It is nothing." He will not be an atheist, but a theist all the more. The superior conception of God always nullifies the inferior conception.

Thus as the world grows in its development, it necessarily outgrows its ancient ideas of God, which were only temporary and provisional. As it goes forward, the ancient deities are looked on first as devils; next as a mere mistaken notion which some men had formed about God. For example, a hundred years ago it was the custom of the learned men of the Christian church to speak of the Heathen deities, — Jupiter, Apollo, Venus, and the rest, — as Devils. They did not deny the actual existence of those beings, only affirmed them to be not Gods but devils or "fallen angels;" at any rate, evil beings. Some of the heretics among the early Christians said the same of the Hebrew Jehovah, that he was not the true God, but only a Devil who misled the Jews. Now-a-days well educated men who still use the terms, say that Jupiter, Apollo, Venus, and the others, were only mistaken notions which men formed of God. They deny the actuality of the idea; "Jupiter is nothing." A man who has a higher conception of God than those about him, who denies their conception, is often called an atheist by men who are less theistic than he. Thus the Christians, who said the Heathen idols were no gods, were accounted atheists by the people, and accordingly put to death. Thus Jesus of Nazareth was accused of blasphemy, and crucified by men who had not a tithe of the religious development and reverence for God which he possessed. The men who centuries ago denied the actuality of the Trinity, were put to death as atheists, — Servetus among the rest, John Calvin himself tending the flames.

At this day the Devil is a part of the popular Godhead in the common theology, representing the malignant element which still belongs to the ecclesiastical conception of Deity. If a man says there is no devil, he is thought to be, if not an atheist, at least very closely related to an atheist. He denies a portion of the popular Godhead; is constructively an atheist; an atheist as far as he goes; atheistic in kind, as much as if he denied the whole Godhead, when he would obviously be branded an atheist.

I use the word Atheism in quite a different sense. It is the absolute denial of any and all forms of God; the denial of the *Genus;* the denial of all possible ideas of God, — highest as well as lowest.

At this day there are some philosophers, quite eminent men too, who call themselves atheists, and in set terms, deny the actuality of any possible idea of God. They say the idea of God is a mere whimsey of men, and God is not a fact of the universe. Man has a notion of God, as of a ghost, or devil; but it is a pure subjective fancy, — something which he has spun out of his own brain, for there is nothing in the universe to correspond thereto. Man has an Idea of God, but the universe has no Fact of God.

These men do not mean to scoff at others. They teach their doctrines with the calmness and precision of philosophy, and affirm atheism as their Theory of the Universe. It is a conclusion they have deliberately arrived at. They are not ashamed of it; they do not conceal it; do not ostentatiously set it forth.

I am doing these men no injustice in giving them this name, because they claim the style and title of atheists, and professedly teach atheism. They are not always bigoted atheists, but sometimes philosophical. A few of them are in this country, founding schools and sects of their way of thinking. Some of them are men of quite superior ability, men of very large intellectual culture. They seem to be truth-loving and sincere persons; conscientious, just, humane, philanthropic, and modest men aiming to be faithful to their nature, their whole nature. They are commonly on the side of man, as opposed to the enemies of man; on the side of the people, as against a tyrant: they are or mean to be, on the side of truth, of justice, and of love. I shall not throw stones at these men; I shall devise no hard names against them: they will get abuse enough without my giving them any at all. I feel great tenderness towards them, and very great compassion, — which I suppose they would not thank me for. Some of them I know personally; others by their reputation; some by their writings. I think they are much higher in their moral and religious growth than a great many men who are always saying to God, — "I go, sir," — and yet never stir. These are men who have made sacrifices even, to be faithful; and, without knowing it, they have a good deal of practical religiousness of character, both in its subjective form of Piety, and in its objective form of personal and social Morality.

I do not believe that such men are real atheists, though they think themselves so; and I only call them so to distinguish their doctrines, and because they themselves assume the name. I think the philosophical atheist lacks actuality as much as a devil or a ghost.

The Bible says, "The fool hath said in his heart, There is no God." If the Fool says so, I shall believe the fool thinks so; and if the fool holds up his five fingers and says "There is no hand," I shall believe the fool thinks so. But when a Philosopher says there is no God, I do not believe he thinks so, only that he thinks he thinks so. A man may sometimes think he sees a thing when he does not see it; and so a man may think he thinks a thing when he does not think it. A philosophical and consistent atheist is as much an impossibility, I think, as a mathematician who cannot count two; or as a round square, or a three-cornered circle. I shall never believe that a sane man who can understand the multiplication table is an atheist, though he may call himself so. But inasmuch as atheism is set up as a theory of the universe, let us look at it, and see what real Speculative Atheism is. That is the first thing.

There is a mere formal atheism, which is a denial of God in terms. A man says, There is no God; no God that is self-originated, who is the Cause of existence, who is the Mind and the Providence of the universe: and so the order, beauty, and harmony of the world of matter or mind does not indicate any plan or purpose of Deity. But, he says, Nature,—meaning by that the whole sum total of existence,—is powerful, wise, and good; Nature is self-originated, the Cause of its own existence, the mind of the universe, and the Providence thereof. There is obviously a plan and purpose, says he, whereby order, beauty, and harmony are brought to pass; but all that is the plan and purpose of Nature.

Very well. In such cases the absolute denial of God is only formal, but not real. The Quality of God is still admitted, and affirmed to be real; only the representative of that quality is called Nature, and not called God. That is only a change of name. The question is this,—"Are there such Qualities in existence as we call God?" It is not,—"How shall we name the qualities?" One man may call the sum total of these qualities Nature, another Heaven, a third Universe, a fourth Matter, a fifth Spirit, a sixth *Geist*, a seventh God, an eighth *Theos*, a ninth Allah, or what he pleases. Spinoza may call God *Natura naturans*, and the rest of the universe *Natura naturata;* Berosus may call God *El*, and the rest of the Universe *Thebal*. They all admit the existence of the thing so diversely entitled. The name is of the smallest consequence. All those men that I know, who call themselves atheists, really admit the actual existence of the qualities I speak of.

Real Atheism is a denial of the existence of any God; a denial of the *Genus* God, of the actuality of all possible ideas of God. It denies that there is any Mind, or Being, which is the Cause and Providence of the universe, and which intentionally produces the order, beauty, and harmony thereof with the constant modes of operation therein. To be consistent, it ought to go a step further, and deny that there is any law, order, or harmony in existence, or any constant modes of operation in the world. The real Speculative Atheist denies the existence of the qualities of God; denies that there is any Mind of the universe, any self-conscious Providence, any Providence at all. If he follows out his principle he must deny the actuality of the Infinite, deny that there is any Being or Cause of finite things which is self-consciously powerful, wise, just, loving, and self-faithful. To him there are only finite things, — each self-originated, self-sustained, self-directed, — and no more; the universe, comprising the world of matter, and the world of mind, is a finite whole, made up of finite parts; each part is imperfect, the whole incomplete; the finite has no Infinite to depend on as its Ground and Cause; there is no plan in the universe or any part thereof.

Now see the subjective Effect of this Theory. By subjective, I mean the effect it produces on the sentiments and opinions within me.

I. Look at it first as a Theory of the World of Matter.

In respect to the Origin of matter, both theist and atheist labor under the same difficulty: neither knows any thing about that. I know men, chiefly theologians, pretend to understand all about the creation of matter originally; and to hear them talk you would suppose it was as easy to comprehend how "God made a world out of nothing," as it is to understand how a tailor makes a coat out of broadcloth or velvet. But if a man looks with a philosophical eye, he sees this is an extraordinarily difficult thing. The philosophical theist admits the existence of the universe, and the atheist does the same; but in the present state of our knowledge neither atheist nor theist knows the mode of origination. You may go back a good ways and study the formation of an egg, a fish, seed, tree, or rock, or the solar system after the fashion of La Place; but the manner of originating matter, out of which the egg, fish, seed, tree, rock, and solar system are made, is just as far off as ever; and it seems to be beyond the reach of the faculties of man. I will not say that it is so, only, in the present stage of man's development and scientific acquirements, it seems so. The origin of Body,—of any specific form of matter,—may be made out, but the origin of Matter, the primitive, universal substance whence Body comes, still eludes our search. I know that ecclesiastical theists often call the philosophical atheist very hard names because he denies that we can understand this process at present; the charge is gratuitous.

But the real speculative atheist must declare that Matter, the general substance whereof Body is made, is eternal but without thought, or will; and the specific forms of existence,—of egg, fish, seed, tree, rock, and solar system,—all came with no forethought preceding them; came "by chance;" that is to say, by the "fortuitous concourse of atoms" which has no thought or will, and that they indicate no mind, no plan, no purpose, no providence. That is the atheistic theory of the universe; compare it with facts.

See how this scheme works on a great scale in the material world. The solar system has a sun and numerous planets; they are all distributed in a certain ratio of distance; they move round the sun with a certain velocity, always exactly proportionate to their distance from the sun; this holds good with regard to the nearest and the furthest. They move in paths of the same form; they are ruled by the same laws of motion; they receive and emit light in the same way. The laws, which are the constant modes of planetary operation, when we come to study them, are found to be exceedingly intricate; yet they are uniform, and the same for one planet as for another; the same for a satellite as for a planet. They are perfectly kept, and so uniform in action that if you go back to the time of Thales, five hundred years before Christ, you can calculate the eclipse of the moon, and find that it took place exactly as the historians of that day relate; or you may go forward five days, or five years, or five thousand years, and calculate with the same precision. So accurate are these laws, that an astronomer studying the perturbations of a remote planet, the phenomena of its economy not accounted for by the attraction of bodies known to be in existence, conjectures the existence of some other planet which causes the phenomena not accounted for. Nay, by mathematical science he determines its place and size, inferring the fact of a new planet outside of the uttermost ring of the solar system; at a certain minute he turns his telescope to the calculated spot, and, for the first time, the star of Leverrier springs before the eye of conscious man!

Now the atheist must declare that all this order of the solar system, was brought about by the fortuitous concourse of atoms, and indicates no mind, plan, or purpose in the universe. This is absurd. A man might as well deny the fact of the law of the solar system, or the existence of the sun, or of himself, as to deny that these facts, thus coördinated, indicate a mind, denote a plan, and serve a purpose calculated beforehand.

See the same thing on a smaller scale. The composition of the air is such that first it helps light and warm the earth; is a swaddling garment to keep in the specific heat of the earth, and prevent it from radiating off into the cold, void spaces of the universe. Next, by its free circulation as wind, it helps cleanse and purify the earth. Then, it promotes vegetation; carries water from the Tropics to the Norwegian pine, furnishes much of the food of plants, their means of life. Next, it helps animal life, is the vehicle of respiration: all plants which grow, all things that breathe, continually suck the breasts of heaven. Again, it is a most important instrument for the service of man; through this we communicate by artificial light and artificial sound. Without it all were motionless and dumb; not a bird could sing or fly, not a cricket creak to his partner at night, not a man utter a word; and a voiceless ocean would ebb and flow upon a silent shore. The thought-mill would be as idle as the windmill. Man kindles his fire by the air; it moves his ship, winnows his corn, fans his temples, carries his balloon.

Now the air is capable of these, and a great many other functions in virtue of its peculiar composition, — so much nitrogen, so much oxygen. No other combination of elements could ever have accomplished this. Vary the composition, have a little more nitrogen or oxygen, and you alter its powers as a vehicle of radiation, evaporation, vegetation, purification, respiration, communication, and combustion. The atheist must believe that this composition is not the result of any mind, that it serves no plan and purpose, and came by the fortuitous concourse of matter; no more; that it is all chance.

If I should say that this sermon came by the fortuitous concourse of matter, that last Monday I shut up pen, ink, and paper in a drawer, and to-day went and found there a sermon, which had come by the fortuitous concourse of pen, ink, and paper, — every man would think I was very absurd. And yet I should not commit so great a quantity of absurdity as if I were to say "the composition of air came by the fortuitous concourse of atoms;" for it takes a much greater mind to bring together and compose the air which fills a thimble than to produce all the sermons, yea, literature, in the world.

If the atheist says there is mind in matter which arranges the planets, controls their distances, their revolutions, their constant modes of operation, that this mind in matter arranges the elements in the air so as to perform all the functions which I have named, and many more, — then he is false to his atheism, and becomes a theist; for he no longer denies the Qualities of God, but only calls them by a different name.

With atheism as the theory of the universe, the world ought to be a jumble of parts with no contexture; for the moment you admit the existence of order in the very least form, a constant mode of operation on the very smallest scale, — why, you must admit the existence of the mind which devised the order and the mode of operation; and if you call the mind *Geist*, or, God, or Nature, or Jehovah, it makes small odds: the question is not about the name, but about the fact.

Now the world is nowhere a jumble. Things are not "huddled and lumped together" in the composition of the eyeball of the emmet, or of the solar system.

Every part of the universe is an argument against atheism as a theory thereof.

II. Look next at atheism as the Theory of Individual Human Life. According to the atheistic scheme there is no Conscious Power which is the Cause of me and of my life, which is the Providence thereof; no Mind which arranges the world in reference to me, or me in reference to the world. Does that conclusion satisfy the instinctive desires of human nature, any better than it accounts for the facts of material nature?

Look at human life from this point of view. I see but little ways behind, around, or before me; and yet, in all directions, my power of knowledge is greater than my power of work. I know little of the consequences which will follow from my action. I invent an alphabet; I organize the elements into gunpowder, the printing-press, the steam-engine, or men into a representative form of government, with a written constitution. I know very little of the effect which these vast forces will produce in the world of man. I know that the steam-engine will turn my mill, that the printing-press will print my newspaper, that gunpowder will explode at the touch of fire; but I do not know the effect which these organizations, newly introduced to the world, are to have on the families, the communities, the churches, the states of mankind, and on the general development of the human race.

The atheist says there is nothing which knows any better, or which knows any more about it; nothing which uses these inventions as forces for the advancement of any purpose. "The universe," says he, "has no self-conscious mind except the mind of man, and he is only 'darkly wise and meanly great.' Nothing in the world," says our atheist, "knows what a day may bring forth. The universe is drifting in the void inane, and knows nothing of its whence, its whither, or its whereabouts. Man is drifting in the universe, and knows little of his whereabouts, nothing of his whence or whither. There is no mind, no providence, no power, which knows any better; nothing which guides and directs man in his drifting, or the universe in the wide weltering waste of time. Nothing is laid up for to-morrow. My life also tends to nothing."

I am joyful: joy is very well, but nothing comes of it. I am sorrowful, and suffer: this is hard, but it is no part of a plan which is to lead to something further. And when my manhood falls away, and my body dissolves, all that is to lead to nothing better. My baby-teeth fall out, giving way to my man-teeth, but that is all chance indicating no forethought of a mind which provided for the man before the baby was born!

I serve men, and get their hate and scorn: the Sadducee grumbles because I tell him of his soul and immortality; the Pharisee, because I demand that he devour widows' houses no more, nor for a pretence make long prayers; and both of these hunkers, the hunker Sadducee and the hunker Pharisee, throw stones at me, and put me to death. It all comes to nothing for me; I am a dead body, and not a live man: that is is all I get for my virtue!

I am a brave man, and my country needs me to repel the Spanish Armada, or to keep imperial Nicholas, or Francis, or papal Pius the Ninth, or the little-hearted President Napoleon, from kidnapping my liberty. I go out to do battle, and I come home scarred all over with heroism, half my limbs hewed off, aching at every pore.

Or I die on the spot; I carry no heroism, no manhood with me; I am a heap of dust which other dust will soon cover, but the manhood which once enchanted this dust with valiant life, is put out and quenched forever, — it is all gone; it is nothing. My brother in that time of peril was a coward; and when war blew the trumpet and his country called on him, he crept under the oven. When all is over, and quiet is restored, he comes out with a whole skin, and over my unburied bones he marches into peace and carousing, and says, "A pretty fool was this man to lay down his life for me and get nothing for it!" And the atheist says, "He is right."

The patriot soldier gets his wounds and crutch, the martyr his fagot and flame, Jesus his cup of bitterness and cross of death, — and that is all. Dives has his purple and fine linen, faring sumptuously every day, more heedless than the dogs are of the beggar at his gate. Lazarus has his sores and the medical attendance of the hounds in the street, but death ends all.

The mother, whose self-denial leads her to forget every thing but her feeble, crippled child, has nothing but her transient affection and watching; she dies and all is ended. Another mother abandons her sickly, pestilential child to die of her neglect, and she lives forty years longer in joyous wantonness and riot; and when she also passes away it is to the same end as the other; only she for her falseness has had forty years of animal joy, and the noble mother for her faithfulness has had nothing but an instantaneous death. And my atheist says, "There is no future world to compensate the mother who died for love."

My life is a great disappointment, let me suppose; — and for no fault of mine, but for my excellence, my justice, my philanthropy, for the service I have rendered to mankind. I am poor, and hated, and persecuted. I flee to my atheist for consolation, and I ask, "What does all this come to?" And he says, "It comes to nothing. Your nobleness will do you no good. You will die, and your self-denial will do mankind no service; for there is no plan, or order in all these things; every thing comes and goes by the fortuitous concourse of atoms. If you had been a hunker you might have had money, ease, honor, respectability, and a long life, with the approbation of your minister. You had better have been so."

I lay in the ground one dearest to me; some only daughter — her life but a bud, not a blossom, yet mere bud as it is, the better part of my life. In the agony of my heart I flee to my atheist for comfort; and he cannot give me a drop of water from the tip of his finger, while I am tormented in that unutterable grief. "A worm," says he, "has eaten up your rose-bud. Get what comfort you can. This is the last spring day, no leaf will be green again for you."

I come myself to die. I have labored to extend my existence, which every man loves to do; and so I reached back and sought to find out who my fathers and grandfathers were, and trace out my pedigree. I wished to extend myself collaterally, and reached forth toward Nature, and linked myself with that by science and art, and with man by love. The same desire to extend myself urges me to go forward, instinct with immortality, and join myself again to my dear ones, and to mankind, for eternal life. But my atheist stands between me and futurity. "Death is the end," says he. "This is a world without a God; you are a body without a soul; there is a here but no Hereafter; an earth without a Heaven. Die, and return to your dust!"

"I am a philosopher," says he, "I have been up to the sky, and there is no Heaven. Look through my telescope: that which you see afar off there is a little star in the nebula of Orion's belt; so distant that it will take light a thousand million years to come from it to the earth, journeying at the rate of twelve million miles a minute. There is no Heaven this side of that; you see all the way through; there is not a speck of Heaven. And do you think there is any beyond it?

"Talk about your soul! I have been into man with my scalpel in my hand, and my microscope, and there is no soul. Man is bones, blood, bowels, and brain. Mind is matter. Do you doubt this? Here is Arnoldis' perfect map of the brain: there is no soul there; nothing but nerves.

"Talk of Providence! There is no such thing. I have been through the universe, and there is no God. God is a whim of men; Nature is a fortuitous concourse of atoms; man is a fortuitous concourse of atoms; thought is a fortuitous function of matter, a fortuitous result of a fortuitous result, a chance-shot from the great wind-gun of the universe, — which itself is also a chance-shot, from a chance-charge of a chance-gun, accidentally loaded, pointed at random, and fired off by chance. Things happen; they are not arranged. There is luck, and ill-luck; but there is no providence. Die into dust! True, you sigh for immortality; you long for the dear arms of father and mother, that went to the ground before you, and for the rose-bud daughter prematurely nipped. True, you complain of tears that have left a deep and bitter furrow in your cheek; you complain of virtue not rewarded; of nobleness that felt for the Infinite; of a mighty hungering and thirst for everlasting life; a longing and a yearning after God: —

All that is nothing. Die, and be still!" Does not that content you? Does this theory square with the facts of consciousness?

III. Now look at Atheism as a Theory of the Life of Mankind. Man came by chance; the family by chance; society by chance; nations by chance; the human race by chance. Man is his own sole guide and guardian. No Mind ever grouped the faculties together and made a cosmic man,—it was all chance. There is no Mind which groups the solitary into families, these into nations, and the nations to a world,—it is all chance. There is no Providence for man, except in human heads; Politicians are the only legislators; their statutes the only law—"There is no Higher Law." Kings and presidents are the only rulers: there is no great Father and Mother of all the nations of mankind. There is no Mind that thinks for man, no Conscience to enact eternal laws, no Heart to love me when father and mother forsake me and let me fall; no Will of the universe to marshal the nations in the way of wisdom, justice, and love. History is the fortuitous concourse of events, as Nature of atoms; there is no plan, nor purpose in it which is to guide our going out and coming in. True, there is a mighty going, but it goes nowhere. True, there has been a progressive development of man's body and mind, and the functions thereof; a growth of beauty, wisdom, justice, affection, piety; but it is an accident, and may end to-morrow, and the next day there may be a decay of mankind, a decay of beauty, intellect, justice, affection; science, art, literature, civilization may be all forgot, and the naked savage come and burn up Boston, New York, London, and Paris, and drown the last baby of civilization in the blood of the last mother. You are not sure that any good will come of it; there is no reason to think that any good will come of it. Says Atheism, "Everywhere is instability and insecurity."

Look on the aspect of human misery, the outrage, blood, and wrong which the earth groans under. Here is the wife of a drunkard, whose marriage life is a perpetual violation. She married for love a man who once loved her; but the Mayor and Aldermen of the city insisted that he should be made a beast. A beast, did I say? Ye fourfooted and creeping things of the earth, I beg your pardon! Even the swine is sober in his sty. The Mayor and Aldermen of the city made this man a drunkard; and the poor wife watches over him, cleanses his garments, wipes off the foulness of his debauch, and stitches her life into the garments which some wealthy tailor will sell, — giving her for wages the tenth part of his own profit, — and which some dandy will wear, — thanking the "Gods of dandies" that he is not like that poor woman, so ill-clad and industrious. She will stitch her life into the garments, working at starvation wages, and yet will pay the fines to keep the street drunkard out of the House of Correction, where the city government hides the bodies of the men it slays. She toils till at length the silver cord of life has got loosed, and the golden bowl begins to break. She goes to my atheist, and asks, "What comes of all this? Am I to have any compensation for my suffering?" And the Atheist says, "Nothing comes of it; there is no compensation. You are a fool. You had better have got a license from the Mayor and Aldermen to prey on other men's wives about you; and then you might have had wealth and ease and respectability. You ought to drink blood, and not shed your own."

"Abel's blood cries out of the ground;" continues our Atheist, "but there is no ear of justice to hear it, and Cain, red with slaughter, goes off welcomed to the arms of the daughters of Nod; the victims of nobleness rot in their blood; booty and beauty are both for him. The world festers with the wounds of the hero; but there is no cure for them: the hero is a fool, — his wounds prove it. Saint Catherine has her wheel, Saint Andrew his sword, Saint Sebastian his arrows, Saint Lawrence his fire of green wood; Paul has his fastings, his watchings, his scourge, and his jail, his perils of waters, of robbers, of the city and the wilderness, his perils among false brethren, and Jesus his thorny crown, his malefactor's death; Kossuth gets his hard fate, and Francis the Stupid sits on the Hungarian throne; the patriots of France broil in the tropic marshes of Cayenne, and Napoleon, surrounded by cultivated women who make him merchandise of their loveliness, and by able men who make merchandise of their intellect, Napoleon fills his own bosom and the throne of France with his debauchery; Europe is dotted with dungeons, — Austrian, Hungarian, German, French, Italian, — they are crowded with the noblest men of the age, who there do perpetual penance for their self-denial, their wisdom, their justice, their affection for mankind, and their fidelity to God. These die as the fool dieth. There is no hope for any one of them, in a body without a soul, in an earth without a heaven, in a world without a God. Does not that content you?"

"All the Christian world over, Oppression plies its bloody knout, — its well paid metropolitan Priest blessing the scourge before it is laid on. The groan of the poor comes up from the bogs of Ireland, and from the rich farms of England, and her crowded manufactories. Men make circumstances in London, which degrade two hundred thousand people below the Cannibals of New Zealand, and starve the Irish into exile, brutality, or death. The sighing of the prisoner, breaks out from the jail of the tormentor, who

> ——— ' Holds the body bound,
> But knows not what a range the spirit takes.'

"The iron gripe of kings chokes the throat of the people. Every empire is girded at the loins with an iron belt of soldiers, which eats into the nation's flesh. Siberia fattens with Freedom's noble dead, and in America three millions of men drag out a life in chains, bought as cattle, sold as cattle, counted as cattle, only not prayed for in the Christian churches, as cattle are; and the little commissioner who kidnaps at Boston, and the great stealers of men who enact the statutes which make American women into marketable things, are honored in all the 'Christian' churches of the land. Most of 'the great men,' all the 'citizens of eminent gravity,' all the 'unimpeachable divines,' are on the side of wrong. Cry out, blood of Abel! there is no ear to hear you. Victims of nobleness, rot in your blood! it will enrich the ground. Ye saints, — Catherine, Andrew, Sebastian, Lawrence, Paul, Jesus, — bear your rack and gibbet as best your bodies may! Kossuth, stoop to Francis the Stupid! Ye patriots of France, kneel to Napoleon the Little, and be jolly in the Sodom which he makes. Ye that groan in the dungeons of the world, who starve in its fertile soils, who wear chains in free America, — yield to the Jeffries, the Haynaus, the slave-hunters, and the priests! for there is a body without a soul, an earth without a heaven, a world without a God. Atheism is the Theory of the Universe; and there is no God, no Cause, no Mind, no Providence."

The Atheist looks on the lives of the noble men

> "Who in the public breach devoted stood,
> And for their country's cause were prodigal of blood,"

and he says, "these men were fools; every man of them might have been as sleek, as comfortable, and as fat as the oiliest priest that Mammon consecrates. They were fools, and only fools, and fools continually. To the individual hero there comes nothing but blood and wounds."

He looks on the nations that failed in their struggle against a tyrant's chain: Poland fell, and Kosciusko went to London, only "Peter Pindar" to welcome the exile; Greece went down in Turkish night; Italy and Spain must bow them to a tyrant's whim, — and the Atheist has no hope. The States which fail read no lesson to mankind, and have no return for their unblest toil. He looks on the nations now in their agony and bloody sweat, sitting in darkness and iron; he sees no Angel strengthening them. What a picture the world presents: Heroism unrequited, paid with misery, vice on a throne, and nobleness in chains. Want, misery, violence, meet him everywhere; and for his comfort he has his creed — a body without a soul, an earth without a heaven, a world without a God!

The Atheist sends out his Intellect to seek for the controlling mind, which is the Cause of the created, the Reason of the conceivable, the ground of the true, and the loveliness of things beautiful. His intellect comes back, and has brought nothing, has found nothing, but the reflection of its own littleness mirrored on the surfaces of things. He saw matter everywhere; he met no causal and providing Mind.

He sends out his Moral Sense to seek the legislating Conscience which is Justice in what is right, the Ground of good, and the Altogether Beautiful to the Moral Sense, the Equitable Will which rules the world. But his Moral Sense returns silent, alone, and empty; there is no Equitable Will, no Altogether Beautiful of moral excellence, no Ground of Good, no Conscience which enacts Justice into an unchanging law of right; there is only the finite will of man, often erring and always feeble, man an animated and self-conscious drop of dew in the Sahara of the world, conscious of desire, of will, but of such feebleness that soon he will exhale into thin air, and be no more a drop in all the world,— will evaporate into nothing Everywhere is material fate, material chance: spiritual order, spiritual providence,— that is a dream.

He sends out his Affections on the same quest, seeking his heart's desire. They have grown strong by love of Nature,— the crystal, the plant, and animal; they have been educated by loving man — parent and friend, and wife and child, and all mankind; refined by loving noble men, who attract ingenuous youth as loadstones draw the iron dust. Now his Affections fly forth with trembling wing, and seek the All-perfect Ideal, the object of their love, to stay the hunger of the heart which craves the Infinite to feed upon and love. But the affections also come back to the sad man with no return. "There is nought to love," say they; "nothing save man and the ideals of his heart; they are beautiful, but only bubbles; his warm breath fills them for a moment; how fair they shine, — they cool, they perish, and are not! The breath was but a part of the windy cheat which blows along the world, — the bubble breaks, and is nothing. There are only finite things for you to love; only finite things to love you in return." He presses the frail object of his affection closer and closer to his heart. "This, at least," say I, "is secure, and is a fact — the dear one is a reality, and not a dream." Still there is a sadness in my eye, whence speaks the unrest and wasting of the heart which longs for the unchangeable lovely. Death comes down to separate me from the best beloved. Beauty forsakes the elemental clod, the lip is cold; the heart is still; the eye — its lovely light all quenched and gone. Where is the mind which once spoke to me in hand and lip; the affection which loved me, finding its delight in loving, serving, and in being loved? It is nothing, all gone — like the rainbow of yesterday, no trace thereof still lingering on the sky. "But what!" say I, "is there nothing for me to love which will not pass away?" "No: love gravitation, if you like, cohesion, the primary qualities of matter; nought else abides." I look up, and an ugly Force is there, alien to my mind, foreign to my conscience, and hurtful to my heart, and wantonly strikes down the One I valued more than self, and sought to defend with my own bosom; then I die, I stiffen into rigid death. So the heathen fable tells that Niobe clung to her children with warding arms, while the envious deities shot child after child, daughters and fair sons, till the twelve were slain, and the mother, all powerless to defend her own, herself became a stone!

Last hope of all, as first not less of all, the atheist

sends out his Soul, to seek its rest and bring back tidings of great joy. Throughout the vast inane it flies, feeling the darkness with its wings, seeking the Soul of all, which at once is Reason, Conscience, and the Heart of all that is, which will give satisfaction to the various needs of each. But the soul likewise comes back — empty and alone, to say, " There is no God; the universe is a disorder; man is a confusion; there is no Infinite, no Reason, no Conscience, no Heart, no Soul of things. There is nought to reverence, to esteem, to worship, to love, to trust in, nothing which in turn loves us, with all its universal force. I am but a worm on the hot sand of the world, seeking to fly — but it is only the instinct of wings I feel; striving to walk, but handless and without a foot; essaying then to crawl, so it be only up. But there is not a blade of grass to hold on to and climb up by, not a weed to shelter me in the intolerable heat of life."

Thus left alone I look at the ground, and it seems cruel, — a mother that devours her young. No voice cries thence to comfort me; it is a force, but nothing more. Its history tells of tumult, confusion, and continual change; it prophesies no future peace, tells of no plan in the confusion. I look up to the sky, there looks not back again a kind Providence, to smile upon me with a thousand starry eyes, and bless me with the sun's ambrosial light. In the storms a vengeful violence, with its lightning sword, stabs into darkness, seeking for murtherable men.

There is no Providence, only capricious, senseless Fate. Here is the marble of human nature, the atheist would pile it up into palace or common dwelling; but there is only the fleeting sand to build upon, which the rains wash away, or the winds blow off; nowhere is there eternal Rock to hold his building up. No, he has not daily bread, — nothing to satisfy the hunger of his mind, his conscience, and his heart, the famine of his soul, only the cold, thin atmosphere of fancy. Does he believe in immortality, — it is an immortality of fear, of doubt, of dread. Experience tells him of the history of mankind, a sad history it seems, — a record of war and want, of oppression and servility. He sees that pride elbows misery into the kennel and is honored for the merciless act, that tyrants tread the nations underfoot, while some patriot pines to oblivion and death; he sees no prophecy of better things. How can he in an earth without a heaven, in a soul without a body, a world without a God?

Atheism sits down on the shore of Time; the stream of Human History rolls by, bearing successively, as bubbles on its bosom, the Egyptian civilization, and it passes slowly by with its myriads of millions, and that bubble breaks; the Hebrew, Chaldean, Persian, Grecian, Roman, Christian civilization, and they pass by as other bubbles, with their many myriads of millions multiplied by myriads of millions. Their sorrows are all ended; they were sorrows for nothing. The tears which furrowed the cheek, the unrequited heroism, the virtue unrewarded, — they have perished, and there is no compensation; because it is a body without a soul, an earth without a heaven, a world without a God. "Does not that content you?" asks our atheist.

No man can ever be content with that. Few men ever come to it, —

> "Thanks to the human heart by which we live!"

Human nature stops a great way this side of that.

I am not a cowardly man; but if I were convinced

there was no God, my courage would drop as water, and be no more. I am not an unhopeful man; there are few men who hope so much; I never despair of truth, of justice, of love, and piety; I know man will triumph over matter, the people over tyrants, right over wrong, truth over falsehood, love over hate; I always expect defeat to-day, but I am sure of triumph at the last; and with truth on my side, justice on my side, love on my side, I should not fear to stand in a minority of one, against the whole population of this whole globe of lands: I would bow and say to them, —"I am the stronger; you may glory now, but I shall conquer you at last." Such hope have I for man here and hereafter, that the wickedest of sinners, I trust, God will bring face to face with the best of men, his sins wiped clean off, and together they shall sit down at the table of the Lord, in the Kingdom of God. But take away my consciousness of God, and I have no hope; none for myself, none for you, none for mankind. If no Mind in the universe were greater than Humboldt's, no ruler wiser than presidents, and kings, and senates, and congresses, if there were no appeal from the statutes of men to the Laws of God, from present misery to future eternal triumph, on earth, or in Heaven,—then I should have no hope. But I know that the universe is insured at the office of the Infinite God, and no particle of matter, no particle of mind shall ever suffer ultimate shipwreck in this vast voyage of mortal and immortal life.

I am not a sad man. Spite of the experience of life, somewhat bitter, I am a cheerful, and a joyous, and a happy man. But take away my consciousness of God; let me believe there is no Infinite God; no infinite Mind which thought the world into existence, and thinks it into continuance; no infinite Conscience which everlastingly enacts the Eternal Laws of the Universe; no infinite Affection which loves the world; loves Abel and Cain,—loves the drunkard's wife and the drunkard; the Mayors and Aldermen who made the drunkard; which loves the victim of the tyrant, and loves the tyrant; loves the slave and his master; loves the murdered and the murderer, the fugitive, and the kidnapper,—publicly griping his price of blood, the third part of Iscariot's pay, and then secretly taking his anonymous revenge, stealthily calumniating some friend of humanity; convince me that there is no God who watches over the nation, but "forsaken Israel wanders lone;" that the sad people of Europe, Africa, America, have no guardian,—then I should be sadder than Egyptian night! My life would be only the shadow of a dimple on the bottom of a little brook,—whirling and passing away; all the joy I have in the daily business of the world, in literature and science and art, in the friendships and wide philanthropies of the time, would perish at once,—borne down in the rush of waters and lost in their headlong noise. Yes, I should die in uncontrollable anguish and despair.

A realizing sense of atheism, a realizing sense of the consequences of atheism,—that would separate our nature, and we should give up the ghost; and the elements of the body would go back to the elements of the earth. But—God be thanked!—the foundation of religion is too deep within us. There is a great cry through all creation for the Living God. Thanks to Him, the evidence of God has been ploughed into Nature so deeply, and so deeply woven into the texture of the human soul, that very few men call themselves atheists in this sense. No man ever willingly came to this conclusion: no man; no, not one! Those men, who have arrived at this conclusion,—we should cast no scorn at them; we should give them our sympathy; a friendly heart, and the most affectionate and tender treatment of their soul.

Religion is natural to man. Instinctively we turn to God, reverence Him, and rely on Him. And when Reason becomes powerful, when all the spiritual faculties get enlarged, and we know how to see the true, to will the just, to love the beautiful, and to live the holy, —then our idea of God rises higher and higher, as the child's voice changes from the baby's treble pipe to the dignity of manly speech. Then the feeble, provisional ideas of God which were formed at first, pass by us; the true idea of God gets written in our soul, complete Beauty drives out partial ugliness, and perfect Love casts out all partial fear.

SERMON II.

OF ATHEISM AS ETHICS.

LUKE XVII. 5.

INCREASE OUR FAITH.

II.

OF PRACTICAL ATHEISM, REGARDED AS A PRINCIPLE OF ETHICS.

LAST Sunday I said something of Speculative Atheism, that is, of atheism considered as a theory of the universe; with some of the effects on the feelings, and the views of Nature, and individual and general human life, which come thereof. To-day I ask your attention to a sermon of Practical Atheism; that is to say, of Atheism, considered as the Principle of practical Ethics.

If a man starts with the idea that there is a body and no soul, an earth without a heaven, and a world without a God, that idea needs must become a principle of practice, and as such it will have a quite powerful effect on the man's active character; it will come at length to be the controlling principle of his life. For as in human nature the religious is the foundation-element of man, as I showed the other day, so any misarrangement in that quarter presently appears at the end of the hands, and affects the whole life of man.

Speculative Atheism will not be fully reduced to practice all at once, but in the long run it will assuredly produce certain peculiar results; just as certainly as any seed you plant in the ground will bear fruit after its own kind, and not after another kind. You and I are not very consistent, it may be, and we therefore allow something to come between our first principle and the conclusion which would follow from it; but the Human Race is exceeding logical, and carries out every principle into practice, making its earnest thoughts into very serious things: only the idea is not carried out at once, but in long ages of time, and by successive generations of men. Every theological idea, positive or negative, that is firmly believed in by mankind or by nations, will ultimately be carried out by them to its legitimate, practical effect, and will appear in their trade, politics, laws, manners, — in all the active life of mankind. We think that the litany which we repeat in the church is our confession of faith. Often, that reaches very little ways in; but the real confession of the world's faith is writ in its trade and politics, in its wars and hospitals, in its armies and school-houses, better than in its "pious literature." The history of America, is the publication of our real theology, the confession of our actual creed. Each intentional act comes from a sentiment or idea. It is well to see what our ideas are before the thought becomes a thing.

Last Sunday I showed that there was a mere formal speculative atheism, which was only a denial of God in terms, or the denial of the actuality of a certain special idea of God, but yet contained an affirmation of the quality of God under another name; while real speculative atheism was the denial of the quality of God under all names, a denial of the actuality of any possible idea of God. And I showed also that there were reputed atheists, who denied some specific notion of God, because they had a better one; and because they were really more theistic and more religious than the men about them.

The same distinction is to be made in respect to practical atheism. Real practical atheism is the living of speculative atheism as a practice; that is, the living as if there was no God, who is the Mind, Cause, and Providence of the world; and that is living as if a man had no natural obligation to think and speak true, to do right, to feel kind, and to be holy or faithful to himself; living as if there were no soul, no heaven, no God. That is real, practical atheism.

There is a formal practical atheism, which is merely formal, and is based on formal speculative atheism. As the mere formal speculative atheist denies the name of God, but affirms the quality of God, and ascribes that quality to Nature,—so the mere formal practical atheist denies that man owes any natural absolute obligation to God, to think true, to do right, to feel kind, and to be holy; but he affirms that he owes this natural and absolute obligation to Nature; either to all Nature, represented by the universe, or to partial Nature, represented by mankind, or by the individual man, or some special faculty in man. In this case the atheist really affirms the absolute obligation of man to the quality of God, only he gives that quality of God another name, and is no practical atheist at all; though he thinks he is so, and calls himself by that hard name. For only the semblance of real practical atheism can be built on the semblance of real speculative atheism. If a man confesses that he has a natural and absolute obligation to think true, to do right, to feel kind, and to be holy, it is comparatively of little consequence whether he says that he owes this obligation to Nature or to God; because in such a case he means the same by the word "Nature" that another man means by the word "God;" and the obligation is the same, the consciousness of it is the same, and the duty which comes therefrom will be just the same.

I dislike to hear Nature called God, or God called Nature. Let each thing have its own name. In due time I will show what evils are like to follow from this confusion of terms, miscalling the finite and the Infinite. Still that confusion is not atheism.

Real practical atheism, I say, is the carrying out of real speculative atheism into life, living as if there were no natural obligation on man to think true, to do right, to feel kind, and to be holy; no obligation, therefore, to be faithful to himself as a whole, or to any part of himself as a part.

This real practical atheism is divisible for the present purpose into two forms.

First, the Undisguised practical Atheism. Here the practical atheist openly and undisguisedly denies the quality of God, denies that he owes any natural obligation to think true, to do right, to feel kind, or to be self-faithful; and on the contrary affirms speculative atheism as his practical principle and motive of life, and then endeavors to live up to it, — or live down to it. That is one form.

Second, the other is Disguised practical Atheism. Here the practical atheist acts on the idea that he has no natural obligation to think true, to do right, to feel kind, and to be holy; and thus really and in act denies the idea of God; but suppresses the formal denial of God and the affirmation of atheism; or he even goes so far as to affirm his belief in God, and deny his assumption of atheism as a principle of action. That is the other form.

Now in truth these two men, the undisguised professor of atheism, and the disguised practiser thereof, if they were consistent, would act pretty much alike in most cases, and do the same thing; only the undisguised atheist would do it overtly, with no denial of the fact and motive, but with the affirmation of each; and the disguised atheist would do it covertly, denying both the fact and the motive, thus adding hypocrisy to atheism. The undisguised atheist will be the more manly, because he is more thorough-going in his manhood; and such a person will always command a certain degree of admiration, because it is manly in the man to say right out what he thinks right in; and if he is going to live after a certain principle, to declare that principle beforehand. There is a consistency of manhood in that, and the very assertion is therefore often a guarantee of the man's honesty. But the disguised atheist will be the more atheistic, because he is really the more thorough-going in his atheism. One is true to his natural character as man, the other to his conventional character as atheist, for as atheism is the negation of Nature, so the negation of itself is a legitimate function of atheism. The reason of this will appear presently.

I said last Sunday that there never was any complete, real speculative atheism in the world; for complete, real speculative atheism is so abhorrent to human nature, that if a man had a realizing sense thereof and of its speculative consequences, he must needs die outright. I may say the same of complete, real practical atheism. There is no complete and real practical atheism; for I think nobody could ever be perfectly consistent with real speculative atheism, and live as if he felt absolutely no obligation to speak true, to do right, to feel kind, and to be holy. That, therefore, is an extreme which man cannot possibly reach. Human nature would give up before it came to such a conclusion. It is conceivable — but neither actual nor possible.

But yet there is a great deal of practical conduct which logically rests on this basis, and on no other, and though no man was ever fully false to his nature, and fully true to his atheism, yet very many are partially false to their nature, and partially true to atheism; and so there is a good deal of practical atheism in the world; much more than there appears of real speculative atheism; and though no man is a complete practical atheist, yet there are many with whom practical atheism preponderates in their daily life, and turns the balance. I mean to say they live more atheistically than theistically. The man does not clearly say to himself, "There is no God;" he only half-says it, and little more than half-acts on that supposition. He does not say out, "There is no God, and hence no obligation to speak true, act right, feel kind, and be faithful to myself;" because, first, there is some theism left in the man, — I think nobody can ever empty himself wholly of the consciousness of God; — or next, because the man is not fully self-conscious of his consciousness, so to say, and does not really and distinctly bring to light the principles which are yet the governing principles in his nature; — Or, finally, if he is thus conscious, he does not dare to say it, but yet acts mainly on that supposition. Now there is a great deal of this in the world; very much more than appears at first sight.

I mentioned the other day that some men whom I knew, calling themselves atheists, were yet excellent men; true, just, loving, and holy men; full of a certain religiousness, eminently faithful to themselves, keeping the integrity of their conscience at great cost of self-denial, and feeling more strongly than the majority of men the absolute obligation they were under to be faithful to every limb of their body and every faculty of their spirit. These were only formal atheists, not real atheists. They did not think there was no God; they only thought that they thought so. Some of these men have really a higher idea of the quality of God than the Christians about them; only they do not call it God, but Nature; for the "Nature" of the physical philosopher, or the "Mind" of the metaphysical philosopher is sometimes higher in some particulars, than the notion of the "Trinity," or the notion of the "Unity," which the general run of Christians have formed. I am bound as a faithful man to confess this. So some of these who are called atheists, and who name themselves so, are in reality more theistic and more religious than the general run of Christians about them. Such men as these do not show the practical characteristics of real atheism, but of the real theism which they have disguised to themselves by the name of atheism.

Thus one of these in America says, "It will do very well for Christian Doctors of Divinity and deacons, who believe in an angry God that will damn mankind forever, to declare there is in the universe no Law higher than the Baltimore Platform, and the Compromise Measures of the American Congress. It will do very well for them to declare that an angry God has given politicians authority to make such statutes, and declare them binding on men, and so 'suppress' and 'discountenance all agitation' for the welfare of one sixth part of the population of the country. But atheists, who believe in Nature, — the material world, — in Mind, — the spiritual world, — they must declare that there is a Higher Law; to wit: the Law of Nature, seen everywhere in the ground, and in the sun; and the Law of Mind also, felt everywhere in the consciousness of Man."

It is very plain that this man, though he calls himself an atheist, has really an idea of God, and consequently of man's obligation to speak true, act right, feel kind, and be holy, much higher than the Christian divine who would send his mother into bondage to keep the Compromise Measures; a much higher idea than the man who would renounce his reason for the sake of his creed, and who would give up his humanity in order to join a church, or to keep the wicked statutes which men make in their parliaments. Here you perceive the man calling himself by that ugly name, was only a formal atheist, and had really an idea of God which vastly transcended that of the churches about him. I am bound in justice to say this.

The actual consequence of atheism as a principle of action is something very different from that. The practical atheist, starting from his speculative principle that there is nothing which is the Mind, the Cause, and the Providence of the universe, or of any part thereof; and accordingly that Nature and Man are, respectively, the only mind, cause, and providence of themselves, — he must necessarily believe that man is under no natural and absolute obligation to think true, to do right, to feel kind, and to be holy. He must deny that there is any such obligation to God, because he denies the existence of God, or because he denies the existence of the quality of God, and he must deny that he owes this obligation to himself; for as man is his own mind, cause, providence, lawgiver, and director, so every propensity of the man is likewise and equally its own cause, its own mind, its own providence, its own lawgiver and director. Accordingly passion is no more amenable to reason and conscience, than reason and conscience are amenable to passion. The parts are no more amenable to the whole, than the whole to any one of the parts. Man is finite, and there is no Higher Being above man; and so there is no Higher Law above the caprice of any passion or any calculation. The man may will any thing that he will, and it shall be his law. For reason there stands the arbitrary caprice of man, the arbitrary caprice of each instinctive desire, or of any calculated act of will, and no more.

If the atheist admits there is in human consciousness an Idea of Right, he must declare it is not any more binding upon man than the Idea of Wrong. We form an Idea of Absolute Right: "it is a mere whim," says the atheist; "there exists no substance in which the Absolute Right can inhere. It is an abstract quality which belongs to no substance. It is a nothing; only it differs from an absolute transcendental nothing in this, that it is a thinkable nothing; not real, — an actual thing; not possible, — a thing to become actual; yet conceivable — an actual thought in the mind. You may distribute *nothing* into various heads, and say there is a pure nothing, which cannot be conceived of at all. You can have no notion of a pure nothing — it is not even thinkable; that is absolute transcendental negation — a denial of subjective conceivableness, as well as of objective actuality. Then you may say, there is also another form of nothing, which is the thinkable nothing. According to an atheist, God is a thinkable nothing, and the Idea which men have of God, has no more objective actualness to support it, than the Idea of Light would have if all material light, all actual, and all possible light, were blotted out of being. Then all the necessary attributes of God fall into the same class — thinkable nothings. So do all the transcendent attributes of man. Truth is a thinkable nothing, Justice a thinkable nothing, and any excellence which surpasses the excellence of Thomas, and Richard, and Henry, or all actual men, is also nothing; only it is a thinkable nothing, not a transcendental nothing.

This being the case, there is nothing for me to aspire after. Ideal wisdom, justice, love, holiness, each is but a thinkable nothing; — I should not aspire after that, more than I should marshal ghosts into an army to go out and fight a battle; or put in battery a non-existent but yet thinkable cannon, which is no cannon, and good for nothing. And then, all reverence must, of course, be weeded out from the mind of the practical atheist. He can only reverence something that he sees with his eye or feels with his hand, or reverence himself. This faculty of reverence which is born in us, — so delightful as a sentiment, as a principle so strong, — must take one of two forms: that of servility, crouching down before a man; or of self-esteem, strutting proudly in its own conceit. There is no other form possible for it.

The practical atheist denies God, and of course denies religion in all its parts; absolutely denies all obligation; to him the idea of obligation and of duty must lack actuality. He must deny my obligation to conform to my reason, conscience, affections. There is no reason therefore why I should speak and think true, do right, feel kind, and be holy, if it is agreeable to me to do otherwise. Therefore if I am an atheist, and if atheism be unpopular, my atheism will justify me in denying atheism itself and in affirming theism. So atheism, in this way, is self-destructive; its development is its dissolution. So to deny atheism, under such circumstances, will be more atheistic than to affirm it. The atheist who denies it is false to his manhood; there is no atheistic reason why he should be true to it; and the more he denies it, the more he is faithful to his atheistic opinion. So the expedient must take the place of the true and the right; the agreeable must take the place of the beautiful; desire, the place of duty; and *I will* must take the place of that solemn word, *I ought*. There can be no *ought* in the grammar of atheism.

But as the atheist in denying God denies the soul, and in doing that denies the immortality of man, his range of expediency must be limited to this life; and not only must it be limited to the earthly life of the human race, — which may be eternal for aught we know, — but it must be limited to the life of the particular atheist who thinks it, and even to the humbler faculties and lower wants of his nature; and so the highest thing he can desire must be his own present comfort. That is the highest real thing that he knows. So speculative atheism reduced to practice, must logically lead to complete material selfishness, and can lead to nothing else.

But as human nature will not allow complete speculative atheism as a theory of the universe, so it will not any more allow complete practical atheism, or complete selfishness, as a principle of life. There is a margin of oscillation around every man, and we are allowed to vibrate a little from side to side. This margin seems sometimes pretty wide, but complete practical atheism or complete speculative atheism lies a great ways beyond the limit of human oscillation. It is a thinkable nothing, — conceivable but not actual, or even possible. Still practical atheism actually tends to that conclusion.

All this which I have said is general in its application; is universal — it will apply to all forms of life. Now see how this atheism will manifest itself in the practical conduct of men in the various forms of Individual, Domestic, Social, National, and General Human Life. Let me say a word of each of these in its order.

I. I will speak first of the Individual Life.

As by the atheistic theory of the universe there is no such thing as moral obligation, no such thing as Duty, no Absolute Right, — as Man is the highest Mind in the universe, his own Cause, his own Providence, his own Originator, his own Sustainer, and his own Director, — so he is perfectly free to do exactly as he pleases. Duty will resolve itself into caprice of selfishness. Each man is to concentrate himself particularly upon the desire that is uppermost at the time; for as I am my own end, and to seek my own welfare at all hazards, so each particular propensity in me is its own end, and to seek its own welfare, — that is, its own gratification, — at any or all hazards.

So in my Period of Passion, the gratification of the passional propensities will be the chief thing which I am to seek. I recognize no Higher Law, in me or out of me; no law to prescribe a rule of conduct for me as a whole, or to prescribe a rule of conduct for any particular part of me, — any special passion. To acknowledge an imperative and extra-human law from without, which has a natural right to claim allegiance from me and to rule me as a whole — that would be to confess a God; not in terms, but in fact. To acknowledge an imperative and extra-passional law within me, to which I owe allegiance and which has a natural right to rule over any one passion, is to acknowledge God in degree; for what has a natural right to rule absolutely over any one particular propensity is God, so far as that propensity is concerned; and as I deny the actuality of the Infinite, and do not acknowledge a God who is the Reason and Conscience of the Universe and has the right to rule over me as a whole, no more do I acknowledge that my own personal reason and conscience have the right to rule over me or over any special appetite or desire. There is no extra-personal and Infinite Norm to prescribe a rule of conduct for me; there is no intra-personal and finite norm to prescribe a rule of conduct for any appetite or passion. So I am to let my passion have its swing in its quest for pleasure. If I have got rid of the great God of the universe, and acknowledge no absolute obligation to think true, to do right, to feel kind, and to be holy, — it will be ridiculous in me to set up a little God in my own consciousness, and acknowledge the obligation of my members to conform thereto in any one particular.

So the negation of religion as a whole carries with it the negation of control over any one particular passion. As the universe is a "fortuitous concourse of atoms," without any thing to rule it, with no mind to direct it, self-originated, self-directed, self-sustained, so my consciousness must be a fortuitous concourse of passions with no harmony therein; every passion self-originated, self-directed, self-sustained, its own end, and to seek its own gratification wholly regardless of its neighbor, or the whole body.

Accordingly in the Period of Passion I may give loose to my instinctive appetites. You come to me and say, "There is a God. You must not break his law." I deny this. "At least there is something that is right, and you must do that." I deny that also; I say there is no such thing as right. "At any rate you must control your passions for the good of your whole nature, during a long life." But, why should I do that? What right have I to control this or that passion, and debar it of its temporary lust, for the sake of giving the whole man a lasting delight? The passion has no norm but itself; what right has the whole man to control any part of him, or one part to hold another in check? or put off pleasure to-day for more pleasure to-morrow? So at this period of life anarchy of passions is the only atheistic self-government.

In the Period of Ambition — which in New England is commonly by far the more dangerous of the two, as its perils lead to fortune, and the ruin it brings is deemed "eminent success" — I am to let the other selfish propensities seek each its own object, and not hinder them. I am covetous: I am not to restrain my avarice by my reason, my conscience, my affections; I am to seek my own gain in all ways, at all hazards, and in derision of reason, of conscience, and of affection. There is no principle to stand between me and the dollar, or the office which I covet. I am to be wholly unscrupulous in my zeal, and in the means I make use of to achieve my end. I have a great love of power, fame, ease; and I am to let each of these desires have its full swing. There is no higher power to prescribe a rule of conduct for my ambition, more than for my passion. Here all must be a fortuitous concourse of ambitions, the anarchy of ambitions is the only atheistic self-government at this period.

So there is nothing to prevent my life from being the mere selfishness of passion in youth, seeking pleasure as its object; or the selfishness of ambition in manhood, seeking profit as its goal; for nothing has any right to stand between me and the object of my ambition, more than between me and the object of my passion. Atheism must be universal anarchy!

Now each of these forms of atheism may assume two modes. One is that of Gross Selfishness, that is, gross sensualism of pleasure in the period of passion, or gross calculation of profit in the period of ambition. It will terminate in the gross voluptuary or the gross hunker. That is one form. It is the rude, coarse, vulgar form. It is the shape in which atheism would manifest itself with the poor, with the uneducated, with the roughest of men. It is the atheism of savagery,—the practical atheism of St. Giles' parish in London.

The other mode is that of Refined Selfishness, that is, refined sensualism of pleasure in the period of passion, or the refined calculation of profit, in the period of ambition; and so here it will terminate in the delicate and subtle voluptuary, or else in the delicate and subtle hunker;— This is the atheism of civilization, the atheism of St. James' parish in London. The mode will depend on the temperament and circumstances of the man. And yet you see these two are generically the same; with unity of idea and unity of purpose, both seek a selfish object, and both come to the same end, only one in the delicate and the other in the gross form.

In either case the aim of life is to be the rehabilitation of selfishness; I mean the enthroning of selfishness as the leading practical principle of life. The atheist is to look on every faculty as an instrument of pleasure or profit; to look on his life as a means of selfishness and no more; to look on himself as a beast of pleasure or a beast of prey. Behold the man of atheism! — his controlling principle selfishness; his life "poor, and nasty, and short!"

Now man is not selfish by nature. We have self-love enough to hold us together. Self-love, the conservative principle of man, is the natural girdle put about our consciousness to keep us from falling loose, and spreading, and breaking asunder. In human nature self-love is not too strong. When all the faculties act in harmony there is no excess of this. But if you deny that faculty which looks to the Infinite, which hungers for the ideal true, the ideal just and lovely and holy, then self-love, conservative of the individual, degenerates into selfishness, invades others, and each man becomes merely selfish.

This fact implies no defect in the original constitution of Man; for it is a part of the plan of human nature that religion, the consciousness of God, should be the foundation-element of spiritual consciousness, and so the condition of manifestation for all the high faculties put together: and as roses will not bloom without light and warmth, or as ships cannot keep the sea without keel and rudder and a hand upon the helm, no more can the high qualities of humanity come forth without we put in its proper place the foundation-element of man, and let the religious faculty lay its hand upon the helm. The individual atheist, if consistent, must practically live in utter selfishness — material selfishness, selfishness bounded by the short span of his own earthly existence. And that is individual ruin.

II. See next the effect of practical atheism on Domestic Life, in the Family. The normal basis and bond of union in the family is Mutuality of Love in its various forms: connubial — between man and wife, — parental, affiliative or kindly between kith and kin, — and friendly love.

Connubial love in its normal state consists of two factors, — passion, seeking the welfare of the lover, and affection, which seeks the welfare of the beloved. In normal connubial love these two, the plastic and the pliant are coördinated together. Each aims to delight the other more than to enjoy himself, and finds his satisfaction less in enjoying than in delighting. Passion is then beautiful and affection is delightful. Self-love is subordinate to the love of another, the special to the universal. The love of the true, the just, the ever beautiful, and the holy, comes in, and prevents even the existence of selfishness. This condition affords an opportunity for developing and enjoying some of the highest qualities of man. Passion is instinctive, and affection also is instinctive at first; but as man develops himself by culture, as the human race enlarges in its progressive unfolding, so the affections become larger and larger, more powerful in the individual and the race, and the joy of delighting becomes greater and more.

But in practical atheism the family must rest on Mutuality of Selfishness, not on mutuality of love. And this must appear in all its forms, in the relation between acquaintances or friends, between kith and kin, between parent and child, between man and wife. Marriage must be only for the selfishness of transient pleasure, or the selfishness of permanent profit. The parental and filial relation must be only a relation of selfishness, the parents wanting the child to serve them as a beast of burden or as a toy, and the children wanting the parent to serve them, and valuing father or mother only for what they get therefrom. The relations of kinship, of brother and sister, of uncle and nephew, of aunt and niece; the relation of friendship must also be of selfishness, and no more. Passion must be all lust, and affection die out and give place to selfish calculation. The wife must be the husband's tool or his toy, and the husband the toy or the tool of the wife.

Marriage is then possible for the sake only of three things; first, for animal gratification; next for pecuniary profit; last for social respectability. It is a union of passions in the one case, of estates in the next, of respectabilities in the last; at any rate it is the conjunction of bodies without a soul, of selfishness without self-denial, for a here with no hereafter, and in a world with no God. Behold the family of practical atheists! Atheism gone to housekeeping! the housekeeping of atheism like the individual life thereof, — must be what Hobbes said of it, — "poor, and nasty, and short!" Expect no self-command here for conscience' or affection's sake; no self-denial to-day, for dear and lasting delight to-morrow; no self-sacrifice for another's joy or another's growth: mutuality of selfishness is all; and the stronger selfishness must carry the day; and that is the ruin of the family. No family life of joy is possible without self-denial on all sides. The wife must deny herself for the husband; the husband, himself for the wife; the parent for the child; kith for kin, and friend for friend. The stronger and nearer I fold another to my bosom, the nearer and stronger is the demand on me for self-denial, yea for self-sacrifice for the sake of the object that my arms enfold.

Now there is much partial practical atheism which appears in this domestic form. The present position of woman is only justified on the ground that there is no God: men do not understand it as yet; one day they surely will. Every marriage which is not based on mutuality of affection, — where good is to be taken and good is to be given, and man and wife both are to take and both are to give, — is bottomed at last on practical atheism; only on that. The other day I said it was impossible for a man to be a complete speculative atheist. It is impossible for him to be a complete practical atheist. But grant that there was a complete practical atheistic man, and a complete practical atheistic woman; — would marriage be possible between the two? By no means! Not at all! Juxtaposition of bodies is all that would take place. Selfishness is never a bond of real wedlock.

Philosophers in the last century, in France, thought that the Spider had not yet developed all its economy, but might be used for nice purposes of fabric and manufacture amongst men. They thought they could get the filament of a web finer than that of the silk-worm's weaving, out from the spider's mouth. The spider is not gregarious. The philosophers gathered together an innumerable host of the insects and shut them up in one room, and left them to their weaving, feeding them with flies and other food which the spider's appetite longed for. After a few days there was only a single spider left. They fought with each other, and slew one another, till the king-spider was the only one left, and selfishness had eat itself up.

III. See how practical atheism will appear in a larger form of action,—the Social Form, in the Neighborhood and Community.

The normal basis of society is first the gregarious instinct, which we have in common with sheep and kine.

Next, comes the social will, which is peculiar to man, and has this superiority over the gregarious instinct,—it is to join men together in such a way that the individuality of each shall be preserved, while the sociality of all is made sure of. That cannot take place with the animals; and for this reason,—because they are not persons, and free spiritual individuality does not seem of so much value among sheep and kine as amongst men. Each particular Ox may be only "so much of the ox-kind;" this Bison only so much of the bison-kind, and that Buffalo so much of the buffalo-kind; and the individuality of either is of no great value for the development of the ox or the ox-kind. But when you come to man, Thomas is one man, and Oliver is another, and Jason is a third; and it is just as necessary to preserve the free spiritual individuality of each one of these as the individuality of the whole human race. Therefore this social will must so control the gregarious instinct that the individual shall be kept whole while sociality is made sure of.

Then there is a third thing; namely, the religious aspiration, which desires the absolutely true, just, and lovely; and this desire can only be brought out in full action in the company or society of men.

Accordingly in a normal society there will be, first, individual self-love, seeking to develop and enjoy itself:

then the social affection, seeking to delight and develop others about us; and these two may be so coördinated that the individual is kept in society, and the mass also is developed and blessed by the concurrent desire to enjoy and to delight: then there will also be the religious love of God, the ideal True, Just, Loving, and Holy, involving as it does the religious love of men. In short, that will be a society shaped by the Golden Rule.

But the society of atheism must be a mutuality of selfishness; a society of bodies without souls; ruled by selfishness, not conscious affection; for an earth without a heaven, in a world without a God; and in a world, too, without actual reverence, which comes instinctively into every person above the rank of the idiot; — for with atheists reverence must take either the outward form of servility and baseness, or the inward form of gross self-esteem. So this must be a short-sighted selfishness, which lays out for to-day, but never lays up for to-morrow.

Each conjunction of selfishness must needs be a battle. The individual is a warfare of contending passions, lust striving against acquisitiveness, and ambition against amativeness. The family must be a warfare of men and women striving for mastery. Society must be a warfare of great and little, of cunning and foolish, rich and poor, cultivated and ignorant, — contending for mastery. Amongst all these, the strong passion will carry it in the individual, the strong person in the family, and the strong class in society; and therefore no peace is at all possible till the strong passion has subdued the weak in the individual, the strong man the weak men in the family, and the strong class has got its heel on the throat of the weak class in society. Then there will be unity, and the conquering passion will proclaim peace where it has made a solitude. The social aim will be to rule over others, and make them serve you; to give them the least and get the most from them; and then he will be thought the most fortunate man and so the most "respectable" in the community, and "honorable" in the state, who does the least service for mankind, and gets the most pay and the most power from them. Society will be controlled by selfish propensities, not moral ideas, affectional feelings, or religious aspirations for ideal perfection.

See how this principle will work practically in social affairs. Such is the distribution of faculties amongst men that a few persons always control the mass of men. We may deny this because we are Democrats, but it is a fact which everywhere stares us in the face. It is so with gregarious animals: the strong barnyard-fowl is always cock of the walk, and rules the roost just as he will, only as he has but a small margin of individual oscillation, little individual caprice, he rules according to the law of his nature, not the caprice of his will. The actual preponderance of the few men over the many has hitherto prevailed in every form of state government, whether it be called a despotism, an aristocracy, or a republic. Six hundred men, self-appointed almost, meet together in two Conventions at Baltimore, and select two men, and then say to the people,—"One of these is to be your President for four years." And the twenty millions fling up their caps and say which of the two it shall be; and the majority thinks it has made the President. If the conventions had selected two notorious kidnappers,—the Philadelphia kidnapper on one side, and the Boston kidnapper on the other,—one of these would as assuredly be President as either of the actual nominees will be. This, I say, is so at present. It is a fact all over the world, in Republics as well as in Despotisms. The political "democrat" has commonly been also a despot.

But the principle on which atheistic society must needs be founded will be that of mere private selfishness. So all the rulers must of necessity be tyrants, ruling with cruel and selfish aims. Oppression, which is a Measure in the practice of men, must be also a Principle in the theory of the atheist, the accidental actual of human history will then become the substantial ideal of human nature. The most appropriate nomination in that case would be the nomination of the kidnappers. The capitalist wishes to operate by his money; that is his tool to increase his power of selfish enjoyment. The operative wishes to act by his hand and head; these are his tools to increase his power of selfish enjoyment. But both must be thoroughly selfish in principle, and so they will be natural and irreconcilable enemies waging a war for mutual extermination. Accordingly the capitalist will aim to get the operatives' work without giving them his money; and the operatives will aim to get the capitalist's money without giving him their work; and so there will be a perpetual "strike" and warfare between the two, each continually laying at the other with all his might. The harmony of society will be the equilibrium of selfishness; and that will be brought about when the strong has crushed down the weak, has got him under his foot and has destroyed him. Harmony will take place when the last spider has eaten up all his coadjutors. The social peace of atheism is solitude.

In trade the aim will be to accumulate money, — no matter how it is got, by fraud, by lies, by rack-rent on houses, by ruinous usury on land, or less ruinous piracy on the sea. The man will allow nothing to stand between him and the dollar he covets, no intellectual idea, no moral principle, no affectional feeling, no religious emotion. Mr. New England is greedy for money; Mr. South Carolina greedy for slaves. Mr. New England steals men in Africa, or in Massachusetts, and sells them to his brother, Mr. South Carolina, getting great pay. You say to both of these, This is very wrong; it is inhuman, it is wicked. But the atheists say, "What do we know about right and wrong?" "I only know," says Mr. New England, "it brings me money." "I only know it brings me slaves," says Mr. South Carolina. "All we want is money and slaves." You can have nothing further to say to these two gentlemen.

Mr. Salem sends cargoes of rum to Africa, and when it gets there dilutes it with half its bulk of water, drugs it to its old intoxicating power, and then sells it to the black man, who is made just as drunk, and a little more poisoned than if he had the genuine article, the only thing to which New England has characteristically given its name. He sells this to the black man, and sells him also powder and balls to use in capturing his brother men; and when they are caught he "prudently" leaves some other American to take and transport them to market at Rio, or Cuba, with the sanction of the American government. You say to Mr. Salem, This is all wicked. "What do I care for that?" says he. "It brings me very good money, very good honor, the first respectability. You do n't think it's righteousness I am trading for, that I baptize Negroes with poisoned rum for the sake of their 'Salvation!' I leave that matter and the 'Justification of Slavery' to the Christian clergy. It is quite enough for the merchant to make slaves; I leave it to the ministers to prove it is right. You think I am aiming at 'Heaven,' do you? You are very young, Sir!"

But, say you, you are false to your natural obligations to do right, to speak true, to feel kind, and to be holy. "Obligations of that sort!" adds he, "I know no such obligations. This is consciousness without a conscience." At least you must fear the judgment passed against wrong in the next life! — say you, almost driven to your last appeal. "But I know no next life," says he; "here is the present life; I am sure of that." But at least you reverence God? "Not at all," says Mr. Salem, "it is a world without a God!"

If a man starts with such a theory of the universe, and such principles of practice, what can you say to him? Call on that man for heroism when your country is in danger, and he creeps under the oven. Call on him for charity when the country is starving, and he sells bread for a dollar a pound. You can get nothing from him but selfishness. An atheistic community could not build a free School-house, or an Alms-house, or a Hospital, only a Jail. Behold atheism carried into society!

Now, as I said the other day, there is not much acknowledged speculative atheism, — acknowledged to one's self, — but there is a great deal of partial practical atheism, which lets houses at rack-rent, to the ruin of the tenant; which lets money at rack-usury, to the ruin of the borrower; sells rum to the ruin of the buyer; it deals falsely in honorable goods, — there may be as much baseness in the dealing, as danger in the merchandise, — and then with the profits it builds up great houses, which are palaces for selfishness. I look on them as on the rude hovels of the buccaneers of Jamaica and the Caribbees, who went down to the shore of the Spanish main and murdered the crews of the ships they took, and then carried the ships to port and broke them to pieces to build up their own houses from the fragments. You ask these men to forbear from destroying their brothers. You appeal to their humanity, — and they are true to their practical atheism. You appeal to justice, — they know it not; to respect for conscience, — they have none of it; to their consciousness of God, — they recognize no such thing. Tell these men of some absolute right, of their immortal soul, — it is all a dream.

Am I speaking mere fictions? When Boston had kidnapped Thomas Sims, and carried him away, two members of a Christian church in this city, both merchants, met accidentally in its chief business street, and talked the matter over. Both disliked the deed; but one thus justified it, and said, "If we did n't do this we should n't get any more trade from the South, and I remember we have got to live *here*." "So do I," said the other, "remember we have got to live *hereafter*." There were practical atheism and practical religion looking one another in the face. Boston went to the side of practical atheism, as you know, thinking, as her prominent ministers declared, there was no "Higher Law."

There is a great deal of social practical atheism which appears under the guise and with the name of religion. This is the most ghastly, the most deadly kind. It is concealed, — a wolf in sheep's clothing; still a wolf, and his jaws are there under the innocent covering of the lamb. It is Satan transformed "into an angel of light," but still the old devil, spite of usurping the angel's wings. The more consistent atheist will join the church.

Here is an example of that. A man of property in this city dishonestly failed; dishonestly, and yet legally became a bankrupt; paid his creditors sixpence or a shilling on the dollar; and secured to himself considerable property, getting a discharge from all his creditors except one. Afterwards he became rich. The poor man who had refused to compound his debt claimed his due. The rich man did not deny that it was justly due, only declared it was not legally due. There was no redress. At length our defaulting debtor "experienced religion," as they say; — I call it experiencing theology, and very poor theology besides; "experienced religion" at one of the sectarian churches of Boston, — and became what is there called "a religious man;" and came up before a communion table, and professed to commune with God, and Christ, and Man, through the elements of bread and wine. Our poor creditor goes to him again, and says, "Now I hope you will pay me, since you have become a 'religious man' and have joined the church." Quoth the debtor, "Business is business, and religion is religion. Business is for the week and religion for Sunday" — and paid him not a cent. There was social practical atheism in the guise of religion, all the more consistent in that garb.

Sometimes practical atheism gets into the pulpit as well as the pews, and then it is tenfold more deadly; for it poisons the wells of society, and next diffuses the contents abroad as the waters of life. It cries out, "Ho! every one that thirsteth, come up here and be comforted in your sins. Slavery is a Christian Institution." Ask such a man, of that denomination, to preach against any popular wickedness which shakes the steeple over his head, and which jars the great Bible on his pulpit's lid; ask him to preach against wickedness which turns one half his congregation into voluptuaries,— victims of passion,— and the other half into hunkers,— victims of ambition,— and he only cries, "Save us, Good Lord!" Tell him of some noble excellence that is going abroad into society, and is ready to be struck down by the wickedness of the world, and ask him to speak only a word in its favor over the cushions of his pulpit, and he mumbles, "Miserable Offenders! Save us, Good Lord." That is all he can say.

All these practically deny the Higher Law. I am not speaking of momentary errors. You all know I am far more charitable than most men to all errors of that sort. I know myself how easy it is to do wrong; how many depraved things may be done without any depravity in the human heart. But atheism of this sort, disguised or undisguised,— I cannot express the abhorrence and loathing that I feel for the thing. Offences are one thing, but the theory which makes offences— that is the baser thing.

Look about you and see how much there is, however, of practical atheïsm not confessed to itself. The Sadducee comes forward and says, "There is no Angel, nor Resurrection;" and men cry out "Atheist!" "Away with him!" The Pharisee devours widows' houses, and then struts into the temple, drops with brassy ring his shekel into the public chest, and stands before the seven golden candlesticks and prays, "God, I thank thee that I am not as other men are, extortioners, unjust, adulterers, or even as this publican. I fast twice in the week; I give tithes of all that I possess." Men cry out, "This is a Saint! a great Christian!" — and run over the poor widow who is dropping into the alms-box her two mites, all the living that she has, and tread her down. This practical social atheism is the death of all heroism, all manliness, all beauty, all love.

IV. See this practical atheism in the Political Form, in the Nation. The normal motive of national union is the gregarious instinct and the social will, acting in their larger modes of operation, and joining men by mutuality of interest, and mutuality of love. This is the foundation of all real patriotism. Then the union will be for the sake of the universal good of all, and the particular good of each. National institutions, constitutions, and statutes will be the result of a national desire for what is useful to-day, and for what is absolutely true, just, lovely, and holy. There will be a coordination of the particular desire of Thomas and Jane, each seeking his own special good in the action of personal self-love; and of the general desire of the nation seeking the united good of all in the joint action of self-love and of benevolence. All of this let me represent by one word, Justice, a symbol alike of the transient and eternal interests of both all and each. All national statutes will come from the conscience of the nation, which aims to make them so as to conform with the conscience of God, as that is shown in the constitution of the Universe, in the unchanging laws of Human Nature, which represent the Justice and the Love of God. Then every statute will be a part of the intrinsic law of human nature writ out in human speech, and laid down as a rule of conduct for men. Every such statute will be human and conventional in its form, but yet divine and absolute in its substance, as all true science is the divine and absolute Fact of Nature expressed in human speech. Then the reason for obeying the human statutes will be the natural obligation to speak true, do right, feel kind, and be holy; for so far as the statutes of men represent the natural law of God, obedience is moral, and it is obligatory on all to observe them; but beyond this point obedience to those statutes is obligatory on no man, but is immoral, unmanly, and wicked.

But the politics of practical atheism must be based on selfishness. As selfishness obtains in the individual, establishing a personal anarchy of desires; in the family, establishing a domestic anarchy of its members; in the community, establishing a social anarchy in the classes thereof; so it must prevail in the state, establishing a national anarchy in its various parts. Political morality is impossible in the atheistic state; there can be only political economy, which aims to provide merely for the selfishness of men. For by this hypothesis, there is a body without a soul, a here but no hereafter, a world without a God. Men will be consciously held together, in a negative manner, by the mutual and universal repulsion of selfishness, not at all, positively, by the mutual and universal attraction of Justice. All men will be natural enemies, joined by mutual hatred, huddled together by Want and Fear.

Government is a contrivance whereby a few men control the rest. In a democracy, the majority of the people determine what great or little man shall perform this function; or rather they think they determine this, and at least can say who shall not officially attempt this function. In a despotism the majority have not that privilege — but the great or little man himself determines who shall control the nation. In the state of practical atheism, in either case, the government must be one of selfishness — the controlling power seeking the most for itself and the least for the people. So the government will be a tyranny, representing only the selfishness of the ruling power. In all cases the appeal must be to Superior Force — to that as the proximate appeal, to that the ultimate. Now it will be Force of Body, then Force of Cunning. The government may assume various forms, — the controlling power may be a king, a monarchy of selfishness; a few great families, an aristocracy of selfishness; or the majority, a democracy of selfishness: but the substance is still the same, — tyranny and despotism, subjecting the world to monarchic, aristocratic, or democratic force; a rule of the strong over the weak, and against the transient and permanent interests of the weak. To the individual whose natural rights are destroyed, it is of small consequence whether the destroyer is single-headed, several-headed, or many-headed. Political atheism in one, in few, or in many, is still the same.

Special maxims and special aims will vary with special forms of government. Is the controlling power a monarch, he will say, "The king can do no wrong," and above all things will aim to protect the conventional privilege of kings. Is it an aristocracy of long descent, the maxim will be, "Birth before Merit;" "the nobility cannot err." They will make all the power of the people serve to rock the cradle for men of famous line, scorning the common mortal's "puddle-blood." Is it a company of capitalists, the maxim will be "Property, before persons;" "let the State take care of the rich, and they will take care of the people;" "money can do no wrong." They will aim to oppress the poor and make them servants, serfs, or slaves. Is it the mob of proletaries, "Property is theft;" "the majority can do no wrong;" "Minorities have no rights," will be the maxim, and to plunder the rich the aim.

Political atheism is the exploitation of the people,—by the selfishness of the king, the nobles, or the majority; all right must yield to might. There is no moral element in the laws—in making, administering, or obeying them; for atheism itself knows no obligation, no duty, no right, only force and desire. All government is a reign of terror.

In the atheistic state there must be another class. As the formal negation of atheism, and the affirmation of the opposite thereof, is one form of its practical profession, so the Priesthood of Atheism, an atheistic clergy, is philosophically as possible, and historically as real, as the monarchy, the aristocracy, or the democracy of atheism. The clergy will be the ally of the tyrant, the enemy of the oppressed, of the poor, the ignorant, the servant, the serf, the slave. In the name of the Soul which it rejects, of the Hereafter which it denies, of the God whom it derides, the Atheistic Church will declare, "There is no law above the pleasure of King Monarch, or King Many. Obey or be damned." So in the atheistic state the atheistic church will be supple to the master, and hate the slave; will cringe to power, and abhor all which appeals to the Eternal Right; will love empire, and hate piety. Now it will praise royalty, now nobility, now riches, now numbers, claiming always that the actual power holds by divine right; quoting Scripture to show it. This is the most odious form of practical political atheism,—the negation of itself, the affirmation of its opposite; crushing man while it whines out its litany—"Save us, good Lord, miserable offenders."

Hobbes of Malmesbury, was right when he said "Atheism is the best ally of despotism," for it denies the reality of Justice; takes Conscience out of human consciousness, the soul out of the body, Hereafter away from here, and dismisses God from the universe — selfishness the only motive, force the last appeal. That politician was a crafty man who said of religion — "in politics it makes men mad," for it bids them speak true, do right, feel kind, and be holy against the consent of governments when they stand in its way. Alexander at a feast slew Clitus, both drunk with Bacchic wine. One of the flatterers, not drunk but sober, said "It is all right; there is no law above the king!" That was practical political atheism — the sober flatterer exalting a drunken murderer above the eternal God; the exceptional measure of a king, raging with wine and anger, was made a universal principle for all time.

Here in this nation there is much partial practical atheism in the political form. Look at the corruption, the bribery of eminent men, sometimes detected, acknowledged, and vindicated; at the conduct of political parties, no one seeking to govern the nation for the joint good of all the citizens, only for the peculiar good of the party in power; at the tyranny of the majority, striking down the obvious right of the lesser number; at three million men made slaves by the people of America: — what is it all but partial practical atheism? I am glad political men boldly declare the speculative principle which lies at the basis of their practical measures and tell the people, "There is no Natural Law above the statutes which men enact:" no God above King Monarch, or King Many. I am glad they "define their position," all atheistic as it is. Look at the political and clerical defences of the most enormous public wickedness, and you see how deep this practical atheism has gone down into the people, how widely it has spread. But the hope which I have for this nation is built on the Character of God, and on the consciousness of God in the people's heart.

V. You may see how practical atheism must work in the form of General Human Life, the Life of the Human Race taken as a whole. Mankind is a Family of Nations, amenable to the constitution of the universe, and normally to be ruled by the laws of human nature, by Justice, — by the moral obligation to speak true, to do right, feel kind, and be holy. As the members in the body form a harmonious person; as the individuals in a house form a harmonious family; as the families in society form a harmonious community; as the communities in a nation form a harmonious state; so the nations in the earth are to form a harmonious World, with human unity of action for all, with national variety of action for each state, social variety of action for each community, domestic for each family, and individual for each person. Justice is to be the rule of conduct for individual, domestic, social, national, and general human conduct. Thus the ideal of human life in these five forms will be attained and made actual.

But practical atheism makes selfishness, material selfishness, the motive, and material desire the rule of conduct for the nations which make up the world, as for communities which compose the state, or for persons who join in families. So the World of atheism, like its state, society, family, and man, must be only an anarchy of conflicting elements, the strong plundering, enslaving, or killing the weak. The proximate and ultimate appeal will be to force, now force of body, then force of brain.

Here I will not repeat what I have said before in another form; but practical atheism will do on the large scale for the world what it did on the small in the state, community, and home. Each nation will be deemed its own exclusive cause, its own sustainer, director, mind, and providence. "There is no law of God above the nation's will," says the Atheist; "no God above the peoples of the earth. Let us bite and devour one another."

There is much practical atheism of this form in the world. See how Russia oppresses the feebler nations of the East and West. See how this great Anglo-Saxon tribe, with its American and its British head, invades the other feeble nations, — the yellow men in Asia and the islands of the sea, the red men in America, and the black men in Africa. It is only practical atheism which in England justifies her treatment of Ireland, of India, China, Africa, and yet other regions of the world: in America it is only by practical atheism that we can vindicate our treatment of the Mexican and the Spaniard; still more of the red man and the black. Atheism bids the powerful exploiter the weak — now with the sword alone — the heathen way of Rome; now with commerce and the sword — the Christian way of the Anglo-Saxon.

I would gladly say much more that burns in my bosom to be spoken, respecting atheism in its Political and General Human Form, atheism making laws, atheism crushing down the people. I would gladly show how this manifests itself in wicked wars. I could never look on an army invading another country to do it wrong, without asking, "Are the men who send the army abroad atheists before men, as well as before God?" I would gladly speak of this in its Universal Form, — arraying nation against nation, making the strong tread down the weak. But yonder silent finger warns me that I must not trespass too long.

Speculative atheism is a thing human nature revolts at. So of speculative atheists, who have a full consciousness of complete atheism, there are at most but few; I think not one. Practical atheism would be just as impossible, if one could be thoroughly conscious thereof. But without knowing it, there are men who thus act, and move, and live, and have their being, as if there were no God; as if man had no soul; as if there was no special obligation to speak true, to do right, to feel kind, and to be holy. But there are many depraved things done which indicate no depravity in the man— excesses of instinct not yet understood, errors of passion untamed as yet, nay of ambition, not knowing itself. But there are depraved things which come out of conscious and systematic wickedness, — the deliberate frauds of theology and trade, and the confessed wrong in domestic, social, national, and general human life. These are the fruits of practical atheism, though the man knows not what tree it is which bears them.

We see atheism in two forms: One speculative, denying that there is any God. I shudder at that. I see men of large culture attempting to found schools of speculative atheism in this land. My bosom burns with pity and love for those men. Others may throw stones at them; I shall throw none. Abuse enough from every hireling clergyman they will have, and every unreasonable sect; they shall have no abuse from my lips; for I see how the creed and the conduct of the churches of our land, and of the Christian world, have helped drive these men to their speculative atheism. Yet I am bound to warn every man against this; against its beginning, for at first there is something rather attractive in the freedom of thought which it allows. Let us have all that freedom of thought and exercise every faculty of the intellect, and never fear. Little thought stops at Atheism; much thought does not turn out of the way in that direction; or if it do, it comes rounding home, and so returns to God.

But I see practical atheism far more abundant, and far more dangerous; by deeds, men denying there is any God, any soul, any everlasting life, any obligation to speak true, to do right, to feel kind, and to be holy. This is a sad sight.

Speculative Atheism sits down, as I said last Sunday, on the shore of Time, and the stream of Human History runs by, bearing the various civilizations,— Egyptian, East Indian, Chaldean, Grecian, Roman; each seems a bubble, though it contains the birth and life, the groans unheard, the virtue unrewarded, the prayers unanswered, of millions of millions of men. Yet the remorseless stream, which comes from no whence, and goes to no whither, swallows all these down, —love unrequited, heroism not paid, virtue unrewarded.

Practical Atheism does not sit down in this way; it goes out into the storm and tumult of active life, and there it stands, this Cerberus of selfishness, with its three heads;—Lust, which hungers and barks after pleasure; Ambition, that thirsts for fame and power;

and Avarice, which is greedier than all the rest. And this monster of three heads stands there, making havoc of the individual, the family, the community, the church, the nation, and the world.

But, thanks be to Almighty God! not only is the religious element so strong in us, but the moral and affectional are so powerful, the intellectual so mighty, that human nature must stop a great ways this side of complete Atheism. A body without a soul, a here but no hereafter, a history without a plan, an earth without a heaven, a universe but no God — no man can have a realizing sense of it and live. Only let us be warned in season, and freely develop the moral, affectional, and religious faculties, and have their blest reward.

SERMON III.

OF THE POPULAR THEOLOGY, AS THEORY

7

MATTHEW XV. 9.

TEACHING FOR DOCTRINES THE COMMANDMENTS OF MEN.

III.

OF THE POPULAR THEOLOGY OF CHRISTENDOM, REGARDED AS A THEORY OF THE UNIVERSE.

On the last two Sundays I spoke of Atheism. First of Atheism as Philosophy, — a theory of the universe; and next of atheism as Ethics — a principle of practical life. To-day I ask your attention to a sermon of the Popular Theology of Christendom, regarded as Philosophy, a theory of the universe; and next Sunday I hope to speak of it as Ethics, a principle of practice.

From the beginning of human history there has been a progressive development of all the higher faculties of man; of the religious powers, which connect man with God, as well as of the other faculties, which connect man with the material universe and men with one another. There has been a progress in Piety, in Morality, and in the Theories of these two. Of course, then, there has been a progress in the visible results of this development of the religious faculties. The progress appears in the rise, decline, and disappearance of various forms of religion. Each of these has been necessary to the welfare of the human race; for at one time it represented the highest religious development of the persons who embraced that form of religion. Sometimes it was a sect; sometimes a nation; sometimes a great assemblage of nations: but in each case the form of religion which the people accepted represented the highest development of the religious faculties of those people at that time. As the science of a nation represents its intellectual development, so the form of religion shows how far men have got on in their piety and morality. But as each form of religion, when it is once established, is a thing which is fixed and does not change, and as the religious faculties are not fixed, but go on with increasing power from age to age, so it happens that men must necessarily outgrow any specific and imperfect form of religion whatever, just as they outgrow each specific and imperfect form of science. Human nature continually transcends the facts of human history, so new schemes of science, new forms of religion continually crowd off the old.

This work of making a form of religion, and then outgrowing it and making a new one is continually going on. On a small scale it takes place in you and me, who are constantly transcending to-day the form of religion which satisfied us yesterday; it takes place on a large scale in the human race as a whole. Sometimes a man distinctly and suddenly breaks with his form of religion, or no religion, and takes a new one. Sometimes a nation does so. This is called a Conversion of the individual, a Reformation of the nation; in either case it is a Revolution in religion. But in general there is nothing sudden or abrupt about this; the whole change takes place silently and slowly, with no crisis of revolution; but insensibly, little by little, the boy's religion passes away and the man's religion takes its place. A nation improves in its religion as in its agriculture, its manufactures, its commerce, and its modes of travelling; and the improvement is not by a leap, which Nature abhors, but by a gradual sliding upwards, almost insensible. It has been so with the human race.

Two thousand years ago our fathers in the heart of Europe were Pagans. Ten or twelve hundred years ago they put off their Paganism and accepted Papal Christianity. Three hundred years ago they put off Papal Christianity and accepted Protestant Christianity. Each of these obvious changes, from Paganism to Papacy, from Papacy to Protestantism, was sudden and violent, a crisis of revolution. But before that crisis came about, a yet greater change had taken place, silently and slowly, the Pagans getting ready for Papalism, and the Catholic getting ready for Protestantism. That was unobserved. First they grew up to Paganism, then to Papal Christianity, and then to Protestant Christianity. Shall mankind stop at Paganism? at Papal Christianity? at Protestant Christianity? You and I may perversely stop, we may stand still, — at least try to do so; but mankind never stops. The soul of the human race constantly unfolds; it does not pause. Like the stars in their courses without haste and without rest it goes ever on. There is a continual and silent change taking place at this day, and it must for ever take place. It is not possible for the human race to stand still in its religious development; no more than for the matter of the Earth to cease to attract the Moon and be itself attracted thereby.

The leading nations of the Caucasian race have thus far outgrown, first, the savages' rude Fetichistic worship; then classic Heathenism; then patriarchal Deism;

then the Mosaic worship of Jehovah; and now the most enlightened portion thereof have come to what is called "Christianity." That is the form of religion which they have reached to-day. Shall we stop with the present form of religion called "Christianity?" Mankind never surrenders to time. There is a progress in what is called Christianity, a continual change of the thing, though the name abides the same. Protestantism is clearly, on the whole, a step in advance of Catholicism — and Protestantism has advanced very much since the death of Martin Luther. A change is going on at this day within Catholicism and Protestantism.

What is called Christianity embraces three things, namely: first Sentiments, next Ideas, and third Actions. It is chiefly of the Ideas that I shall speak to-day. These Ideas united together I shall call the Popular Theology.

This Popular Theology is not wholly nor in chief the work of Jesus of Nazareth, or of his immediate followers; for, though called by his name, it is no more his production than modern philosophy is the production of Socrates, or modern medicine the production of Galen. What is called Christianity in this sense, — the Popular Theology I mean, — is the result of the religious and philosophical development of mankind up to this day. The development of mankind — in matters pertaining to the sentiment of religion, the idea of religion, the practice of religion, — has gone on a great deal more rapidly since the time of Jesus than before or at his time. The change which is now taking place in the religious world — the change in the sentiments of religion, the ideas of religion, and the actions of religion — is greater by far than the change from Judaism or Heathenism to the Christianity of Paul and Tertullian. I mean to say distinctly that between the Ideas of the foremost religious men of this age and the popular theology of the churches, there is a greater chasm, a wider and deeper gulf, than there was between the ideas of Saint Paul or Tertullian and those of the Jews and Pagans who were around them.

If Jesus of Nazareth were to come back and preach his ideas of theology as he set them forth in Judea, they would not be accepted as Christianity. I think no one of the apostles even would be thought Christian in any church in the world. For, first, there has been a real progress of mankind since their day; and the average preachers have dropped some errors of the apostles, and have got some new truths pertaining to the sentiment, the idea, and the action of religion; and thus there has been a real progress in religious growth.

But then again there has been a change without any progress, as well as a change with progress; and the caprice of individuals of to-day has taken the place of the caprice of the individuals who lived ten, twelve, or eighteen hundred years ago—one error taking the place of another. A change of caprice does not always indicate a progress; but the acceptance of new truths — of sentiment, of idea, and of action,— does represent a real progress.

This progress has been influenced very much by the genius of certain great men, some of them remarkable for feelings of piety, some for ideas of philosophy, some for actions of philanthropy. Jesus of Nazareth has had an immense influence in giving mankind a start in the direction which has been taken since his time. When he declared that love of God and love of Man was the sum of human duty to God and to man, then he made a statement which can never be gainsaid, nor transcended, for in that he came upon the eternal substance of religion. That idea can no more fade out of the religious consciousness of mankind than the multiplication table be dispensed with in Mathematics, the Alpha bet in Literature, or the continent of America fail and be left out of the Geographies which describe the Earth. Jesus of Nazareth appears to have summed up religion in these two things, namely, — in Piety, the love of God; and Morality, the keeping of the laws of God, and especially in keeping the law which commands us to love our brother as ourselves. But that is at the present day thought to be a very small part of Christianity; and it is thought in all the great sects, Catholic or Protestant, to be the least important part thereof.

I do not mean to say that I think Jesus had a complete and analytic comprehension of all which is included in his own words, nor that he did not demand other things inconsistent therewith, only that he made Love to God and Man, the chief thing in his religious teaching. I make a distinction between his theology and his religion. His theology seems to have had many Jewish notions in it, wholly untenable in our day, though commonly accepted by wise men in his. It was in his religion that he surpassed his age.

If any one of the gospels, or if all of them represent his thoughts correctly, then his theology contained a considerable mixture of error, which indeed is obvious to any man who will read those records without prejudice. With those works in our hands it would be absurd to maintain that Jesus entertained no theological error, in matters of importance; that he had all theologic truth; or all the theologic truth known to any or all persons of his own time. From the time of

Moses to Jesus there was a large intellectual and religious development of mankind, a marked progress in the religious sentiments, ideas, and actions of individual men, and of the leading nations of mankind. From the time of Jesus to our time this progress, both in individuals and in nations, has been yet more rapid. Old errors have been cast away, new truths have been added to the consciousness of mankind. The theology of the most eminent Catholics or Protestants at this day represents the thought of Jesus as it appears in the oldest of the four Gospels, no more than a common plough represents the thought of the man who first broke up ground with oxen. No man is so great as mankind. If the great genius at first is so far before his brothers as to be incomprehensible, by and by they overtake him, pass by him, and go still further on till they become incomprehensible to the man who stands where the genius once stood. I know it is thought very wicked to say this in its application to the historical development of religion, as it would be thought very foolish to deny it in its application to the historical development of agriculture, manufactures, or commerce, to any science, to any art. Every great genius for religion will add new facts to the world's experience of religion, just as much since the death of Jesus as before his time. The road is easier after a saint has trod it, and no saint travels the whole length thereof.

Look at the Ideas of Christendom, the doctrines. There is one great scheme of doctrines called "Christian Theology." It contains some things held in common with every other system of theology that has ever been; they are the generic element of the popular theology. Then it contains likewise other things peculiar to itself, which do not belong to any other form of religion; these are the specific element of the popular theology. The first denote the agreement thereof with other schemes of theology, and the next its difference therefrom.

This great scheme of theology is common to all Christendom as a whole, with few individual exceptions. The Christians in general agree in a belief of this common theology, and are thereby distinguished from men of all other modes of religion. The Protestant has departed from the Catholic theology a little, separating therefrom on the question of the authority and functions of the Church — the Protestant affirming the power of the individual as against the power of the great body of Christians. The Unitarian has separated from other Protestants in his doctrine as to the arithmetic of the Godhead, reducing the deity to one denomination, instead of three which the Trinitarians affirm. The Universalist differs from the rest in his doctrine of the final destination of man. But still the great "body of divinity," — the mass of doctrines called "Christian theology," and "Christianity," — has escaped untouched, at least unhurt by Protestants, — Unitarians or Universalists. So Protestants and Catholics, Unitarians and Trinitarians, Universalists and Partialists, agree in the main parts of their theology: they all substantially unite in their idea of God, their idea of Man, and their idea of the Relation between God and Man. The root is the same, the trunk the same, the fruit the same in kind, only the branches are unlike in their form, and direction.

Some of these doctrines, called Christian, were old

at the time of Jesus; some were new at that time: — some of these latter were, doubtless, added by Jesus himself; others by his followers; — a great many have been added since that age, taken either from the transient caprice of men, or from the permanent truths which man has arrived at.

Take an example of the doctrines since formed out of the transient caprice of men, and then regarded as Christian.

First it was declared that the "immaculate conception," the supernatural birth of Jesus, should be a doctrine of the Church. This has become fixed in the Church, and there has been no sect for sixteen hundred years at least, venturing to deny it. All sects, even including the Unitarian and Universalist, affirm the super natural birth of Jesus — that he had no human father; or are supposed to affirm it, stoutly enough denouncing such as doubt or deny it.

Then men went further and affirmed the supernatural birth of Mary, the Mother of Jesus; and, after twelve or thirteen hundred years, that became a doctrine fixed in the Catholic Church which had two "immaculate conceptions." But at the Reformation the Protestant churches rejected this latter doctrine with all their might, staving it off with both hands, thinking it as great an error to believe the supernatural birth of the mother as to doubt that of the son.

Men did not stop there; they went further, and presently declared the supernatural birth of the Mother of Mary to be an essential doctrine, — and they called that mother Anna. That idea is now in the process of fixation; it is getting formulated, — to use a philosophical phrase. That is to say, it has been accepted by a portion of the Catholic Church; and some of the leaders are now insisting that it shall become a fixed doctrine, a point of Catholic theology which all are to believe, or "perish everlastingly."

This process of doctrinization by caprice may go on; there is no reason it should stop here. By and by it may be said that the Grandmother, the Great-grandmother, and the Great-great-grandmother were all born supernaturally; and then in addition to Anna, the fictitious mother of Mary, there may be a Joanna, a Rosanna, a Roxanna, and a Susanna, and each of these declared to have a supernatural birth. It may become a doctrine of some future Church that a man must believe in all the seven "immaculate conceptions," or else "perish everlastingly." Why should Catholics stop with three while the Hindoos have so many? There is no historical evidence that Jesus of Nazareth ever believed himself supernaturally born or his mother supernaturally born; and Anna, the mother of Mary, is a person as purely fictitious as Joanna, and Rosanna, and Roxanna, and Susanna, whom I have just invented. That is one example of the process of forming a doctrine out of caprice and fixing it in the Church; the popular theology contains many more. The Mohammedan theology equally abounds in doctrines derived from caprice. Nay, all the mythologies of the world are full of such fancies; for human nature is the same in Gentile, Jew, and Christian.

Some doctrines of Christian theology are Biblical, and were taught by Jesus; some Biblical and were not taught by him. After the death of Jesus there was a great development of theological doctrines quite foreign to him, as any one may see who will read the book of Revelation, — which has very little religious feeling in it, — or the fourth Gospel, full of religious feeling, each containing a theology widely unlike that which is taught in the words of Jesus in the former three gospels; nay, directly antagonistic thereto. But the greater part of what is called Christian theology is post-Biblical, and would be as strange to Paul and Apollos, as much of their teaching would be foreign to the ear of Jesus. Some of its doctrines at his time lay latent in the mind of the world, and have since become patent, so to say; others have been added anew.

In the popular theology there are comprised some of the greatest truths of religion which man has attained thus far.

There is, for example, the doctrine of the Existence of God, as Creator and Governor of the world, a Being different in kind from matter, and from man.

Next, there is the great doctrine of the Immortality of every man, and the certainty of retribution.

As a third thing, there is the doctrine of the moral Obligation of every man to obey the Law of God.

As a fourth thing, there is the doctrine concerning the Connection between Man and God, whereby man receives from God inspiration, guidance, and blessing.

And as a fifth thing, it is affirmed that there is this Connection between man and man,—a duty on the part of one to love another, of all to love each, and of each to love all.

These are great doctrines, of immense value to mankind.

I am by no means disposed to underrate science, the grand achievements of human thought, which have brought the stars down to the astronomer's mirror, and have brought up to common knowledge the little things which millions of years ago were laid away and embalmed in the unchanging rock. Man has formulated the sky and knows the whereabouts of the stars; has formulated the rock and knows the habits of the little insects which you find in a piece of slate from Berlin, in the chalk of Dover Cliff, in the sands under our feet, or in the slime that skirts our wharves as each receding tide goes out. All these are grand triumphs of human thought. But these five great doctrines which I have spoken of,—the existence of God, the immortality of man, the moral obligation of man to obey the law of God, the connection between man and God, and the connection of love between man and man,—these I think are by far the most important speculative doctrines known to the human intellect.

But the popular theology has very great defects as a scheme of the universe, and it teaches great errors. Fifteen or sixteen hundred years ago Arnobius and Augustine, with other great teachers of Christianity, pointed out the follies of Heathenism in the most bitter polemics. It would be just as easy and just as appropriate in bitter sermons, at this day, to point out the errors of the popular theology of the churches. I wish with no bitterness to expose the error. Bitterness is always out of place in philosophy, in theology, in philanthropy. The Heathens before Christ meant to be right, and as a whole did the best they could; and so the Christians after Christ have meant to be right, and have done the best they could as a whole. Aristotle and Augustine seem to me equally honest, and equally mistaken in many matters. Individuals have purposely gone wrong, but ninety-nine out of a hundred of the men who have taught theology before Jesus or after him, it seems to me, meant to learn the truth and teach the truth. Let us thank all of these for the good they did, and let us do better if we can; hoping that somebody, by and by, will come and do better than we, and will efface our errors, seeing truths clearly which we have but dimly seen, and the truths dimly which we have not seen at all.

I say there are great errors in the popular theology of the Christian churches, regarded as a Theory of the Universe; great errors in the Idea of God; in the Idea of Man, and next in the Idea of the Relation between the two.

I. Look at the Idea of God. In the popular theology God is represented as a finite and imperfect God. It is not said so in words; the contrary is often said; nevertheless it is so. He is actually represented as imperfect in power, imperfect in wisdom, imperfect in justice, in love, and in holiness. It is so represented in facts, or alleged facts, related in the Bible, in the Old and New Testament both. It is so in the Catholic Church and the Protestant Church; with the Unitarian and the Trinitarian, with the Partialist and the Universalist.

In terms, religious writers very rarely speak of God as malignant, but they continually represent Him so in act. I say they rarely speak of God as malignant; now and then a writer does. Some "divines" have distinctly declared that God was malignant; and not long ago, in a sister city of New England, a clergyman preached a sermon to his people with this title: "On the Malevolence of God;" If you study the popular theology as a whole, you will find that it regards God as eminently malignant, though it does not say so in plain words. The Tyrian idolaters, I think, called Baal merciful and beneficent, even when they thought he demanded the sacrifice of their children.

According to the popular theology there are three acknowledged persons in the Godhead.

First, there is "God the Father," the Creator of the universe, and all that is therein; the great Being of the world, made to appear remarkable for three things,—first for great power to will and do; second for great selfishness; and third for great destructiveness. In the popular theology God the Father is the grimmest object in the universe; not loving and not lovely. In the New Testament, in the Gospels of Matthew, Mark, and Luke, there are some dreadful qualities ascribed to God, which belonged to the Hebrew conception of Jehovah: but a great many exceeding kind and beautiful qualities are also assigned to Him;—witness the Parable of the Prodigal Son; witness many things put into the mouth of Jesus. The book of Revelation attributes to the Deity dark and malignant conduct which it is dreadful to think of. But the popular theology in the dreadful qualities assigned to God has gone a great ways beyond the first three Gospels, and the book of Revelation. It has taken the dark things and made them blacker with notions derived from other sources.

Then there is "God the Son," who is the Father in the flesh, but with more humanity in him, and with very much less selfishness and destructiveness than is attributed to the Father. Still in the popular theology the love which the Son bears towards man is always limited: first limited to Believers, and next to the Elect.

It is no doctrine of the popular theology that Christ actually loves transgressors, and as little that God loves them.

Then, thirdly, there is " God the Holy Ghost," the least important person in the Trinity, who continually " spreads undivided and operates unspent," but does not spread far or operate much, and is easily grieved away. The Holy Ghost is not represented as loving wicked men, that is, men who lack conventional faith, or who are deficient in conventional righteousness. No one of these three persons of the Godhead has any love for the souls of the damned.

All this is acknowledged and writ down in the creeds of Catholic and Protestant, and in this they do not differ. A few heretical Unitarians have differed from the main church on the arithmetic of deity, not on the ethics or psychology thereof.

It is commonly said there are only three persons in the Deity. But there is really a fourth person in the popular idea of God, in the Christian theology, to wit, the Devil; for the Devil is really the fourth person of the popular Godhead in the Christian churches, only he is not so named and confessed. The belief in the devil is almost universal in Christendom. It is a New Testament doctrine, and an Old Testament doctrine. Catholic and Protestant, Trinitarian and Unitarian, Partialist and Universalist, agree in this. No Christian sect has ever denied his existence; they cannot whilst they believe in the " Infallibility of the Scriptures." Says a writer of undoubted soundness, who represents the popular theology of the English and American sects, " The devil is the implacable enemy of the human race, and especially of believers, whom he desires to devour." He is represented as absolutely evil, without any good in him. When Origen, sixteen hundred years ago, declared that the devil would be saved in the final redemption, if there were a spark of goodness in him, he was declared a heretic by the churches, and all Christendom rung with accusations against him, because he thought the devil might be saved. It was a heresy in Robert Burns when he said he was loath to think of the pit of darkness even for the devil's sake, and wished he might "take a thought and mend."

Well, now, this absolutely evil Devil, if there were such a being, must have come from God, who is the only Creator; and of course, therefore, is as much a part of God's work and design as the Eternal Son after he was "eternally begotten," or the Eternal Holy Ghost after he had "eternally proceeded;" and the existence of the devil, therefore, is as much a work of God as the existence of the Son or the Holy Ghost; and all the evil of the devil must have originated with God. God, therefore, must have made the devil absolutely evil, because He wanted to make the devil absolutely evil. If the devil were made partially good, with a nature which, under the circumstances he was placed in, would develop into absolute evil — all of that must be so, because God the Father wished it to be so. The devil must be "the implacable enemy of the human race," with this extraordinary appetite for "believers," because God wished him to be so. God therefore is responsible for the devil; and the character of absolute evil, which is in the devil, must have been in God first.

The power assigned to the devil and the influence over men commonly attributed to him, is much greater, since the creation, than that of all the three other Persons put together. And so the devil is really therefore the most effective person of the popular Godhead, only not so confessed. There is no mistake in this reasoning, strange as it may seem. It takes all these four Persons to make up and represent the popular theological notion of God.

Then God as a whole is represented as angry with mankind as a whole. There is, on the one side, an offended God, and on the other an offending human race. God the Father is angry with mankind; God the Son, and God the Holy Ghost are both angry with mankind; and the devil, "the implacable enemy of the human race," as a roaring lion walks about seeking whom he may devour, "especially believers."

But there are a few whom the devil will not be able to devour, who will be saved, whom the Holy Ghost will inspire, whom the Son will ransom and the Father bless. These are only the smallest fraction of mankind, and the devil gets all the rest: so that really, according to the practical teaching of this theology, the devil, the unacknowledged person of the Godhead, is, after all, stronger than God the Father, God the Son, and God the Holy Ghost, all united.

To speak of the deity as a Unit, God is represented as not working by law, that is, by a constant mode of operation — in the most important cases, — but by miracle. So God and the universe are not completely at one, but He acts in it by miracle; that is, by an irregular and capricious mode of operation, reversing its laws; for example, in the Flood, in the storms and earthquakes of the material world, in the creation of woman, the birth of Jesus, the inspiration of the prophets and apostles. All these are theologically represented as results of the spasmodic action of God, now a spasm of wrath, then of love. This theory does not properly belong to that idea of God — original perhaps with the Hebrews — which makes Him independent of matter and transcendent over it. Much better does it cohere with the notion of the classic deists, with whom God and Matter were both eternal and irreconcilable forces, always a little at feud. However the absurd theory has crept in to the Christian theology, where it appears yet more absurd than in the schemes of Socrates and Aristippus.

The authors of the popular theology had no conception of a uniformity of force, no conception of a universal law, whereby God works in the world of matter and of spirit — in short, no conception of the Infinite God. So theologians make two forms of operations in the universe. One is the "work of Nature," by means of law — a constant mode of the operation of a constant force; the other is the "work of Grace," by means of miracles — inconstant modes of the operation of an inconstant force. Wheat grows out of the ground by the law of Nature, and is not thought, in theology, eminently to show the goodness of God; but when Jesus made, as it is said, five loaves feed five thousand men, besides women and children, and leave twelve baskets of broken bread, that is thought a miracle, a revelation of the immense power of God, which shows much more of his goodness than all the wheat that grows from the bosom of the earth, century out and century in, furnishing food for the whole human race! Newton writes the Principia of the Universe; he writes by the "light of Nature" and describes only the "work of Nature," and his masterpiece is considered, theologically, a small thing. St. Jude writes an epistle of twenty-five verses, and it is claimed that he wrote by the "light of miraculous inspiration;" his book is a "work of Grace;" a miracle; and that poor production of Jude is thought to be incomparably greater than the Principia of Newton, with the Mécanique Celeste of La Place thrown in. "Newton and La Place," says this theology, "write by the carnal reason, and their works are fallible; while Jude wrote by miraculous inspiration, and his writings are infallible."

The doctrine concerning Man is no better. Man is represented after this wise: He was so made by God and furnished with such surroundings that as soon as he tried to go alone he "fell from a state of innocence into a state of sin," and has transmitted "original sin" to all his posterity. Men are born with a sinful nature, and if not "totally depraved" they are so nearly so that the fraction of goodness is infinitesimal and not worth estimating. Sin does not consist in sinning, but in being born of Adam after the fall; for his offence wrought an attainder in the soul of all his children, forever. Man of himself, it is said, has no power to find out moral or religious truth, and to secure his own religious or moral welfare. He is naturally wicked and hates God, hates other men, hates truth with his reason, justice with his conscience, love with his affections, holiness with his soul; loves falsehood, injustice, hate, and wickedness, all for their own sake, not as means to an end;—hates God the Father, God the Son, and God the Holy Ghost, and only loves the Devil. In his flesh there dwells no good thing. The natural desires are sinful, and men are first wicked by nature and next also by will. There is none that doeth good, not one. Men are evil and evil continually; their heart is as prone to wickedness as the sparks to fly upward; they are conceived in sin and shapen in iniquity. If they do something that seems good, even their righteousness is as filthy rags.

All things which God made work well except human nature; and that worked so badly that it fell as soon as it was put together. God must start anew, and so he destroys all, except eight persons. But, so bad is human nature, the new family behave no better; they must be cast aside; and God discards all excepting the posterity of a single man. But they turn out as bad as the rest, and must be thrown over. No good comes of human reason, and human nature; so at length "a New Dispensation" is established. But the new dispensation has worked scarcely better than the others. The human race does not turn out as God designed, or expected. It is a failure.

This is taught in every great scheme of theology, Protestant or Catholic.

Note next the doctrine of the Relation between God and Man. God is the sovereign lord, the king of the human race, and is represented as creating and ruling the world not for the world's good, but for his own good or glory. Jesus calls God "THE FATHER," — the favorite name with that great noble heart, — and does not call Him King. In the third Gospel God is the Father who sees his penitent prodigal son a great way off, and goes out to meet him, and falls on his neck and kisses him, and rejoices more over one sinner brought to repentance than over ninety and nine just men. The author of the Epistle ascribed to John, says — "God is Love." It is the bravest word in the whole Bible. But by the popular theology God is King; Catholics and Protestants represent Him as a despotic king. There are three elements, as I just said, conspicuous in his character. The first is Power, — force of hand, force of head; next, Selfishness, — love of his own glory; and third, Destructiveness. Like other kings He cares little for the welfare of his creatures, though He pretends to care much. Men must fear this king; this is the highest thing you can do. You must pray to God only by attorney. Your prayer will make Him alter his mind and change his purpose, if you employ the right attorney in the right way; for though this king is said to be unchangeable, it is thought He will be moved by the poor petitions you and I put up. Divines talk of "constraining prayer," — a prayer that will constrain God to alter his will! The classic mythology represents the ancient Heathen gods as selfish in their ruling propensity; and the popular theology represents God as selfish in his love of power and of glory, and terribly selfish in his wrath. Accordingly, such actions are ascribed to the Deity, in the popular theology, as in almost any country of Christendom would send a man to the gallows. The God of the popular theology is the exploiterer of the human race.

In this theology God is represented as having made and finished a miraculous communication of his will to a small portion of mankind, — the Jews and Christians: that is the "law of God" written in the Bible; the Old Testament is his first word, and the New Testament is his last word. But in fact the two are in many fundamental teachings exactly opposite; yet men are told to believe them exactly alike. A man must believe every word in the Old and New Testament, and keep every command there. Does his reason stand in the way? — "down with reason!" does his conscience, his affection, or his soul stand in the way? — "down with them all!" cries the popular theology, "down with human nature!" The universe is not thought to be the word of God at all, that is "Nature;" and here again the old heathen notion of a discord betwixt God and the world comes up anew. The laws written in this marvellous body; the laws of the understanding, the conscience, the affections, the soul,—they are not thought to be the word of God; they are not imperative, ultimately binding on men. We are to obey only an arbitrary and capricious command.

But man has not kept this command. Men could not keep it; God knew they could not and would not keep it when He made them. Of course He wished to make such a law and such men as are thus unfit for one another—Nature unlawful, and law unnatural. And when men do not keep the law that He told them to keep, and which he had made it impossible for them to keep, straightway He is angry with them, and hates them, and will destroy them in wrath. So He makes the earth bring forth thorns and thistles for the first offenders, and provides eternal torments for the erring sons of men.

This theology declares, Every sin is an infinite evil, because it is a violation of the absolute command of God. In a moment of time you can commit an infinite sin, and if you have once transgressed any commandment of God, even in the smallest particular, you are guilty of violating the whole law of God, and are under the infinite wrath of God; and all you can do, all you can suffer, will not reconcile God to you: He hates you with all his power, all his selfishness, all his destructiveness. But if you do not commit any of these sins, at least you are born of the first sinner, and accordingly were as much hurt by the "fall" as he. But, the theology continues, an atonement has been made, a sacrifice for the sin of the world. God the Father eternally begot God the Son, and sent him into the world, going voluntarily, and had him crucified as a sacrifice for the sin of the world. Thus God the Father is appeased by the sacrifice of God the Son, who has made atonement for men and taken all the sins of men upon himself, and so pacified the infinite wrath of God the Father.

But he did this only for such as would comply with certain doctrinal and liturgical conditions: that is, they must believe certain doctrines which are repugnant to the whole nature of a good and cultivated man; repugnant to his reason, his conscience, his affections, and his soul. Then they must do certain sacramental deeds, which have no connection with practical life; nothing to do with natural piety and natural morality. The belief of these doctrines and the doing of these deeds is called "Christianity," or "religion." It is represented as wholly unnatural and all the more valuable for that reason, for the natural heart is at enmity with God. Thus some men are to be "saved;" such as comply enjoy eternal happiness, the rest "perish everlastingly."

The theoretic and principal design of this theology is not to make better men,—better fathers, husbands, brothers, sons; better mechanics, merchants, farmers,—only to get them "saved;" that is, to insure them a good time in the next world. Morality and its consequent welfare on earth is only incidental to the end of religion. So religion is positively selfish—not for its own sake, but for salvation's sake.

But very few come to that salvation; it is only a few that are saved,—look at the list of mankind,—only the Christians and a few of the eminent Hebrews before Christ, no Hebrew since; and of the Christians, none but the Elect in the Protestant Church, and in the Catholic Church only such as die in its communion. Well, to speak approximately, in round numbers, at this day there are a thousand million men on the earth. Two hundred and fifty millions are "nominal Christians." To take the Protestant view, — of these nominal Christians perhaps one in forty is what might be called a real Christian; that is an ecclesiastical Christian, or actual member of a church with the doctrinal and liturgical qualifications just referred to. That gives us six and a quarter millions of real ecclesiastical Christians. According to the theology of the prevailing Protestant sects, none can be saved unless he is of that company. But this number must be winnowed down still further; for only the Elect are to be saved. What is the ratio of the elect Christians to the non-elect? I do not find it put down in the theological *arithmetic*, and have no means of ascertaining. But all the rest are to be damned to everlasting woe; that is, all men now living who are not Christians, namely, seven hundred and fifty millions; and of the nominal Christians ninety-seven and a half per cent., or two hundred and forty-three millions and a quarter more; and of the real Christians I know not how many; and of men long ago deceased, all the non-elect of the real Christians, all the merely nominal Christians, and all who were not nominal Christians; — so that not more than one out of a hundred thousand men could ever taste of Heaven.

The Catholic doctrine on this point condemns all who are out of the Catholic Church. The distinction sometimes made by tender-hearted and pious Catholics, between the Body of the Church which is visible, and the Soul of the Church which is invisible, is only an individual departure from the doctrinal tradition of the Church itself.

The first Gospel represents the way to Heaven as narrow and strait, and found by few; and the other, the way to Hell, is represented as broad and abundantly travelled. Says the Methodist hymn, which incarnates in a single verse the teaching of the popular theology,

> "Broad is the road that leads to Death,
>   And thousands walk together there;
> But Wisdom shows a narrow path,
>   With here and there a traveller."

Those that are saved are not saved by their character; virtue has no virtue to save your soul. Tell the Catholic priest you expect Heaven for your good works, and your faithfulness to yourself, — he assures you that you are in the bond of iniquity. Tell the Protestant priest the same thing, he is certain you are in the broad way to destruction. You must be saved only by the sufferings of Christ as the divine cause; and by belief in this theology, as the human condition. Piety and Morality, "natural religion," is no condition of salvation; good works are bad things for that. The elect are no better than other men; they are saved by virtue of the Decrees of God, who has mercy on whom He will have mercy, and rejects whom he will, and takes his elect to heaven by a short path through "grace," not over the long, flat, dull road of "works." It is supposed that man has no right towards God, and that God's mode of operation is infinite caprice. Laws of Nature are no finality with their Maker!

The Holy Ghost is represented as going about seeking to inspire men with the will to be saved. He does not come into assemblies of men of science, who are seeking to learn the laws of God. It would be deemed impious to speak of the Holy Ghost as attending the meetings of the French Institute, or the Academy of Arts and Sciences in Boston. He does not come into assemblies of men trying to make the world better off, and men better. It would be deemed blasphemy to speak of the Holy Ghost as attending a meeting for the prevention of pauperism or crime; a peace meeting, a temperance meeting, a meeting against capital punishment, an anti-slavery convention, or a Woman's Rights' meeting. If somebody should say of the Convention that met at Syracuse, day before yesterday, to commemorate the rescue of a fugitive slave out of the hands of the kidnappers, that "the Holy Ghost descended upon it," what would the clergymen say? Why, that would be thought a greater atrocity than even I have ever yet committed. The Holy Ghost is not represented as inspiring philosophers like Leibnitz, Newton, and Kant, or philanthropists like the reformers of old or modern times. He attends camp-meetings, is present at "Revivals," frequents tract societies, and the like. You never saw a picture of the Holy Ghost coming down upon a chemist inventing ether, on Columbus thinking America into life, or on Faustus making a printing-press — it is the Devil that is said to have inspired him, and by no means the Holy Ghost. Oh no, the Holy Ghost is not represented as descending on Franklin, flying a kite into a thundercloud and taking out the lightning with a string, founding academies, and hospitals, and libraries; but he comes down upon monks, and nuns, and ascetics, praying with their lips; not on common laborious men and women praying with their hands. It would be thought impious to paint the "gentle spirit" coming down on a New England school-house, where an intelligent young woman was teaching children the way they should go; or to paint the "Heavenly Dove" fluttering over the head of John Pounds, the British shoemaker, sitting in his narrow shop amid paste-horns and swine's bristles, and bits of leather,

> "His lapstone over his knee,
> Drawing his quarters and sole together,"

whilst teaching the little boys and girls to read and write after he had picked them out of the streets. The Holy Ghost of theology has nothing to do with such things at all; nothing to do with schemes for making the world better, or men better.

Then it is represented that God once inspired men, Hebrews and Christians. Now he inspires no man as of old; he only sends you to a book and the meeting-house. It is thought God inspires nobody now. He has spoken his last word, and made his last will and testament. There can be no progress in Christianity, none out of it. We have got all the religious truth God will ever give us. The fount of inspiration is clean dried up, and God is so far off that the human soul may wander all its mortal life and never come near him. All it gets must be at second-hand.

Such, my friends, is the popular theology as a Theory of the Universe. This is the theology which lies at the basis of all the prevailing sects. I have taken pains not to quote the language of particular sects or particular persons. Let no one be answerable for the common vice. The Universalists have departed widely from this theology in the doctrine of damnation; the Unitarians have departed less widely in the doctrine of the threefold personality of God. But with the mass of theologians God is still represented as finite and malignant; man the veriest wretch in creation, with a depraved nature; the relation between him and God is represented as a selfish rule on God's part, and a slavish fear on man's part;—one man is saved out of a hundred thousand, and ninety-nine thousand nine hundred and ninety-nine are damned to eternal ruin. God exploiters the human race. Man is a worm, and God is represented as a mighty heel to crush him down to hell, not to death but to writhings without end.

This being so, see how the world looks from this theological point of view.

God is not represented as a friend, but the worst foe to men; existence is a curse to all but one out of a hundred thousand; immortality is a curse to ninety-nine thousand nine hundred and ninety-nine out of every hundred thousand on earth; religion a blessing to only ten in a million, to all the rest a torment on earth, and in hell, the bitterest part of the bitter fire which burns everlastingly the immortal flesh and quivering soul.

Is this popular theology a satisfactory Theory of the Universe? Does it correspond to the facts of material Nature, under all men's eyes; the facts of human history, the facts of daily observation? Does this idea of God, of Man, and of their Relation — of God's providence and man's destination — does this agree with the natural sentiments of reverence and trust which spring unbidden in the living heart; with the spontaneous intuitions of the True, the Beautiful, the Good, the Holy; with the results of the highest reflective consciousness? No, it is a theory which does not correspond with facts of material Nature and human history, facts of daily observation; it does not agree with natural sentiments, spontaneous intuitions, or with voluntary reflection! It is a theory without facts, without reason, a theory whose facts are Fancies, and its reason Caprice. It swings in the air at both ends. So it bids us ignore the facts of the outer universe and deny the powers of the inner world; then where it has made a solitude it proclaims a peace, and calls it the Peace of God.

The other Sunday I spoke of Speculative Atheism as a Theory of the Universe. I hope I did no injustice to atheism, or the atheist. But which is the worst, to believe that there is no God who is Mind, Cause, and Providence of this universe, that all comes by a fortuitous concurrence of atoms, the world a chance-shot; or to believe there is a God who is Almighty, yet omnipotently malignant, who consciously aims the forces of the universe at the wretched head of his own child? Which is the worst, to believe that I die wholly, absolutely, irrecoverably, and go down to be a brother to the worm of the dust, or to believe that, immortal, I go to curl and stretch and writhe in tortures forever and ever? Which is the hardest, to believe that your only child, which fades out of your bosom before the rose-bud is fully blown, is no more in all the earth, in all the sky, in all the universe, or that she goes to torment unspeakable, unmitigable, which can have no end when the universe of worlds shall have passed away, and left no wrinkle on the sky that has also grown old and passed out of being? Which, I ask, is the worst, to believe that there is no ear to hear Abel's blood crying against Cain, or to believe that there is an ear which hears it, One who will damn Cain and millions on millions of men, guilty of no sin but birth — the act of God; — will damn all these forever and ever, and then will look down with the Eye which never slumbers nor sleeps, and see the innumerable millions of men, women, and babes, all lie there a mass quivering with torment, which He had inflicted of his own freewill, and made them for the sake of inflicting it, while Himself feels not a twinge of pity, nor lets fall a single tear-drop of love, but rolls all the universe of hell as a sweet morsel under his tongue! Which I say, is the worst— to declare with the atheist "There is no God, all possible ideas thereof lack actuality," or to paint the Cause, the Mind, and Providence of all this world as a hideous Devil — and the universe itself an odious and inexorable hell?

Yet the atheist, I suppose, has been faithful to himself; and the men who have taught these horrid and odious doctrines, I cannot say they have not been faithful. But I must say that as I hate atheism, so I hate this other doctrine, which represents religion as a torment, immortality a curse, and God a fiend.

Atheism, as I said the other Sunday, sits down on the shore of Time, and sees the stream of Humanity pass by. All the civilizations which have enfolded so many millions of men in their arms, seem but frail and brittle bubbles, passing into nought, — virtues unrequited, tears not wiped away, sufferings unrecompensed, and man without hope.

Look again. The Popular Theology sits down on the same spot by the shore of Time, and the great river of Human History sweeps by, fed by a thousand different streams, all mingling their murmurs into one great oceanic harmony of sounds, as it rolls on through Time, passing to Eternity. I go up before Theology and ask, "what is this?" "It is the stream of Human History." "Whence does it come?" "It flows from God." "Where is He?" "There is God! Clouds and thick darkness are about Him. He is a consuming fire, a jealous God, and the breath of his nostrils and the wrath of his heart are poured out against mankind. In His hand is a twoedged sword, and out from His mouth there goes forth fire to wither and destroy." "Where does this stream end?" ask I. "Look!" is the answer; "there is the mouth and terminus of this great stream." On the right Theology points to Jesus, standing there with benignant face,—yet not all benignant, but cruel also; Theology paints the friend of publicans and sinners with malicious pencil, making to the right a little, thin, narrow outlet, which is to admit a mere scantling of the water into a shallow pool, where it shall gleam forever. But on the other hand a whole Amazon pours down to perdition the drainage of a continent, into the bottomless pit, which Hell is moved to meet at its coming, and a mighty devil—the vulture of God's wrath, tormentor and tormented,—sailing on horrid vans, hovers above the whole. And there is the end! No,—not the end, there is the beginning of the eternal torments of the vast mass of the human family—acquaintance and friend, kith and kin, lover and maid, husband and wife, parent and child.

Which—Atheism or Theology—gives us the fairest picture? Atheism, even annihilation of the soul, would be a relief from such a Deity as that; from such an end.

I said the other day there were atheists in America seeking to spread their notions. But for one who denies a deity there are a hundred ministers who preach this other doctrine of a jealous and an angry God; the exploiterer of the race, who will drive down the majority of men to perdition, and go on his way rejoicing! The few atheists will do harm with their theory of the universe; but not a hundredth part of the harm which must be done by this view of God, and Man, and the Relation between the two. Atheism is taught in the name of philosophy, in the name of Man; this theology is taught in the name of religion, in the name of God. I said I should throw no stones at atheists; that I felt pity for them. I shall throw none at theologians, who teach that religion is a torment, immortality a curse, and God a devil. I pity them; they did not mean to go astray. Mankind is honest. Most of the men who teach the dreadful doctrines of atheism, and of the popular theology are alike honest. Lucretius and Augustine, d'Holbach and Calvin, I think, were all sincere men, and honest men — and perhaps equally went astray.

Do men really believe these doctrines which they teach? The fool hath said in his heart, "There is no God!" and I can believe the fool thinks so when he says it. Yes, if the fool should say what the theologian has said, — "God is a devil, Man is a worm, hell is his everlasting home; immortality the greatest curse to all but ten men in a million," I should believe the fool thought it. But does any sober man really believe all this of God, and Man, and the Relation between them? He may say so, but I see not how any man can really believe it, and have a realizing sense of this theology, and still live. Even the men who wrote this odious doctrine, — the Basils and Gregories and Augustines of old time, the Edwardses and Hopkinses of the last generation, and the Emmonses of this day,—they did not believe it, they could not believe it. The atheist thinks that he thinks there is no God, and theologians think that they think religion is a torment, immortality a curse, and God a devil. But, God be thanked, Nature cries out against this odious doctrine, that man is a worm, that religion is a torment, immortality a curse, and God a fiend.

From behind this dark and thundering cloud of the popular theology, how beautifully comes forth the calm, clear light of natural human religion, revealing to us God as the Infinite Father, as the Infinite Mother of all, perfectly powerful, perfectly wise, perfectly just and loving, and perfectly holy too! Then how beautiful is the Universe! It is the great Bible of God;—Material Nature is the Old Testament, millions of years old, spangled with truths under our feet, sparkling with glories over our head; and Human Nature, is the New Testament from the Infinite God, every day revealing a new page as Time turns over the leaf. Immortality stands waiting to give a recompense for every virtue not rewarded, for every tear not wiped away, for every sorrow unrecompensed, for every prayer, for each pure intention of the heart. And over the whole,—Old Testament and New Testament, Mortality and Immortality,—the Infinite Loving-Kindness of God the Father, comes brooding down as a bird over her nest; aye, taking us to His own infinite arms and blessing us with Himself.

Look up at the stars, study the mathematics of the heavens writ in those gorgeous diagrams of fire, where all is law, order, harmony, beauty without end; look down on the ant-hill in the fields some morning in early summer, and study the ethics of the emmets, all law, order, harmony, beauty without end; look round on the cattle, on the birds, on the cold fishes in the stream, the reptiles, insects, and see the mathematics of their structure, and the ethics of their lives; do you find any sign that the First Person of the Godhead is malignant and capricious, and the Fourth Person thereof is a devil; that Hate preponderates in the world? Look back over the whole course of human history; you see war and violence it is true, but the higher powers of man gaining continually on the animal appetites at every step, the race getting fairer, wiser, juster, more affectionate, more faithful unto justice, love, and all their laws; look in you, and study the instinctive emotions of your own nature, and in some high hour of self-excitement when you are most yourself, ask if there can be such a horrid God as the popular theology so blackly paints, making his human world from such a selfish motive, of such a base material, and for such a purpose, — to rot its fiery immortality in hell?

Is this dreadful theology to continue? The days of its foul doctrines are numbered. The natural instincts of man are against it; the facts of history are against it; every advance of science makes this theology appear the more ghastly and odious. It is in a process of dissolution and must die. The popular theology,

"Mouldering with the dull earth's mouldering sod,
  Inwrapt tenfold in slothful shame,
Lies there exiled from eternal God,
  Lost to her place and name;
And death and life she hateth equally,
  And nothing sees for her despair,

But dreadful Time, dreadful Eternity.
No comfort anywhere;
Remaining utterly confused with fears,
And ever worse with growing time,
And ever unrelieved by dismal tears,
And all alone in crime
Shut up as in a crumbling tomb, girt round
With blackness as a solid wall,
Far off she seems to hear the dully sound
Of human footsteps fall;
As in strange lands a traveller walking slow,
In doubt and great perplexity,
A little before moon-rise hears the low
Moan of an unknown sea,
And knows not if it be thunder, or a sound
Of stones thrown down, or one deep cry
Of great wild beasts; then thinketh, 'I have found
A new land, but I die!'"

SERMON IV.

OF THE POPULAR THEOLOGY AS ETHICS.

MATTHEW VII. 19.

A CORRUPT TREE BRINGETH FORTH EVIL FRUIT.

IV.

OF THE POPULAR THEOLOGY OF CHRISTENDOM, REGARDED AS A PRINCIPLE OF ETHICS.

LAST Sunday I spoke of the popular Christian Theology, as a Theory of the Universe. To-day I ask your attention to a sermon of this Theology, regarded as a Principle of Ethics; that is to say, of the practical effects thereof when the Idea shall become a Fact. I am not now to speak of the practical effects of the Christian Religion; that is to say, of Piety and Morality: I am to speak of something very different; namely, of the Popular Theology, with its false idea of God, its false idea of Man, and its false idea of the relation between the two.

I shall not speak of this theology, with these three false ideas, as a fraud, but as a mistake. The worst doctrines thereof, which make man a worm, religion a curse, immortality a torment, and God a devil, I take it, once represented the honest thought of honest men, or what they thought was their thought. John Calvin was an honest man; Augustine and St. Thomas were honest men; Edwards and Hopkins and Emmons, — they were all honest men. The greatest may easily be mistaken, especially if they throw away their reason when they start. The Hebrew theology, the Greek and Roman theology, the Mahometan theology, — all these are the productions of honest men, who meant to be right and not wrong. So the errors of alchemy, in the Middle Ages, of astrology, — they also were the mistakes of honest men.

This theology — very much miscalled Christian — has been made a practical principle of Christendom for many hundred years. It is set up as Religion; for though religion and theology are as different from one another as breathing is different from the theory of breath, or as slumber is different from the philosophy of sleep, yet it is taught that this theology is religion, is Christianity, and that without this there can be no adequate piety and morality, no sufficient belief in God, and no happiness in the next life. This theology declares, "There is no stopping betwixt me and blank atheism."

Since religion is represented as thus unnatural and unreasonable, there are many who "sign off" from conscious religion altogether: they reject it, and will have nothing to do with it. It seems to war with their reason, with their conscience, their affections, their soul; and so far as possible, they reject it. They mean to be true to their noblest faculties in doing so. The popular theology, with its idea of God and Man, and of their Relation, is the philosophy of unreason, of folly. How can you ask men of large reason, large conscience, large affections, large love for the good God, to believe any one of the numerous schemes of the Trinity, the Miracles of the New or Old Testament; to believe in the existence of a Devil whom God has made, seeking to devour mankind? How can you ask such men to believe in the existence of an angry God, jealous, capricious, selfish, and revengeful, who has made an immeasurable hell under his feet, wherein he designs to crowd down ninety-nine thousand nine hundred and ninety-nine out of every hundred thousand of his children? Will you ask Humbolt, the greatest of living philosophers, to believe that a wafer is "the body of God," as the Catholics say? or Mr. Comte, to believe that the Bible is "the word of God," as the Protestants say? Will you ask a man of great genius, of great culture, to lay his whole nature in the dust, and submit to some little man, with no genius, who only reads to him a catechism which was dreamed by some celibate monks in the dark ages of human history? You cannot expect such men to assent to that: as well might you ask the whole solar system to revolve about the smallest satellite that belongs to the planet Saturn.

A methodist minister explained the success of his sect by saying, "We preach religion without philosophy." That is to say, religion without reason; resting on the authority of the priest who preaches it. An eminent Unitarian minister says, "We also must preach religion without philosophy." That is, religion without reason, resting on the authority of the minister. What is the effect of it? Men who have philosophy, who have reason, will shun your Unitarian and Methodist churches, and keep to their reason and philosophy; and they will have as little of such "religion" as possible. Will you ask a philanthropic woman to believe that "God hates sinners," and will abandon his own children to the eternal torments of the devil, when the philanthropist would not leave the devil's children to their infernal father's care, but lay down her own life to save them? Shall mortal men believe in a God meaner and less humane than they themselves?

See the effect of this theology. The new literature of our time, the new science of our time, the new philanthropy of our time, have no relation to the popular theology, except that of hate and of warfare. There is a very sad negation and denial of religion in the popular literature. Religion is seldom appealed to in the Houses of Parliament, in Old England or New England. It does not appear as a conscious motive force in any of the great actions of the age, in the great philanthropies, the great philosophies and literatures, in the great commerce. In the most popular writers of England, France, Germany, religion does not appear at all as an acknowledged motive. The ideal Brothers Cheeryble of Mr. Dickens, the actual philanthropists of Europe and America, are God's men, but not the Church's Christians. All the real piety which appears in the works and words of Jesus of Nazareth, all the real philanthropy, is bottomed on something exceedingly different from the popular theology.

The immortality of the soul is represented as a curse; and, accordingly, that immortality is denied by many philosophical and good men. From the damnation of theological immortality they flee away for relief to sheer annihilation; — and it is a good exchange which they make; for if the popular theology were true, then immortality would be the greatest curse which the Almighty God could inflict on mankind; and the whole human race ought to go up in a mass before the Father, and say, "Annihilate us all at once, and make an end of your slow, everlasting, butchery of human souls!"

There is but one denomination of hell, and in respect to this there is no difference between the Catholics and the Protestants — only one quite modern sect of the latter formally and utterly rejecting it. With that exception the modern Christian Church is unitary on the ghastly doctrine of eternal damnation, and it makes small odds whether I quote from Aquinas, Quenstedt, or Edwards. It is a favorite doctrine with the Catholic and Protestant clergy.

According to the popular theology the Elect are very well satisfied with hell as the portion for their neighbors. Listen to Jonathan Edwards, who is commonly reckoned one of the ablest intellectual men New England ever bore in her bosom; a self-denying and good man, a man who would have laid down his life for his brother, if his brother had needed the sacrifice. Hear what he says, following Calvin, Aquinas, and Augustine: "The destruction of the unfruitful" (and the unfruitful are those not elected to eternal bliss) "is of use to give the saints a greater sense of their own happiness and of God's grace to them." The damned "shall be tormented in the presence of the holy angels, and in the presence of the Lamb. So they will be tormented in the presence also of the glorified saints. Hereby the saints will be made the more sensible how great their salvation is. When they shall see how great the misery is from which God hath saved them, and how great a difference He hath made between their state and the state of others, who were by nature and perhaps for a time by practice, no more sinful and ill-deserving than any, it will give them a greater sense of the wonderfulness of God's grace to them. Every time they look upon the damned it will excite in them a lively and admiring sense of the grace of God in making them so to differ." "The view of the misery of the damned will double the ardor of the love and gratitude of the saints in Heaven;" "will make them prize his favor and love vastly the more, and they will be so much the more happy in the enjoyment of it."

A good man on earth cannot eat his dinner, if a hungry dog looks in his face, without giving him a bone, surely the crumbs that fall from his table; but the elect of Mr. Edwards, chosen out of God's Universe, are to whet their appetite with the groans of the damned. What shall we think of the Ethics which makes a Christian Minister anticipate new joy in heaven from looking down upon the torment of his former neighbors and friends, nay, of his own children,—and whetting his appetite for Heaven with the smoke of their torment steaming up from hell! But such is the doctrine of the popular theology of New England and of Old England, and all Christendom. The idea is sufficiently scriptural, and has long been claimed as a "doctrine of revelation." Everybody who denies it from Adamantine Origen of Alexandria to Hosea Ballou in Boston, gets a bad name in the churches. The idea of eternal damnation is the Goliath of the Church. Now I say annihilation is a relief from that form of "everlasting life;" and that is the cause why many men deny the immortality of the soul.

Then God is represented as a tyrant; an omnipotence of selfishness, with a mode of action which is wholly inconsistent with the facts of Nature and the laws of the human mind. Of all the grim conceptions of

Deity which men have ever formed, from Tyrian Melkarth to Scandinavian Loke, I know none more grim and abominable than the conception of God set forth by some of the ablest writers of the Catholic and Protestant Church. It revolts the dearest instincts of human nature.

Accordingly some men deny the existence of God. They not only deny the actuality of the popular theological idea of God, but of all possible ideas of God. There is much excuse for the speculative atheist in his denial.

The popular theological idea of God is not adequate to the purposes of science. God is not represented as really omnipresent, a constant and perpetual power, but as present eminently in one spot called Heaven. A modern Doctor of Divinity declares in an address, well studied, and delivered before scholarly men, that we are not to suppose that God is in all places as he is in some one special place. Accordingly his action is to be regarded as irregular and spasmodic. This doctrine, though seldom plainly put, though often denied in terms, lies deep in the popular theology—which knows no God immanent in the Universe and yet transcendent thereof. It is the Bible doctrine, Catholic and Protestant.

Science knows no limited and local God; it tells us of a power immanent and uniform;

> "As full as perfect in a hair as heart."

So then Science rejects the theological idea of God as not being adequate for scientific purposes.

Then as Theology tells you of a God who loves one and rejects nine hundred and ninety-nine out of the thousand, modern Philanthropy rejects that idea of God, as inadequate to its purpose. Science rejects it because he is impotent; Philanthropy rejects it because he is malignant.

The popular idea of God does lack actuality. It is a conceivable nothing; but impossible, and involving as much contradiction as the notion of a cubical sphere, or of a thing which is and is not at the same time. The atheist is right in denying the existence of an angry and jealous God, who makes ninety-nine thousand nine hundred and ninety-nine for ruin, and only one for bliss. The "atheism" of Comte and Feuerbach, is higher and better than the theological idea of God, as represented by Jonathan Edwards, the great champion of New England divinity. But Edwards only painted full length, and in colors, what Augustine and Aquinas and other great theological artists had faintly sketched, with paler tints, shrinking back a little from the gorgon head they dimly drew.

Now as this theology gives us such an unjust and unnatural idea of God, of Man, and of the Relation between the two, there has followed, as an unavoidable consequence of this, a great denial of religion all over Christendom; a denial of the religious nature of man, of the immortality of the soul, and of the existence of God. The great priests are technical Christians everywhere; the great philosophers and the great philanthropists are not technical Christians anywhere. I mean to say the Church does not recognize them as belonging to its bosom; — and they do not belong to the Church's bosom. What is more — the sincerity of the great priests in their professions of theological belief, is popularly doubted just in proportion to the intellect and education of the priest; while nobody doubts that the denial of the philosopher is sincere and honest. Out of the priesthood the great minds reject the popular theology; many of them I fear reject all theology. Of all the greatest minds of the Germanic race, Humboldt, Von-Buch, Oken, Oersted, Vogt, not one of them is technically a Christian. The great Germanic minds not long ago deceased — Kant, Fichte, Hegel, Göthe, Schiller, and the rest were any thing but "professing Christians;" not one of them could accept the theology of the Church which baptized him. The leaders of the new French literature, — Comte, the Communists, and George Sand, and several popular writers — they are atheistic: I mean speculatively atheistic. I fear that the leaders of English literature are not at all better, only in the English there is a greater amount of national reserve; they do not speak right out, as the French or Germans. The later works of the greatest mind of England at this day, have no religiousness in them, according to the common sense of the word, and he has been led even to go far towards absolute denial of all religion.

In England there is a social aristocracy composed of rich or well-descended men, well instructed also in their intellect; they seem almost entirely destitute of conscious religion; they have no theology which satisfies their intellectual and religious need. Some of them turn round, and follow the dim candle of tradition leading them back to mediæval, or even ante-Christian darkness. Some positively deny the truths of religion which come to consciousness in every age, — mediæval or ante-Christian. The most hopeful it is who feel their way along by the natural instincts of the soul — feeling after God if haply they may find him who lives and moves and has his being in them, as they theirs in him. Near the other extreme of society there is a large body of hardy, able, thinking men who treat the popular theology with well-deserved scoff and scorn; but yet they see no clear light.

On the Eastern Continent, in addition to those classes there is another, — the army of learned men, whose doubts are yet deeper than the English, and their denial less compromising and more public. Since the breaking up of Paganism in Europe, there has never been such a period of distrust, of anarchy, and of chaos in religion.

Is it any better in America? Here the ablest men are so busy in the race for money or for rank, men are so uniformly "up for California," or "up for office," that there seems to be little thought in that quarter directed to theological or religious matters. Among these men compliance with popular opinion and popular forms, I suppose often means the same in America in our time, as in Rome in the days of Cicero.

Newton and Leibnitz two hundred years ago were the tallest heads in Europe; they were the leaders also in the theology of Europe, and a strong consciousness of God pervades all the writings of those mighty men. But the minds that at this day take the place of the Newtons and Leibnitzes of the last age, are silent on the matter, or else mock it to scorn. I do not know a single great philosopher in all Christendom who is, in the technical sense of the churches, a "Christian," or who would wish to be. Of course these men have the elements of religion, — love of justice, love of truth, love of men, and of faithfulness to their own souls; but they do not often make it shape these elements into conscious religion, and seem to have little conscious trust in God.

This theology has led to a great amount of real rejection of religion by men who wish to be faithful to their nature in all its parts. It is of no use to say they are bad men. They are not bad men: they lead the science, and philanthropies of the world; and I am afraid that the average speculative "atheist," as he calls himself, is at this day better than the average speculative "Christians," as they call themselves. The atheist has abandoned religion because it is painted in such a form that it seems worse than atheism. The Church taught him his denial, and it ought to baptize him, and not blaspheme him. I think Calvin and Edwards have driven more men from religion than all the speculative "atheists" have ever done from Pomponatius to Feuerbach.

Then there are bad men who reject religion, reject it in their badness. The popular theology is no terror to the wicked man. The corrupt politician of England, America, Germany, France, the extortioner, the kidnapper, — they pretend to accept this theology, they "join the Church," bring the minister over to their side, and do not fear a single fagot in the great hell of theology. They may laugh at the theological devil, they can beat him at his own weapons. The baron of the Middle Ages living for the flesh, and against the better instincts of his soul, kept clear of the Church till death knocked at his door, then all at once compounded for sin, appeased the clergy, and paid off the old score. The modern freebooters pay as they go. It is the cheaper way. What does the American slave-holder care for the devil, for hell, or for the God of Christian theology? He gets ministers enough to baptize slaveholding, and prove it is "only the application of the golden rule to life." "Christianity" is not a terror to evil doers, but it is a terror to good doers; for at least the American churches launch their feeble thunders in the defence of every popular wickedness.

Now see the effect of this theology on such as accept it.

Note first its effect on the Feelings. Religion is not thought a welcome thing, a thing that is to be loved for its own sake. Men do not love to speak of it; it is a subject almost wholly banished from "good society." It is sad, grim, melancholy; it is not love, it is fear; almost wholly fear. If you take the theological idea of God, you cannot love Him, — I defy anybody to love Jonathan Edwards's or John Calvin's conception of the Deity: you can only fear him as the great jailor and hangman and tormentor of the universe, the divine exploiterer of the race. His world is represented as a great inquisition — the torture-chamber holding in its hideous embrace all but ten in the million! Ask the children brought up in families who believe much in this theology, if they ever liked religion: ask the grown men. Look in the faces of the severe sects who take this theology to heart, and what sad, joyless faces they are. Read the publications of the American Tract Society, read the New England Primer, the popular books treating of religion and circulated in all Catholic countries, and you see that this religion is fear, and not joy. Men hold their breath when it thunders lest God should hear them breathe, and lay at them with his lightning. I once heard an eminent Trinitarian minister preach in this city that it was wholly impossible for God to love any man except just so far as that man believed all the doctrines of the Bible and the New England Primer, and kept every commandment in both of these books. So, then, there could only be a very few millions of the whole world that God cared any thing about. All the rest he would damn; and they would get hell-fire, but no pity from angel, God, or devil. No Abraham would give Dives a drop of water from his finger's tip. Could you love such a God? I should hate him; not as I should dislike a tyrant like Cesar Borgia, or even as I should loathe a New England kidnapper, but as I should hate a devil.

God is represented as selfish and only selfish, and selfish continually. He has the power to bless men, and prefers to curse them. Religion is represented as selfishness, only carried out to all eternity,—and such selfishness, too, as none but pirates and kidnappers ever practise on earth. "Aha," say the blessed Catholics of Aquinas, "Aha," say the elect Puritans of Edwards, as they look on the torture of their brethren, "Let God be praised for the torment of the wicked; so religion bids!"

This crow of fear flies round all the churches of Christendom. Men tremble at death; they are afraid of hell. Read the *Dies Irae* of the Catholic Church, the "Judgment Hymns" of the Protestants, or still worse hear them sung by some full-voiced choir to appropriate music, and you understand what lies at the bottom of the ecclesiastical service. Attend a funeral in one of the stricter sects,—the funeral of the best man you can find, but one who was not a "church-member;"—and how cheerless, how hopeless, how comfortless! You would think that the door which led to the street where the last and loved remains of the friend, husband, father, were to be borne out, opened into the bottomless pit. Men talk of death, and say it is a dreadful thing to come into the presence of the Living God! Are we not always in Thy presence, O Living Father? Are not these flowers thy gift? and when I also blossom out of the body, and the husks of the flesh drop away, is it a dreadful thing to come into thy presence, O Living God; to be taken to the arms of the Mother who bore me?

I once knew a boy of early development in religion, dry-nursed at school, against his father's command, on the New England Primer, and he was filled with ghastly fear of the God represented in that Primer, and the hell thereof, and the devil therein, and he used to sob himself to sleep with the prayer, "O God! I beg that I may not be damned!" until at last, before eight years old, driven to desperation by that fear, he made way with that Primer, and with its grim God, and Hell, and Devil, and found rest for his soul in the spontaneous teachings of the religious sentiment which sprung up in his heart. There are many who have been tortured by it all their lives long, and who have not sobbed themselves to sleep after fourscore years of torment.

You may divide the feelings into two classes: one that seeks a finite object, — father, mother, child, brother, sister, aunt, friend; the other which seeks the infinite Object, the Father and Mother of all. This theology is poison and blight and mildew to both of these classes of feelings. It makes the trembling mother afraid that she shall love her child too well; so the desire of the finite object is balked of its satisfaction. She cannot love the God painted to her in the dark theology of our day — and so the infinite hunger of the soul is yet unstilled.

Note its effect on the Intellect. It debases the mind. Quoth Protestant theology, "Reason is carnal: you must accept the Scriptures as the word of God, the Old Testament as His first word, and the New Testament as His last word; therein God has spoken once for all; you can get nothing further from Him. You must prostrate your mind to the Bible; you must believe it all."

The Roman Church is the great idol of the Catholics: it is infallible. The Pope is the Church in little; he is infallible, and is God, so far as doctrine is concerned. With the Protestants the Bible stands in just the same place; it is God to the Protestant theology, to all intents and purposes, so far as doctrine is concerned.

This theology stands in the way of physical science. Here is the scheme of the Universe which belongs to the popular theology: There is an expanse called the earth with its hills and valleys, rivers, lakes, and seas; next below it, there are the waters which are under the earth; then above it is the firmament, beneath which are the sun, the moon, and the stars, and above it the waters which are over the earth; the sun, moon, and stars move round the earth. This rude notion has long stood in the way of science; it wrung from Alphonso of Castile the exclamation, "If God had asked my advice at the creation, the world would have been more simple and better arranged." Galileo must subscribe to this scheme of the universe, or be burned at the stake. The Jesuits who edited Newton's Principia declare that his theory is contrary to theology — and they publish his mathematical demonstrations of the revolutions of the earth only as a "hypothesis," as a theory not a fact.

The popular theology meets the Geologists at every turn, and denies the most obvious phenomena of sense, and the strictest conclusions of science. An eminent theologian, a professor in the most liberal theological school in America once said: "I can believe that God created all the geological strata of the Earth, with their fossil remains, all at once, just as they are to-day, much easier than I can believe the popular theology is mistaken in its account of the creation in six days!" Geology must give way to Genesis!

It stands in the way of history. This is the theological scheme of human history: About six thousand years ago God created one man, and out of one of his ribs formed one woman. The human race is descended from that pair. About fifteen hundred years later He destroyed by a flood all their descendants except a single family from which all the men now on earth have descended. God chose one family out of all the rest, made a bargain with them, revealed himself to them, and not to others, and loved them while he hated the rest, and protected his chosen by constant miracles, giving Abraham a son miraculously born, then miraculously commanding the father to offer him as a bloody sacrifice; and at last God himself becomes a man, born miraculously, and lives a human life on earth, is put to death, and thence returns to life and divinity once more. Theology sharply opposes every discovery, every fact, and every thought which is at variance with these assumptions. It demands belief therein as the condition of religion and of acceptance with God.

See how this theology affects the Conscience. If

you wish to know what is right, for the standard of ultimate appeal, the theologian sends you to the Bible, — full of blessed things, but no master; it contains the opinions of forty or fifty different men, the greater part of them living from four to ten hundred years before Jesus, and belonging to a people we should now call half-civilized. For example, if you ask, Is it right for the community to kill a man who has slain one of his neighbors, when the community have caught and put him in a jail, and can keep him there all his life, shut from doing harm? — the theologian sends you to the Bible, and tells you that once, (nobody knows when,) somebody, (nobody knows who,) in some place, (nobody knows where,) said, "Whoso sheddeth man's blood, by man shall his blood be shed!" — and therefore to the end of time you shall hang every murderer.

You ask, Is it right to catch a dark-colored man, and make him your slave for life and pay him nothing for his services? and Theology answers, "Yes, for Abraham did so, even with white men, and every thing that Abraham did of course was right;" and next, "Paul sent back a man who had fled from bondage," — only he was not black, but white; and thirdly, — and this is the great argument of all, — "Ham, the son of Noah laughed at his father when he was drunk, and when Noah rose up from his debauch he cursed the son of Ham, saying, 'Cursed be Canaan! a servant of servants shall he be unto his brethren!' and therefore the whites are right in enslaving the blacks." This is the theological argument.

I ask, Must I obey the law statute of men, when it offends my conscience? "Yes," says Theology, "for when Nero was emperor of Rome a poor sailmaker said, 'The powers that be are ordained of God,' and 'whosoever resisteth the power resisteth the ordinance of God.'" The fact that Paul's noble life was a manly resistance to tyrants, and a brave obedience to God, is not taken into the account.

This theology leads men to disregard the natural laws of both body and spirit, in order to keep an arbitrary command. So it underrates the natural morality and natural piety. Men keep the Ten Commandments: therein they do well; but they forget that every faculty of the body, every faculty of the spirit — of the mind, the conscience, the heart, and the soul, — has also its commandments, just as imperative as though they had been thundered forth by the voice of the Most High, amidst the clouds of Sinai. The popular theology denies this.

See the effect of this theology on Practical Life. Religion is largely separated from daily work and daily charity. It has a place for itself, the meeting-house; a time for itself, Sunday or the hour of prayer. It is not thought that "saving religion" has any thing important to do in the chaisemaker's yard, in the tailor's shop, or on the farm of the husbandman, in the counting-room of the merchant, or the banking-house of the capitalist. Religion consists, first, in belief; next in sacraments, — ritual work, attending meeting by passive bodily presence, baptism, prayer in words, and communion, as it is called, by bread and wine. Religion is for eternity; its function is to get souls "saved," "redeemed;" — saved from an angry God, redeemed from eternal torment; not saved from a mean and selfish and wicked life, not saved from this cowardly and boyish fear of death, — by no means that.

A practical philanthropist who picks drunkards out of the mire, gets them washed and clothed and restored to their right mind, once visited a poor widow in a cold winter day. She had no wood to burn, no means to get it. A clergyman was trying to console her; "Have faith in Christ," said he, "He will help you!" Quoth the practical man, "It is not faith in Christ she lacks, she has as much of that as you or I, it is wood she stands in need of. Her faith will not save her, with the thermometer at zero. Do you think the Saviour will come and tip her up two feet of wood at her door? No such thing! She has got faith, but wants fire-wood." The missionary went his way, there was no more that he could do, the practical man had the wood there in an hour!

The Unitarians and Universalists have less of the popular theology than the other sects. I have heard Orthodox men confess the fact that these heretics were the best neighbors, the best friends, the most honest business men, eminent in charity, and all good works; and I believe the praise was pretty just: but, they said, "they are the worst Christians in the world, and all their goodness is good for nothing, except in this life, and God does not value their works a straw; at the last day He will pass by every Universalist and Unitarian in the world, with all their philanthropy, to save some Orthodox deacon who never went out of his way to do a kind deed."

Hence it comes to pass that men who are eminent for theological piety are not to be trusted. Their theology makes them attend to beliefs, rituals, and sacraments, but there it ends. Mr. Screw has the devoutest belief in the popular theology, never fails of a sacrament, never cherishes a doubt. His morning and evening are fringed with a form of prayer, but he will devour a widow's house the next moment, and say grace after the meal. An Arabian proverb says, "A man who has been a pilgrimage to Mecca is not to be trusted again." Men that have much of this theology, and its "piety," generally have a bad name in business. A business man told me he always wanted more indorsement on a note from a long-faced man, eminent *in theology*, than from a common citizen who met him in the street. "Strict Christians" are said to be worse in these matters than other men; I mean more covetous, more sly, more grasping, less to be relied upon. The severe sects are austere in their theology, loose in business; strict in sacrament, lax in charity; instant in prayer, not seasonable in humane works. If you want self-denial to spread abroad the doctrines of their sect, there are no men so ready to make such a sacrifice. The efforts which have been made in the stricter American Churches to carry what they call the Gospel — but which is only their theology — to Heathen lands, are of immense value to the men who have made the sacrifice; whether the Heathen are thereby profited I will not say. But for works in morality, in philanthropy, in charity, these sects are not first and foremost. Of self-denial for a theological purpose they have the manliest abundance, but of self-denial for humanity the meanest lack.

The present position of the clergy is to be attributed to the character of their theology. There are at this day about twenty-eight thousand Protestant clergymen in the United States, and about a thousand Catholic priests. Almost all of them come from the middle class in society, — the class most remarkable for industry, enterprise, charity, morality, and piety, — in a word, for religion. They have the most costly culture of any class in the nation: the professional education of the clergymen has cost the public more than the professional culture of all the lawyers; or all the doctors, or all the merchants and men of science and literature in the country; for most of these latter men pay for their education as they go, or at any rate their fathers pay for it, but a large special outlay is made by public charity, for the education of the minister, — very properly made too. Nine tenths of these, I believe, who accept this calling, come to it from a love of it, from a desire to serve God in it; not from selfishness, but with the expectation of self-denial. Surely at this day there is little from without to attract a man to so thankless a calling, for their average pay does not equal that of a fireman on a railroad. They count it the holiest and most arduous office in the world. But yet, starting from that class, with that education, the costliest in the land, and with such noble motives, — how very little do they bring to pass, in promoting sentiments of love to God and men; how little in diffusing ideas of truth and justice, or in any noble action in any practical department of life! They do exceedingly little for any one of the three. Many of these men stand in the way of the human race, and while mankind is painfully toiling up hill they block the wheels forward and not hindward.

This is not wholly the fault of these men. They are earnest and self-denying, and mean to be faithful, most of them. But it is the bad theology they start with which hinders them, — their false idea of God, of Man, and of Religion, — the Relation between God and Man.

They are working with bad tools, — dull theology, dull sermons. Once a clam shell was the best cutting instrument which the human race had used or discovered. Then it was received with thankfulness of heart. But if a man in these times should go out into the fields to cut grass or corn with a clam shell, how do you think his day's work would compare with that of a man who mowed with scythes, or reaped with sickles or with shears moved by horses cut down his acre in an hour? Verily the fields are white for harvest, the laborers many, but with the clam shell for sickle, they tread down more with their feet than they bind up with arms!

The clergymen cannot defend their theology. Attacks have long ago been made against the philosophical part of it, and they have never been repelled; against the historical part of it, and there is no satisfactory answer thereto. The Unitarians have attacked the divinity of Jesus, the Universalists the eternity of hell, and the assaults have not been philosophically met. There is a breach in the theologic wall, not filled up save with denunciations, which are but straws that a breath blows off, or which rot of their own accord.

Within a few years most serious attacks have been made on the "Inspiration of the Scriptures." Its physics are shown to be false science, its metaphysics false philosophy, its history often mistaken. In England, Mr. Hennell denies the divine origin of Christianity, and writes a labored book to prove that it came as other forms of religion have come, — the best thought of noble men. In Germany, Mr. Strauss, with a troop of scholars before and behind him, denies the accuracy of the history of the New Testament; denies the divine birth of Jesus, his miracles, his ascension, his resurrection — they are what one of the latest writers of the New Testament calls "old wives' fables;" Mr. Newman tells of "the Soul, her sorrows and her aspirations," and shows the "Phases of Faith" which a devout and truthful spirit passes through in the journey after religion, exposing the dreadful famine in the churches, and showing that much of the popular theology is a mere show-bread which it is not possible for a man to feed on. No man shows that Newman is mistaken, none refutes Strauss, no man answers Hennell. Books enough are written it is true: "Lives of Jesus," "Defences of Miracles," "Evidences of Christianity," — to prove that some men wrote some books with such miraculous helps from God that they could make no mistakes, but yet the mistakes are there in the books; — "Voices of the Church," "Eclipses of Faith," and the like, and denunciations "Against Freethinking," without stint. Now and then a feeble charge is repelled, a weak position of the assailant is reconquered, but still the theologians are continually beaten and driven back before the well served artillery of thought.

Church-membership is thought a needful condition of salvation: without that a man is not a Christian in full, and is not sure of any thing good hereafter. But very few join the Church. Of the twenty-three millions of America, there are not three and a half million members of the Protestant Church, not one hundred and thirty to a minister; — a little more than three million Protestant church-members, a little more than three million slaves also. Singular statistics! so many church-members, so many slaves! There were never so many voters with so small a proportion of church-members; never so small a proportionate sprinkling of baptism in the face of the community; never so little taking of the sacraments of the Church.

Ecclesiastical interests do not thrive. Compare the interest men feel in a bank, in a manufacturing company, in a lyceum, with what they take in a Church. And yet the minister tells them that the bank, the lyceum, and the manufactory are only for to-day and tomorrow — for the body while the Church is for the soul, and forever!

What is the reason of this lack of interest? Even clergymen themselves partake of the general dulness, and do not study vigorously as the doctors and men of science; do not plead for the souls of men, as the lawyer for their money; do not toil as the merchant or mechanic for his gain. Ministers do not study the science of their calling as the physician, the engineer, the manufacturer of cloth or leather, the geologist, the watchmaker, studies the science of his calling. Even the almanac-maker is a philosopher; the clergyman, — how seldom does he show any tinge of analogous culture?

In practical affairs the American clergy have but little good influence on public morals and manners; an influence not at all in proportion to the number, the education, the character, the position, and the motives of these men.

Politicians declare there is no law higher than an Act of Congress, which makes it felony to give a cup of cold water to a man fleeing from bondage. What do the clergymen say? "The powers that be are ordained of God, and whoso resisteth the powers that be, resisteth the ordinance of God." "Religion is an excellent thing," says the politician, "for every thing but politics: there it makes men mad." The minister does not say, "I am not mad, most noble Festus, but speak forth the words of soberness and truth:" — not at all. Felix trembled before Paul preaching; now Paul in the pulpit, preaching, trembles before Felix in the pew, slumbering. The statesman says, "Religion must not be applied to politics: there let us be practical atheists." The minister says, "I will not apply religion to politics. Be practical atheists there. I will not disturb you. My Kingdom is not of this world."

Traders apply to business the same principle which the politician applies to the State, and say, "Religion is an excellent thing everywhere but in business: there it makes men mad. The 'golden rule' is the last one that the merchant ought to have in his desk; it is wholly unknown to the official 'sealer of weights and measures.' Let us not apply religion to business." The clergymen answer, "Let us not apply religion to business. Here let us be practical atheists together. The golden rule is for the pulpit desk; for Sunday, not for the counting-house and the merchant's shop. Religion is to get the soul saved, not to prevent the extortion of the usurer, or the tyranny of the oppressor. Business is business, religion is religion."

Different traders make particular application of this rule to their several specialities. The liquor dealer says, "Religion is an excellent thing everywhere but in the rum trade: there it makes men mad. Let us never apply it to the sale of intoxicating drink." The clergyman says, "Let it be so." The dealer in human flesh declares, "Religion is a most excellent thing in all matters except slave-trading: there it makes men mad. Let us not apply religion to the 'patriarchal institution.'" The clergyman answers, "Slavery is of God. Abraham was a slave-holder; Christ Jesus says nothing against the worst evils of Grecian or of Roman slavery, — not a word against buying slaves, breeding slaves, selling slaves, beating slaves, or putting them to death. It is plain that he approved of the institution, and designed that it should be perpetual. The great Apostle to the Gentiles sent back a runaway slave, thus executing the fugitive slave act of those times, and giving an example to Christians 'to fulfil all righteousness.' It is only 'natural religion' which forbids slavery, the heathenism of pagan Seneca and Modestinus. Christians are not in a state of Nature, but of Grace. One of 'the advantages of a revelation' is this — the kidnapper may keep his bondmen forever. Mr. Jefferson said all men are created equal, and endowed by their Creator with certain natural and unalienable Rights, amongst others with the Right to Life, Liberty, and the Pursuit of Happiness. He was an infidel, stumbling by the light of Nature; but we have a more excellent way, and hold slaves by divine revelation which transcends the light of Nature. Let us not destroy slavery by 'natural religion,' but preserve it by 'Christianity.' It is a good thing to have as many slaves as church-members!"

At this day the popular preaching does very little to correct the great popular sins of the people. It does more to encourage them. Here are the vices of the leading class of men in their period of calculation after the period of passion has passed by — covetousness of money, ambition for political and social rank. Both of these are unscrupulous in their modes of action. Does the body of clergymen do any thing to correct this evil, — corruption in trade, corruption in politics? Far more I think to encourage each of these leading vices of the age.

America invades the other nations. The pulpit never stands in front of the cannon. Who preached against the Mexican War? How many ministers, think you, in the twenty-eight thousand Protestant pulpits? Who will preach against the present national lust for land? Extortioners levy their usury to the ruin of the borrower, — the pulpit does not say a word against it. Politicians declare that the great object of government is the protection of property, — the pulpit knows no higher object for government; "take care of the rich and they will take care of the poor." Intemperance floods the cities, fills the Almshouse and the Jail, — the pulpit says but little: thank God, in humble places it does say something, though the metropolitan pulpit commonly "hangs out" for Rum. Licentiousness mows down the beauty of the girl, and prostitutes the manly dignity of the man, — but the pulpit is silent as the house of death. It has forgotten the book of Proverbs. The kidnapper comes to Boston, New York, Philadelphia, to seize our fellow-worshippers, — and most of the churches are on his side. In this city, a man fleeing from slavery, seized by ruffians and confined in our illegal jail, brought into most imminent peril, sends round his petition to the churches for their prayer; the churches are dumb; eloquent ministers come out and defend the stealing of men. The American pulpit is powerless against sin: it is a dumb dog that cannot bark at the wolf. The great Rabbis of the popular theology are on the side of every popular sin. What Roman augur ever opposed a Roman wickedness?

All over the world woman is in a state of subjection to man, almost everywhere counted inferior to him, a tool for his convenience, created only because it was "not good for him to be alone;" throughout Christendom deprived of the ecclesiastical, political, and academic rights or privileges of men, and consequently oppressed by the strong arm. What has the Christian Church to say?

Do not blame the minister too much. He is the victim of his theological circumstances, and is commonly a great deal better than his creed. He is wiser than he dares to preach. His theology tells him that religion is not for the earth but for Heaven; not to make the world better, but insurance on souls, to get them saved from an angry God. What he calls "means of Grace" are not a diligent use of all out faculties of body and mind, each in its normal mode of activity; but the vicarious sufferings of Jesus of Nazareth are the Divine Cause, and a belief in the popular theology is the Human Condition; all our "righteousnesses are as filthy rags," and shelter no man from the wrath of God and the flames of hell. It tells him that the function of the minister is not to promote piety and morality, but first, to intercede with an offended God for the sake of an offending people; next, to administer the sacrament of baptism, — to sprinkle a little water on the face of a baby, — and of the Christian communion, — to give some men a morsel of bread to eat and a drop of wine to drink in the meeting-house; and next to expound the Scriptures according to the standard of his sect. That is the ecclesiastic theological function of a minister, whereby he is "to save souls;" this he thinks is "to preach Christ and Him crucified." So the churches are not chiefly institutions of religion, to teach piety and morality; but institutions of theology, and are controlled not by the blameless religion of Jesus, but by Theology and Mammon. In small country towns where the people are ruled by the clergy, the churches are mainly controlled by Theology; and in large wealthy towns, where another class of men bears sway, they are controlled chiefly by Mammon. The Church sitting on her cockatrice's eggs in the one case, hatches mainly churchlings, and in the other chiefly wordlings.

So the churches are no defence against political tyranny: they are on its side; in old England, New England, France, Germany, Russia, all through Christendom, the churches side with despotic power. They are no protection against practical atheism: if the statesmen say, "There is no Higher Law," the leading clergy answer "Very true! there is none." They are no defence against covetousness: the great ecclesiastical teachers of Christendom are its allies. All the popular vices are sure to have the churches on their side.

None of the great ideas of the times originate with the clergy and the Church: new thought is not generated there. Theology keeps

> "Hawking at geology and schism,"

and hates new ideas. None of the great sentiments of devotion to God are cradled there: Theology mumbles its ritual, and scoffs at the light of Christian sentiment. None of the great philanthropies begin there: Theology is getting men saved from future torment, and kills philanthropy. The temperance movement, the peace movement, the education movement, the anti-slavery movement, the great movement for the elevation of woman, the philanthropy which would heal the criminal, cure the sick, teach the deaf, dumb, blind, and the fool, — all these are foreign to the Church and the clergy, to the popular theology which underlies both.

You know the qualities most valued in a man called

Christian, in all the sects of the sectarian churches:— belief in all the doctrines of his sect; a devout attendance on all the forms thereof; a sad countenance;— much talk on theological matters; the reading of theological books. That makes up what is called "Christianity." Do you think that Jesus would recognize such things as "the essentials of religion" in one of his followers?

How would you judge of the health of a man who proceeded in that way; a man who was thick with the doctors, who was always puddering with medicine, and reading medical treatises, and everlastingly in a fuss about his head, or his heart, or his stomach,—his digestion, or his circulation? Would you think that was a proof that he was sound and healthy? The doctors might say he was a very good patient, but a very silly man.

A celebrated clergyman of America once preached a funeral sermon on a distinguished statesman then lately deceased. The minister claimed the politician as an exemplary follower of Christ, "He had full faith in the leading doctrines of the Gospel." What do you think they were? Jesus of Nazareth would be a little amazed to hear: "the sinfulness of man; the divinity of Christ; the necessity of his atonement; need of being born again, and that his own personal hope of salvation depended on the promises and grace of Christ, and that he now wished to throw himself upon it as a practical and blessed remedy." That was what a Doctor of Divinity took for proof that a famous American statesman, almost eighty years old, was a Christian! He did not ask for piety, not for morality, only for a belief in these doctrines of the popular theology.

If Jesus of Nazareth were to come back, and bear

the same relation to the nineteenth century which he bore so blessedly to the first, it seems to me that the first thing he would preach against is what is called "Christianity" in these days; — I mean the Theology of Christendom.

This theology is the greatest evil of our times. It stands in the way of the emancipation of man. It defends the despotism of the Church, and the despotism of the State, the despotism of the noble over the proletary in Europe, of the master over the slave in America, of the capitalist over the laborer, of the rich over the poor, of the learned over the ignorant, and last of all, the despotism of man over woman. It is a lion in the path of humankind.

This theology rests on two great pillars as its foundation, the Jachin and Boaz of theology.

I. The notion that God is finite in his wisdom, justice, love, and holiness — only infinite in power to damn; that He is a jealous, angry, and revengeful God, with eternal hell behind him, wherein he will torture forever the vast majority of his children, and that Man is wicked by nature, subject to the wrath of God, and utterly incapable, by his own efforts, of escaping from it.

II. The notion that Christ has made an atonement for the sin of the world, and by his sufferings and death has mitigated the anger of the Jealous God who has given a conditional pardon of sin and promise of salvation, and that the condition of this Salvation is a belief in the popular theology, — which is commonly called Faith, "faith in Christ," and "faith in God," — and a compliance with the ritual of the Church.

This Theology makes man a worm; religion a torment to all but ten in a million; immortality a curse to mankind; God a devil omnipotent to damn, and his rule in time and eternity the most selfish despotism which the world ever knew.

This Theology is not always to last: it is in the process of dissolution — there is dry-rot in its limbs. Philosophy shows there is no such dreadful God; criticism that there is no such atoning sacrifice to appease imaginary wrath, no need of such belief, or of such compliance; consciousness knows no such human nature as the popular theology proclaims. No, we are all conscious of a nature quite different from that. Yea, O Father in Heaven, thou hast written of Thyself on the walls of human consciousness, and we feel Thee in our heart, with all thy Infinite Wisdom, Justice, Love, and Holiness.

This dark theology must pass away.

It is at this day in the same condition that Judaism and Paganism were in Paul's time. Then the great priests were Pagans or Jews; the great philosophers, the great philanthropists, were neither Jew nor Pagan. Now the great priests are theological Christians, the great philosophers far otherwise. The new bud is crowding off the old leaf. The great hearts have no confidence in this theology; the great heads have no confidence in it; the great hands have no confidence in it. The social aristocracy of England seems false to religion. A writer, one of the learnedest men in Europe, himself really religious, declares that since the breaking up of Paganism there has never been such a decline of religion in Europe as at this day. Another not at all bigoted declares that in England the foremost classes of the people, — men of birth and riches, — have no regard for religion. The laboring men whose daily toil hardly fills their mouths and satisfies their hunger, — they also have small confidence in it. The intellectual aristocracy of France and Germany have mainly turned their faces not only against this theology, but against conscious religion itself.

Well, how much of religion is there in America? Ask the twenty-eight thousand ministers: ask the three million, three hundred thousand church-members that question: then let the three million, three hundred thousand slaves give answer to the question. "The dark places of the earth are full of the habitations of cruelty;" the American pulpit knows it, and defends the cruelty and the darkness of the dark places of the earth. Ask the politician who says there is no Higher Law for the State; ask the trader who says there is no Higher Law for business, and who wishes to sign off from religion, each in his peculiar vocation, — ask them what respect there is for religion in America!

You and I, my friends, live in an age when mankind has outgrown the popular theology. God be thanked! we have outgrown its idea of God, its idea of Man, and its idea of Religion. Hence comes the confusion of the times; hence the denial of religion in politics, in trade. We live in an age of transition. The old theology will pass away; depend upon it, it will pass away. Philosophers have destroyed its philosophical basis, critics have destroyed its historical basis, and it swings in the air at both ends. That must pass away.

But Religion, — that will not fade out of the human heart: sooner shall yonder sun, which those clouds only hide, fade out of heaven. No! with every advance of man religion shines brighter and brighter, leading onward to its perfect day. Out of this chaos of theology, how beautifully comes up the manly and mild and trusting face of Jesus of Nazareth! Far off, severed from us by two thousand years of time, and five thousand miles of space, we see him with his beatitudes, his parable of the Good Samaritan, of the Father who went after his prodigal son, having more joy in his heaven over the one sinner that repented than over the ninety and nine that never went astray. How beautifully comes up that young Nazarene, proclaiming the one religion, — love to the Father, and love to the Son — to Man here on the earth, for mankind is the Son of God!

Coming out of the popular theology, I feel as one who has wandered long in some dark, subterranean, mammoth cave, where the sound of running water was thunderous and sad, — lit by uncertain torches, led by wandering guides, where lifeless stones grinned as horrible monsters at him, and he hesitated and stumbled at every step, — where the air was contaminated by the smoke of the torches, and his steps faltered and his heart sank. I feel as one coming out into the glad light of day, where the sky is blue over me, and the sun sheds down its golden light, and the ground is green with grass, and is beautiful with summer or with autumn flowers, fragrant to every sense.

God be thanked that we leave the cavern behind us, with its smoky lights, its paths that lead to wandering; that God's heaven is over us and his ground is under our feet, his eternity before us, and his Spirit in our spirit.

"Oh ye, who pined in dungeons for the sake
　Of Truth which tyrants shadowed with their hate,
Whose only crime was that ye were awake
　Too soon, or that your brethren slept too late;
　Mountainous minds, upon whose top the great

Sunrise of knowledge came, long e'er its glance
Fell on the foggy swamps of fear and ignorance;

"The time shall come when from your heights serene,
Beyond the grave, ye will look back and smile,
To see the plains of earth all growing green,
Where Science, Art, and Love repeat Heaven's style,
And with God's beauty fill the desert isle,
'Till Eden blooms where martyr-fires have burned,
And to the Lord of life all hearts and minds are turned.

"The seeds are planted, and the spring is near;
Ages of blight are but a fleeting frost:
Truth circles into Truth. Each mote is dear
To God, no drop of Ocean is e'er lost,
No leaf forever dry and tempest-tost.
Life centres deathless underneath Decay,
And no true Word or Deed can ever pass away."

SERMON V.

OF THEISM AS THEORY.

MATTHEW X. 29.

ARE NOT TWO SPARROWS SOLD FOR A FARTHING? AND ONE OF THEM SHALL NOT FALL ON THE GROUND WITHOUT YOUR FATHER.

V.

OF SPECULATIVE THEISM, REGARDED AS A THEORY OF THE UNIVERSE.

On the last four Sundays I spoke of Atheism, regarded first as a Theory of the Universe, and then as a Principle of Ethics; next of the popular Christian Theology, also regarded first as a Theory of the Universe, and then as a Principle of Ethics. I have spoken of each, as metaphysics and as ethics; as theory first, and then as practice. Both subjects were painful to touch, yet needing to be handled at this day. It is never pleasant to point out and expose a false theory of philosophy, or a false system of practice, and I am glad I have passed by that for the present. A good man hates to kill any thing, — even snakes and hyænas.

I now come to a theme much more pleasant: namely, the Philosophical Idea of God. So I ask your attention to a Sermon of Speculative Theism, considered as a Theory of the Universe; and next Sunday I hope to speak of Theism considered as a Principle of Practice. If what I have to say this morning be somewhat abstract and metaphysical, and closely joined together, and rather hard to follow, I beg you will remember that this dryness belongs to the nature of the subject, which I shall treat as well as I can, and as plain as I may.

I use the word Theism, first, as distinguished from Atheism; that is, from the absolute denial of all possible ideas of God. Second, as distinguished from the Popular Theology, which indeed affirms God, but ascribes to Him a finite character, and makes Him a ferocious God. And third, as distinguished from Deism, which affirms a God without the ferocious character of the popular theology, but still starts from the sensational philosophy, abuts in materialism, derives its idea of God solely by induction from the phenomena of material nature, or of human history, leaving out of sight the intuition of human nature; and so gets its idea of God solely from external observation, and not at all from consciousness, and thus accordingly, represents God as finite and imperfect. I use the word as distinguished from Atheism, the denial of God; from the Popular Theology, which affirms a finite ferocious God; and from Deism, which affirms a finite God without ferocity. So much for the definition of terms.

Some of you may perhaps remember the introductory sermon of last year's course, treating of the Infinite Perfection of God. In that discourse I started from human nature, from the facts of consciousness in your heart and in my heart, assuming only the fidelity of the human faculties, their power to ascertain truth in religious matters, as in philosophical and mathematical matters; and I showed, or think I showed, that those faculties of human nature — the intellectual, the moral, the affectional, and the simply religious — in their joint and normal exercise, led to the idea of God as a Being infinitely powerful, infinitely wise, infinitely just, infinitely loving, and infinitely holy, that is, faithful to Himself.

To-day I start with that conclusion as a fact. I shall not undertake to prove the actuality of this idea,—the existence of the infinite God; I shall take it for granted. I did not undertake to prove the existence of a God against Atheism; nor the non-existence of the ferocious God against the Popular Theology. At this stage of proceeding I shall assume the existence of the Infinite God, relying for proof on what has been said so often before, and still more, on what is felt in your consciousness, without my saying any thing. Only for clearness of conception, let me state some of the most important matters connected with the idea of God.

I. There must be many qualities of God not at all known to men, some of them not at all knowable by us; because we have not the faculties to know them by. Man's consciousness of God, and God's consciousness of himself must differ immeasurably. God's ideas of himself must differ as much from our idea of him, as the constellation called the Great Bear differs from one of the beasts in the public den at Berne. For no man can ever have an exhaustive conception of God,—one I mean which uses up and comprises the whole of God. We have scarcely an exhaustive conception of any thing. Certain properties and forces of things we know; the substance of things is almost, if not quite beyond our ken. But we may have such an idea of God as though incomplete, is perfectly true, and comprises no quality which is not also a quality of God. Then our idea of God is true as far as it goes, only it does not describe the whole of God. To illustrate this, — a thimble cannot contain all the water in the Atlantic Ocean at once, but it may be brimful of water from the Atlantic Ocean; and it may contain nothing but water from the Atlantic Ocean. So our idea of God, though not containing the whole of him, may yet comprise no quality which is not a quality of God, and may omit none which it is needful for our welfare, that we should know. In the self-consciousness of God subject and object are the same, and he must know all his own Infinite Nature. But in our consciousness of God the limitations of the finite subject make it impossible that we should comprehend God as he is conscious of himself. It is enough for us to know of the Infinite what is knowable to finite man.

With qualities not knowable to us I have nothing to do. I shall not undertake to discuss the psychology and metaphysics of God. The metaphysics of man are quite hard enough for me to grapple with and understand.

II. Then as a next thing, God must be different in kind from what I call the Universe; that is from Nature, the world of Matter, and from Spirit, the world of Man. They are finite, He infinite; they dependent, He self-subsisting; they variable, He unchanging. God must include both, matter and spirit.

There are two classes of philosophers often called Atheists; but better, and perhaps justly, called Pantheists.

One of these says, " there are only material things in existence," resolving all into matter; " The sum-total of these material things is God." That is material Pantheism. If I mistake not, M. Comte of Paris, and the anonymous author of the " Vestiges of the Natural

History of Creation," with their numerous coadjutors, belong to that class.

The other class admits the existence of spirit, sometimes resolves every thing into spirit, and says, "the sum total of finite spirit, that is God." These are spiritual Pantheists. Several of the German philosophers, if I understand them, are of that stamp.

One difficulty with both of these classes is this: Their idea of God is only the idea of the world of Nature and of Spirit, as it is to-day; and as the world of Nature and of Spirit will be fairer and wiser a thousand years hence than it is now, so, according to them, God will be fairer and wiser a thousand years hence than he is now. Thus they give you a variable God, who learns by experience, and who grows with the growth and strengthens with the strength of the universe itself. According to them, when there was no vegetation in the world of matter, God knew nothing of a plant; no more than the stones on the earth. When the animal came, when man came, God was wiser, and He advances with the advance of man When Jesus came, He was a better God; He was a wiser God, after Newton and La Place; and was more a philosophical Being, after those pantheistic philosophers had taught him the way to be so: for their God knows nothing until it is either a fact of observation in finite Nature — in the material world, — or else a fact of consciousness in finite Spirit — in some man; He knows nothing till it is shown Him. That is a fatal error with Hegel and his followers in England and America.

Mr. Babbage, a most ingenious Englishman, invented a calculating engine. He builded wiser than he knew; for by and by he found that his engine calculated conclusions which had never entered into the thought of Mr. Babbage himself. The mathematical engine out-ciphered its inventor. And these men represent God as being in just that predicament: the world is constantly revealing things unknown before, and which God had not conceived of. As there is a Progressive Development of the powers of the Universe as a whole, and of each man, so there is a Progressive Development of God. He is therefore not so much a Being, as a Becoming.

This idea of an Improvable and Progressive Deity is not wholly a new thing. The doctrine was obscurely held by some of the ancient philosophers in the time of Plato.

If God be Infinite, then he must be immanent, perfectly and totally present, in Nature and in Spirit. Thus there is no point of space, no atom of matter, but God is there; no point of spirit, and no atom of soul, but God is there. And yet finite matter and finite spirit do not exhaust God. He transcends the world of matter and of spirit; and in virtue of that transcendence continually makes the world of matter fairer, and the world of spirit wiser. So there is really a progress in the Manifestation of God, not a progress in God the manifesting. In thought you may annihilate the world of matter and of man; but you do not thereby in thought annihilate the infinite God, or subtract any thing from the Existence of God. In thought you may double the world of matter and of man; but in so doing you do not in thought double the Being of the Infinite God; that remains the same as before.

That is what I mean when I say that God is infinite and transcends matter and spirit, and is different in kind from the finite universe. This is the great point in which I differ most widely from those philosophers. I find no fault with them; I differ from their conclusion.

III. As a third thing, the Infinite God must have all the Qualities of a perfect and complete Being; must be complete in the qualities of a perfect being, perfect in the qualities of a complete one. To state that by analysis which I have just stated by synthesis: He must have the perfection of Being, self-existence; the perfection of Power, almightiness; the perfection of Mind, all-knowingness; the perfection of Conscience, all-righteousness; of Affection, all-lovingness; of Soul, all-holiness, perfect self-fidelity. Hence, as the result of all these: He must have the perfection of Will, absolute freedom. I mean to say, according to this idea of God, there must be no limitation to his existence, his power, his wisdom, his justice, his love, his holiness, and his freedom; none from any outward cause, or any inward cause whatsoever. The classic, or Greek and Roman Idea of God, represented him as finite, limited subjectively by elements of his own character, objectively limited by the elements of the material world; the popular theological idea in fact represents him as finite, limited subjectively by selfishness, wrath, and various evil passions, objectively by elements in the world of men which continually prove refractory, and turn out as he did not intend. In this matter of the Infinity of God, I differ from the popular theology, as well as from the common scheme of philosophy.

So much for the Idea of God considered as Infinite; so much for its diversity from the common schemes.

Now look at this philosophical Theism, with its Idea

of the Infinite God, as a Theory of the Universe. Let me divide the universe into two great parts. One I will call the World of Matter, and the other the World of Spirit. By the world of matter I mean every thing, except the Deity, known to us that is not man; and by the world of spirit I mean what is man, — both man in his material substance, and in his spiritual substance. Let me say a word of each. For shortness' sake, I will call the world of matter Nature. I begin with this, as it is the least difficult.

In Nature God must be both a perfect Cause, and a perfect Providence.

I. Of God as perfect Cause. Creation itself, the non-existent coming into existence, is something unintelligible to us. But this we know, that the Infinite God must be a perfect Creator, the sole and undisturbed author of all that is in Nature. So there must be a complete and perfect harmony and concord between God and the Nature which he creates, God and his works must be at one; and Nature, so far as it goes, must represent the Will and Purpose of God, and nothing but the will and purpose of God. So, there can be nothing in Nature which God did not put in Nature from himself.

Well, God must have made Nature first, from a perfect Motive; next, of perfect Material; third, for a perfect Purpose or end; fourth, as perfect Means to achieve that purpose. That is — the motive for creation, the purpose of creation, must be in perfect harmony with the infinity of God; in harmony with his infinite power, wisdom, justice, love, and holiness: the material of Nature, and the means therein, with the constant modes of operation thereof — the Laws of Nature, must be perfectly adequate to the perfect purpose, and so must be in complete harmony with the Infinite God; with his infinite power, infinite wisdom, justice, love, and holiness. That is very plain, following unavoidably from the Idea of God as Infinite.

Now a perfect Motive for creation, — what will that be? It must be absolute Love producing a desire to bless every thing which he creates; that is, a desire to confer such a form and degree of welfare on each thing which he makes as is perfectly consistent with the character and nature of that thing made; that is, with its highest form and degree of welfare. Absolute Love is a perfect motive.

A perfect Purpose or end of creation is the achievement of that bliss; not the achievement thereof to-day, but ultimately. Perfect Material and Means are those which perfectly achieve that purpose; not to-day, or when I will, or when the thing created wills, but when the infinite wisdom and love of God wills.

The Infinite God must create all from a perfect motive, for a perfect purpose of perfect material, as perfect means; for you cannot conceive of a God infinitely powerful, wise, just, loving, and holy, creating any thing from an evil motive, for an evil purpose, from evil material, or as evil means. No more can you conceive of the Infinite God creating any thing from an imperfect motive, for an imperfect purpose, of imperfect material, or as imperfect means. Each of these suppositions is wholly inconsistent with the idea of the Infinite God; for He can have only perfect motives, perfect purposes, perfect material, and perfect means to create out of, and to create by. This being so, you see that the selfishness and destructiveness ascribed to God in the popular theology are at once struck out of existence. For such selfishness and destructiveness are absolutely impossible to the Infinite God.

II. Next, of God as perfect Providence. Creation and Providence are but modifications of the same function. Creation is momentary providence; providence, perpetual creation: one is described by a point; the other by a line. Now God is just as much present in a blade of grass, or an atom of mahogany, this day and in every moment of its existence, as he was at the instant of its creation. Men say, "When God created matter he was present therein." Very true! but he is just as present therein, with all his powers, and just as active with all his perfections, at every moment while that matter exists, as he was when it was first created. Men tell us, when they read the Bible, "How grand it must have been to have stood in the presence of God when Moses miraculously smote the rock, which gushed with miraculous water." But every drop of water, which falls from my roof in a shower, or from my finger, thus, as I lift it in this cup,—has as much the presence of God in it as when, in Biblical phrase, "the morning stars sang together, and the Sons of God shouted for joy," at the creation of water itself. It cannot be created without God; it cannot subsist without God.

Here, too, in his Providence, the motive, the end, the material and means, must be infinitely perfect. Let me develop this a moment.

God at the creation must have known the action and history of each thing which he called into being just as well as he knows it now; for God's knowledge is not a becoming wiser by experience, but a being wise by nature. The Infinite God must know every movement of every particle of matter. We generally assent to that in the gross, and reject it in the detail. Let me give an example.

All the powers, and consequently all the action, movements, and history of the whole Universe of matter, whereof this solar system is a part, a single —

> " Branch of Stars we see,
> Hung in the golden galaxy ; "

all the powers, actions, movements, and history of the solar system itself, of its primaries and secondaries, must have been completely and perfectly known to God before the universe, or any single " branch of stars," had its existence. So the powers and consequent history and movement of every particular thing on each of these orbs must have been known. The action and history of the mineral matter on the earth in its inorganic form, in the form of crystal, liquid, gas ; — the action and history of vegetable matter in the fucus, the lichen, and the tree ; — and so of animal matter, in the mollusk, the eagle, and the elephant, — all must have been completely and perfectly known by God before their creation; eternally known to him. The powers, and so the history, of each atom in Nature must have been as thoroughly known to the Mind of the Universe a million million years ago, as at this day; in their cause as well as by their effects.

For example, God must have known, at the moment of creation, the present position of this crescent moon which beautifies the early evening hour; and he must have known, too, the history of these molecules of carbon that make up the cotton thread which binds the sheets of this sermon together.

To say it short, the statics and dynamics of the

universe, and of each atom thereof, must have been eternally and thoroughly known to God. And each atom with its statical and dynamical powers, — the mineral, vegetable, and animal forces of the universe — must have been created by him, from perfect motives, of perfect material, for a perfect purpose, and as perfect means; they must be continually sustained by him, and he must be just as present and just as active in each moment of the existence of any one of these things as at the creation thereof, or at the creation of the all of things. So, then, each of these must have been created with a perfect knowledge of its powers, actions, movements, and history, and created from love as motive, for ultimate good as purpose, of materials proportionate to the motive, and so adequate to the end, and accordingly provided with the means of accomplishing that purpose; for the infinite perfection of God would allow no absolute evil, no absolute imperfection, in his motive, or his material, in his purpose, or his means. If there were any such absolute evil or imperfection in the created, it could only have come from an absolute evil or imperfection in the Creator; that is, from a lack of infinite power, wisdom, justice, or love — because God has not love enough to wish all things well; or justice enough to will them well; or wisdom enough to contrive them well; or power enough to make them well.

Each thing which God has made has a Right to be created from perfect motives, for a perfect purpose, from perfect material, and as perfect means; and a right, also, to be perfectly provided for. I know, to some men it will sound irreverent to speak of the Right of the created in relation to the Creator, and of the consequent Duty and Obligation of the Creator in relation to the created. But the Infinite God is infinitely just, and it is with the highest reverence that I ask, "Shall not the God of all the earth do right?" It is the highest reverence for the Creator to say that "He gives his creatures a Right to him, to him as infinite Cause, to him as infinite Providence;" and I count it impious to say that God has a right to create even a worm from imperfect motives, for an imperfect purpose, of imperfect material, as imperfect means. This right of the creature depends on the nature of the thing, on its quality as a creation of the infinite God; not on the quantity of being it has received from Him. So of course it is equal in all; the same in the smallest "motes that people the sunbeams," and the greatest man; all have a birthright to the perfect Providence of the Infinite God; an unalienable right to protection by his infinite power, wisdom, justice, love, and holiness. This lien on the Infinity of God vests in the substance of their finite nature, and is not to be voided by any accident of their history, for that accident must have been known and provided for as one of the consequences of their powers. Each thing has the infinite perfection of God as guarantee to that right. God is security for the universe, and his hand is indorsed on every great and little thing which he has made. Then, if am sure of God and his infinity, I am sure beforehand of the ultimate welfare of every thing which God has made, for the Infinite Father is the pledge and collateral security, the indorser therefor.

We cannot comprehend the details of this Providence, more than of creating, nor fully understand the mode of attaining the end; the mode of terminating, originating, and sustaining are equally unintelligible to us; but the fact we know from the idea of God as Infinite. As we cannot with a Gunter's chain measure the distance between the sun and the earth, but as by calculation, starting from facts of internal consciousness and external observation, we can measure it with greater proportionate exactness than a carpenter could measure the desk under my hand: — so we cannot understand God's mode of operation as Cause or Providence, more than an Indian baby, newly born, in Shawneetown, could understand the astronomer's mode of operation in calculating the distance between the earth and the sun; but as we have this idea of God, though we know not the mode of operation, the middle terms which intervene betwixt the purpose and the achievement, we are yet sure of the fact that the motive, purpose, material, and means are all proportionate to the nature of the Creator, and adequate for the welfare of the created.

In Nature God is the only Cause, the only Providence, the only Power; the law of Nature, — that is, the constant mode of action of the forces of the material world — represents the modes of action of God Himself, his thought made visible; and as he is infinite, unchangeably perfect, and perfectly unchangeable, his mode of action is therefore constant and universal, so that there can be no such thing as a violation of God's constant mode of action; for there is no power to violate it except God himself, and the infinitely perfect God could not violate his own perfect modes of action. And accordingly there can be no chance, no evil, no imperfection, in motive or purpose, in material or means, or in the modes of action thereof. Everywhere is calculated order, nowhere chance and confusion; everywhere regular, constant modes of action of the forces in the material world, unvarying and eternal laws, nowhere is there an extemporaneous miracle. Men have their precarious makeshifts; the Infinite has no tricks and subterfuges,—not a Whim in God, and so not a Miracle in Nature. Seeming chance is real direction; what looks like evil in Nature is real good. The sparrow that falls to-day does not fall to ruin, but to ultimate welfare. Though we know not the mode of operation, there must be another world for the sparrow as for man.

So much for this Theism as a Theory of the World of Matter. Now a word for it as a Theory of the World of Spirit, of the World of Man. This shall include man so far as he is matter; and so far as he is matter and something more.

Look at this first in the most general way, in relation to Human Nature,—to Mankind as a whole; then I will come down to particulars. Here the same thing is to be said as of Nature; namely, the Infinite God must be a perfect Cause thereof, and have created the world of man from perfect motives, for a perfect purpose, of perfect material, as perfect means. God has no other motive, purpose, material, or means. The perfect motive must be Absolute Love—producing the desire to bless the world of man, that is, the desire to confer thereon a form and degree of welfare which is perfectly consistent with the entire nature of man. The perfect purpose must be the attainment of that bliss; the ultimate attainment not to-day, or when man wills, but when the Infinite God wills. Perfect material is that which is capable of this welfare; and perfect means are such as achieve it.

So much for God considered as a perfect Cause in

the world of man. I need not here further repeat what I just said of creation in the world of matter.

But God must be also perfect Providence for the world of man; He must be perpetually present therein, in each portion thereof. Men think that God was present in some moment of time, at the creation of mankind. Very true! but in each moment of mankind's existence since, God is just as present; for providence is a continuous line of creations, and God is as much present, and as much active, at every point of that line as at the beginning or end thereof. I know men speak of yielding up the spirit and going out of the body, going to God. Is not God about, within, and around us, while we are in the body, just as much as when we shake off the known and enter on that untried being?

God must have known at the creation all the action and history of the world of man as well as of Nature. It is not to be supposed that ten thousand years ago God knew less of human history than he knows to-day. That would be to make God imperfect in his wisdom, growing wiser by experience. Napoleon's *coup d' etat* was a surprise to mankind ten months ago. Do you think it was an astonishment to God ten months ago? was it not infinitely known hundreds of millions of years ago; eternally known? It must have been so.

I know the question is here more complicated than in Nature, for in Nature there is only one force, the direct statical and dynamical action of matter; and accordingly it is easy to calculate the action and result of mechanical, vegetable, electrical, and vital forces. But in the world of man there is a certain amount of freedom, which seems to make the question difficult. In that part of the world of Nature not endowed with animal life, there is no margin of oscillation; and you may know just where the moon will be to-night, and where it will be a thousand years hence. The constant forces, with their compensations, may all be known; and so every nutation of the moon is calculable with entire certainty. The modes of action there are as little variable as the maxims of geometry. The moon's node is an invariable consequent of material necessity. When a star with fiery hair came splendoring through the night, it filled mediæval astronomers with amazement; and celibate priests, divorced from Nature, shook with superstitious fear as it wrote its hieroglyphic of God over Byzantium or Rome: was God astonished at his wandering and hairy star?

In the world of animals there is a small margin of oscillation; but you are pretty sure to know what the animals will do, that the beaver will build his dam and the wren her nest just as their fathers built; that every bee next summer will make her six-sided cell with the same precision and geometric economy of material and space wherewith her ancestors wrought ten thousand years ago, solving the problem of isoperimetrical figures.

But man has a certain amount of freedom; a larger margin of oscillation, wherein he vibrates from side to side. The nod of Lord Burleigh is a variable contingent of human caprice. Hence it is thought that God could not foreknow the oscillations of caprice in the human race, in the Adamitic Cain of ancient poetry, or the Napoleonic Cain of contemporaneous history, till after they took place. But that conclusion comes only from putting our limitations on God. It is difficult for the astronomer's little boy to measure the cradle he sleeps in, or to tell what time it is by the nursery clock; but the astronomer can measure the vast orbit of Leverrier's star before seeing it, and correct his nursery clock by the great dial hung up in heaven itself: yet the difference between the mind of the astronomer's boy and the mind of the astronomer is nothing compared to the odds between finite intellect and the infinite understanding of God. So though the greater complication makes it more difficult for you and me to understand the consciousness of free men, whose feelings, thoughts, and consequent actions are such manifold contingents, it is not at all more difficult for God.

Before the creation the Infinite God, as perfect Cause and Providence, must have known all the powers and consequent actions, movements, and history of the collective world of men, and each individual thereof. For, either man has no freedom at all, or he has some freedom of will.

In the first case, if he has no freedom, no margin of oscillation, the fore-knowableness of his actions does not differ from that of the world of matter; and the nutation of the moon and the nod of Lord Burleigh are equally the invariable consequent of material or human necessity. Then God is the only force in the human world, and of course, without difficulty, knows all its action, for a knowledge of the world is only part of his consciousness of himself; the treachery of Judas and the faithfulness of Jesus are then but facts of the divine self-consciousness.

If there be freedom, then God, as the perfect Cause of man's freedom of will, must have perfectly understood the powers of that freedom; and understanding perfectly the powers, he knew perfectly all the actions, movements, and history thereof, at the moment of creation as well as to-day. The perfect Cause must know the consequence of his perfect creation; and knowing the cause and the effects thereof, as perfect Providence, and working from a perfect motive, for a perfect purpose, with perfect material and by perfect means, he must so arrange all things, that the material shall be capable of ultimate welfare; and must use means proportionate to the nature and adequate to the purpose. So the quantity of human oscillation with all the consequences thereof must of course be perfectly known to God before the creation as well as after the special events come to pass; for to God contingents of caprice and consequents of necessity must be equally clear, both before and after the event. Little boys, under a capricious schoolmaster, learn the constants of his anger's ebb or flow;

> "Full well the boding tremblers learn to trace
> The day's disaster in his morning face."

And do you think the infinite God is astonished at revolutions in Italy, or the discovery of ether? because a hyæna, stealthily and at night, kills a girl in an Abyssinian town, or a kidnapper, as stealthily and also by night, destroys a man in Boston? The hyæna crouching in his den, the kidnapper lurking in his office, are both known to God.

Though human caprice and freedom be a contingent force, yet God knows human caprice when he makes it, knows exactly the amount of that contingent force, all its actions, movements, and history, and what it will bring about. And as he is an infinitely wise, just, and loving Cause and Providence, so there can be no absolute evil or imperfection in the world of man, more than in the world of matter, or in God himself.

So much for this Theism as a Theory of the World of Man as a Whole, in its most general form.

Now see the concrete application thereof in the General Human Life — in the life of nations. In creating mankind God must have known there would come the great races of men, — Ethiopian, Malay, Tartar, American, Caucasian. He must have known there would come such families of the Caucasian as the Slavic, Classic, Celtic, Teutonic; such stocks of the Teutonic as the Scandinavian, the German, the Saxon; of the Saxon such nations as England and America; in their history such events as the American Revolution, the Mexican War, and the like. I mean that God as perfect Cause must have perfectly known all these things from eternity as well as now. History is a surprise to us, not to God. The breaking out of the Mexican War, the capture of Mexico, the failure or success of a general, might be an astonishment to men; God was not wiser afterwards than before. As perfect Cause and Providence, he must have arranged all things so that mankind as a whole shall attain that bliss which his perfect motive and perfect purpose require, which is indispensable to his perfect material and his perfect means. All the powers and consequent actions, movements, and history of mankind must therefore have been known and provided for. The savage, the barbarous, the half-civilized, and the civilized — the feudal and commercial periods, — and others yet in store, must have been known and provided for. The whole religious history of man, Atheism, Fetichism, Polytheism, Monotheism, — the Monotheism of the Hebrews and of the Christians,—must have been known. The rise, decline, and fall, of Egypt, India, Persia, Judea, Greece, Rome, and Byzantium, must have been as well understood by God at creation as now; and as perfect Providence he must have provided for the rise, decline, and fall, thereof, so that they should be steps forward, towards ultimate bliss, and not from it. He must have given man his power of freewill as all other powers, from a perfect motive, for a perfect purpose, of perfect material, and as perfect means; and of course it must achieve that purpose for mankind as a whole, for those great races,—Ethiopian, Malay, Tartar, American, Caucasian; for those families,—Slavic, Classic, Celtic, Teutonic; for those tribes,—Scandinavian, German, Saxon; for every nation,—England, America. The great events of their history,—the American Revolution, the Mexican War,—and every other, must be so overruled and balanced that they shall not contribute to the achievement of the purpose of God. And what is true of the whole must be true of each; God must be perfect Providence for one as well as for another, and so arrange these that they all shall come to ultimate bliss.

Therefore as you look on the sad aspect of the world at present,—on Italy, ridden by the Pope and priest; on Austria, Hungary, Germany, the spark of freedom trodden out by the imperial or royal hoof; on France, crushed by her own armies at the command of a cunning voluptuary; on Ireland, trodden down by the capitalists of Britain; on the American slave, manacled by State and Church,—you know, first, that God foresaw all this at the creation, as a consequence of the forces which he put into human nature; next, you know that he provides for it all, so that it shall not interfere with the ultimate bliss of the Italian, Pope-ridden and priest-ridden; of the Austrian, Hungarian, German, from whose heart the imperial or royal hoof has trod the spark of liberty; of the Frenchman, the victim of a voluptuous tyrant; of the Irishman, trodden down by the British capitalist; and of the American slave, fettered by the American Church and manacled by the American State. God made the world in such a manner that these partial evils would take place; and they take place with his infinite knowledge, and under his infinite Providence. So when we see these evils, we know that though immense they are partial evils compensated by constants somewhere, and provided for in the infinite engineering of God, so that they shall be the cause of some ultimate good. For mankind has a Right to be perfectly created; each race, family, tribe, nation, has a Right to be created from perfect motives for a perfect purpose, of perfect material, and with the means to achieve that purpose; not at the time, when Russia and Montenegro will, or when you and I will, but when infinite wisdom, justice, love, knows that it is best. And sad as the world looks, God knew it all, provided for it all; and its welfare, its ultimate triumph is insured at the office of the Infinite God. His hand is indorsed on each race, each family, each tribe, each nation of mankind. You cannot suppose — as writers of the Old Testament do — that the affairs of the world look desperate to God, and he repents having made mankind, or any fraction of the human race.

See this Theism in its application to Individual Human Life; your life and mine. God is perfect Cause and perfect Providence for me and you. Before the creation he knew every thing that I shall do, every thing that I shall suffer, every thing that I shall be; provided for it all, so that absolute bliss must be the welfare of each of us at last. The evils — that is, the suffering in mind, body, and estate, the imperfect bliss, my failing to attain the outward or inward condition of this welfare, — these must come either from my nature, my human nature as man, my individual nature as the son of John and Hannah; or from my circumstances that are about me; or, as a third thing, from the joint action of these two.

God as perfect Cause must have known my nature, my circumstances, the effect of their joint action; as perfect Providence, he must have arranged things so that nature and circumstances shall work out for me, and for everybody, all this ultimate bliss which the perfect motive can desire as a perfect purpose, which perfect materials can achieve as perfect means. My individual suffering, error, sin, must have been equally foreseen, fore-cared for, and used in the great housekeeping of the Eternal Mother as a means to accomplish the purpose of ultimate welfare.

This must be true of Jesus of Nazareth crucified, and of Judas Iscariot who betrayed him to the cross; of the St. Domingo hero who rotted in his dungeon, and of Napoleon the Great, who locked his dungeon door — himself one day to be jailed on a rock, with Ocean mounting guard over this Prometheus of historic times; of theistic John Huss who blazed in his fire, and of the Twenty-third John, the perjured pope of Rome, who lit that fire five hundred miles from home.

As at the creation of the world of matter God knew where the solar system would be in space, where the molecules of carbon which form the tie that binds my sermon together, would be on this seventeenth of October, eighteen hundred and fifty-two years after the cradling of Jesus of Nazareth;—as He arranged the universe so that the solar system and these molecules of carbon should harmonize together,—as he knew of the rise, decline, and fall of states, and arranged all these things so as to harmonize with the march of man towards greater bliss;—so he must have known where this little atom of spirit which I call Me would be this day,—what thoughts, feelings, will, and suffering I should have, and he must make all these harmonize with my march towards that ultimate bliss, which my finite human nature needs to take, and which his infinite divine nature needs to give.

God is responsible for his own creation, his world of matter, and his world of man; for mankind in general; for you and me. God's work is all warranted. Each man has a right to perfect creation,—creation from perfect motives, of perfect material, as perfect means for a perfect purpose. God has no other purpose, no other means, no other material, no other motive. He is the infinite power, wisdom, justice, love, and is security for the ultimate welfare of the sparrow that falls; for mankind groping its dim and perilous way; for you and me darkly feeling our way along, often falling into pain, want, misery, and sin. God as Cause, and God as Providence has still means to bring us back and lead us home. I have a natural, unalienable Right to the Providence of the Infinite God; this Providence is the Duty of God, inseparable from his Infinity. If I am sure that God is infinite, then all else that is good I am sure of, for every thing which God makes is stamped by his hand with an unalienable Right to Him as infinite Cause and infinite Providence.

As God was present at the creation of matter and of mankind, present with all his infinite perfection, and active therewith,— so is he present and active with me to-day with all his infinite perfections; then as Cause, so now as Providence. And do you think the universe will fail of its purpose with Infinite God as its Providence and its Cause? Do you think any nation, any single human soul can ever fail of achieving this ultimate bliss, with Infinite God as its Cause and Infinite God as its Providence? Why, so long as God is God it is impossible that his motive and purpose should fail to design good for all and each — or his material and means fail to achieve that ultimate good.

Well, since these things are so, how beautiful appears the Material World! There is no fortuitous concourse of atoms, which the atheist talks of; there is no universe of selfishness, no grim despot who grinds the world under his heels and then spurns it off to hell, as the popular theology scares us withal. Every thing is a thought of Infinite God, and in studying the movements of the solar system, or the composition of an ultimate cell arrested in a crystal, developed in a plant; in tracing the grains of phosphorus in the brain of man; or in studying the atoms which compose the fusil-oil in a drop of ether, or the powers and action thereof,— I am studying the Thought of the Infinite God. The Universe is his Scripture; Nature the prose, and Man the poetry of God. The world is a volume holier than the Bible, old as creation. What history, what psalms, what prophecy therein! what canticles of love to beast and man! not the "Wisdom of Solomon" as in this

Apocrypha, but the Wisdom of God, written out in the great Canon of the Universe.

Then, when I see the suffering of animals, — the father-alligator eating up his sons and daughters, and the Mother-alligator seeking to keep them from his jaws, — when I see the sparrow falling at a dandy's shot, I know that these things have been provided for by the God of the alligator and the sparrow, and that the universe is lodged as collateral security to insure bliss to every sparrow that falls.

From this point of view how beautiful appears the World of Man! When I look on the whole history of man, — man as a savage, as a barbarian, as half-civilized, or as civilized, — feudal or commercial — fighting with all the forces which chemistry and mechanical science can offer, and suffering from want, war, ignorance, from sin in all its thousand forms, — from despotic oppression in Russia, democratic oppression in America; when I see the tyranny of the feudal baron in other times, with his acres and his armies, of the feudal capitalist, now-a-days, — the commercial baron, with notes at cent per cent.; when I see the hyæna of the desert stealing his prey in an Abyssinian town, and the hyæna of the city kidnapping a man in Boston, — when I see all this, I say the thing is not hopeless. O no! it is hopeful. God knew it all at the beginning, as perfect Cause; cared for it all, as perfect Providence, with perfect motive, purpose, material, means — will achieve at last ultimate welfare for the oppressor and the oppressed.

I see the individual suffering, from want, ignorance, and oppression; the public woe which blackens the countenance of men, the sorrow which with private tooth gnaws the heart of African Ellen or William, the sin which puts out the eyes of Caucasian Cain or George. Can I fear? O no! though the worm of sorrow bore into my own heart, I cannot fear. The Infinite God with infinite power, wisdom, justice, holiness, and love, knew it all, and made the nature of Ellen and William, of Cain and George, and controls their circumstances, so that by their action and the action of the world of man and the world of matter, the perfect motive and the perfect means shall achieve the perfect purpose of the infinite loving-kindness of God.

Then how grand is human destination! Ay, your destination and mine! There is no chance; it is direction which we did not see. There is no fate, but a Mother's Providence holding the universe in her lap, warming each soul with her own breath, and feeding it from her own bosom with everlasting life.

In times past there is evil which I cannot understand; in times present evil which I cannot solve; suffering — for mankind, for each nation, for you and me; sufferings, follies, sins. I know they were all foreseen by the infinite wisdom of God, all provided for by his infinite power and justice, and his infinite love shall bring us all to bliss, not a soul left behind, not a sparrow lost. The means I know not; the end I am sure of.

> "Whether I fly with angels, fall with dust,
> Thy hands made both, and I am there;
> Thy power and love, my love and trust,
> Make one place everywhere."

In the world of matter there is the greatest economy of force. The rain-drop is wooed for a moment into bridal loveliness by some enamoured ray of light, then feeds the gardener's violet, or moves the grindstone in the farmer's mill, — serving alike the turn of Beauty and of Use. Nothing is in vain; all things are manifold in use.

"A rose, beside his beauty, is a cure."

The ocean is but the chemist's sink which holds the rinsings of the world, and every thing washed off from earth was what the land needed to void, the sea to take. All things are twofold; matter is doubly winged, with Use and Beauty.

"Nothing hath got so far,
But man hath caught and kept it as his prey;
His eyes dismount the highest star;
He is in little all the sphere.
Herbs gladly cure our flesh, because that they
Find their acquaintance there.

"For us the winds do blow,
The earth doth rest, heaven move, and fountains flow;
Nothing we see but means our good,
As our delight, or as our treasure;
The whole is either our cupboard of food,
Or cabinet of pleasure.

"The stars have us to bed;
Night draws the curtain, which the sun withdraws.
Music and light attend our head:
All things unto our flesh are kind
In their descent and being; to our mind
In their ascent and cause."

And do you then believe that the great God, whose motto, "waste not, want not," is pictured and practised on earth and sea and sky, is prodigal of human suffering, human woe? Every tear-drop which sorrow has wrung from some poor negro's eye, every sigh, every prayer of grief, each groan the exile puts up in our own land, and the groan which the American exile puts up in Canada, — while his tears shed for his wife and child smarting in the tropics, are turned to ice before they touch the wintry ground, — has its function in the great chemistry of our Father's world. These things were known by God, and he will bring every exile, every wanderer in his arms, the great men not forgot, the little not less blest, and bear them rounding home from bale to bliss, to give to each the welfare which his nature needs to give and ours to take.

The atheist looks out on a here without a Hereafter, a body without a Soul, a world without a Heaven, a universe with no God; and he must needs fold his arms in despair, and dwindle down into the material selfishness of a cold and sullen heart. The popular theologian looks out on the world and sees a body blasted by a Soul, a here undermined by a Hereafter of hell, arched over with a little paltry sounding-board of Heaven, whence the elect may look over the edge and rejoice in the writhings of the worms unpitied beneath their feet. He looks out and sees a grim and revengeful and evil God. Such is his sad whim. But the man with pure theism in his heart looks out on the world, and there is the Infinite God everywhere as perfect Cause, everywhere as perfect Providence, transcending all, yet immanent in each, with perfect power, wisdom, justice, holiness, and love, securing perfect welfare unto each and all.

On the shore of Time where Atheism sat in despair, and where Theology howled with delight, at its Dream of Hell all crowded with torment at the end, — there sits Theism. Before it passes on the stream of Human History, rolling its volumed waters gathered from all lands, — Ethiopian, Malay, Tartar, Caucasian, American, — from each nation, tribe, and family of men; and it comes from the Infinite God, its perfect Cause; it rolls on its waters by the Infinite Providence, its perfect Protector; he knew at Creation the history of empires, these lesser dimples on the stream; of Ellen and William, Cain and George, the bubbles on the water's face; he provided for them all, so that not a dimple deepens and whirls away, not a bubble breaks, but the perfect Providence foresaw and fore-cared for it all. God is on the shore of the stream of Human History, infinite power, wisdom, justice, love; God is in the air over it, where floats the sparrow that fell, falling to its bliss, — in the waters, in every dimple, in each bubble, in each atom of every drop; and at the end the stream falls into the sea, — that Amazon of human history, under the line of Providence, on the Equator of the world, falls into the great Ocean of Eternity, and not a dimple that deepens and whirls away, not a bubble that breaks, not a single atom of a drop, is lost. All fall into the Ocean of Blessedness, which is the bosom of love, and then the rush of many waters sings out this psalm from human nature and from human history, — "If God is for us, who can be against us?"

SERMON VI.

OF THEISM AS ETHICS.

PSALM XXV. 21.

LET INTEGRITY AND UPRIGHTNESS PRESERVE ME.

VI.

OF PRACTICAL THEISM, REGARDED AS THE PRINCIPLE OF ETHICS.

LAST Sunday I spoke of Speculative Theism as a Theory of the Universe. To-day I ask your attention to a Sermon of Practical Theism; of Theism considered as a Principle of Ethics.

You start with the Idea of God as Infinite in power, wisdom, justice, love, holiness; you consider him in his relation to the universe, as perfect Cause and perfect Providence; you see that from his nature he must have made the world, and all things therein, from a perfect motive, for a perfect purpose, of perfect material, as perfect means thereto; and therefore that Human Nature must be adequate to the end which God designed; that it must be provided with means adequate to the development of men; that all the faculties in their normal activity must be the natural means for achieving the purposes of God. You see that as he gave Nature, the material world, its present amount of necessitated forces, knowing exactly how to proportion the means to the end, the forces to the result which they were to produce;—in like manner he gave to man his present amount of contingent forces, knowing perfectly well what use men would make thereof, what abuses would ensue, what results would come to pass, and ordered and balanced these things, compensating one constant by another, caprice by necessity, so that our human forces should become the means of achieving his divine purpose, and the freewill of men should ultimately work in the same line with the infinite perfection of God, and so the result which God designed should be achieved by human freedom: therefore, that this perfect Cause and perfect Providence has provided human freedom as part of the perfect means whereby human destination is to be wrought out; — which destination is not fate, but providence.

Well, this Idea of God, the consequent idea of the Universe and of the Relation between the two, cannot remain merely a theory; it will affect human life in all its most important details.

It will appear in the Form of Religion. Man must always work with such intellectual apparatus — faculties and ideas — as he has. With the Idea of the Infinite God, he must progressively construct a form of religion corresponding to that idea. That form of religion will comprise the subjective worship, and the objective service of God; and so it will become the Theoretic Ideal of Human Life.

Then that form of religion will appear in the Actual Life of men, and in all the modes and modifications thereof: — for no human force is so subtle as the religious; it extends, and multiplies, and goes into every department of human affairs;

"Spreads undivided, operates unspent."

Let us now look at the theoretic Form of religion which belongs to this idea, and at the Realization thereof in human life. Treating of a theme so vast I must pass over much which I would gladly say, and only briefly touch where I would fain pause long and dwell.

I. First, then, of the Form of Religion. Of Religion there are always two parts; namely, the subjective portion, which is Piety, consisting of emotions that are purely internal; and next the objective portion, which is Morality, internal in part, and external also; rooted in our consciousness of God, and branched abroad into practical action in our houses and farms and shops, our warehouses, our libraries, and our banks. Let me speak of each of these, going over things very much at large, in the sketchiest way.

First of the subjective portion. When fully grown this subjective part must be pure Piety; I mean to say piety not mixed with any other emotion.

There will be no Fear or Distrust of God, because it is known that there is nothing in him to fear: I fear what hurts; never what helps.

Distrust of God rests on the idea that he is something not perfect; imperfect in power, wisdom, justice, love, or holiness: and with that idea of him God may seem good so far as he goes; but not going infinitely, he does not go far enough to warrant infinite trust; and so there is a partial distrust.

Fear of God is worse yet. That rests on the supposition that there is not only in God something not perfect, but that there is in him something which is not good, not kind.

But you cannot fear infinite Love; you cannot fear

infinite Justice, nor infinite Holiness; nor yet infinite Wisdom and infinite Power, when they are directed by infinite justice and animate with infinite love. With the idea of God as infinitely perfect I may indeed have doubts of to-morrow, doubts of my own or another's temporary welfare, for I know not what result the contingent forces of human freedom will produce to-morrow: but I can have no doubt of eternity, no doubts of my own or another's ultimate welfare, because I do know that the absolute forces of God will so control the conditional and contingent forces of men which his plan arranged and provided for, that ultimately the perfect purpose of God shall be achieved for all and each. A silversmith makes a watch, knowing the powers and consequent necessitated action of the materials he puts therein, so that it will keep time corresponding with the dial of the heavens. But he does not know how the purchasers of the watch will use it, whether or no they will fulfil the conditions essential to its action; and so he cannot absolutely foretell and provide for all its action and history; it will be subject to conditions which he cannot control or even foresee. Now the Infinite God, at the creation of man, knew all the powers He put therein; he knew all the conditions into which the necessitated forces of material nature, and the contingent forces of human nature, shall bring mankind and each special person. Accordingly God absolutely knows not only the primitive powers of each man, but the action, movements, and complete history thereof under any and all the conditions of existence. And the Infinite God working with motives proportionate to his nature, and means adequate to his purpose, must needs make man capable of achieving that ultimate welfare which the finite needs to have and the Infinite needs to give. If God be infinite, a perfect Cause and perfect Providence, this conclusion follows as plain as the farmer's road to mill. So I say I can have no distrust and no fear of God; no fear of ultimate failure or future torment. Suffering I may have in another life: I will meet it gladly, and thank God; it is medical, and not malicious. In the popular theology God is represented as a Jesuitical Inquisitor; but the Infinite God is a protector, a Father and Mother.

Then there will be Absolute Love of God, — to the mind God will be the Beauty of Truth; to the conscience the Beauty of Justice, to the affections the Beauty of Love, to the soul the Beauty of Holiness, and to the whole consciousness of man he will appear as the total Infinite Beauty; the perfect and absolute object of every hungering faculty of man; the Cause that creates from perfect love as motive, for perfect love as purpose, and by perfect love as means; the perfect Providence that provides from the same motive for the same purpose, and by the same means. So he will appear as the Father and the Mother of all; operating by necessitated forces in the dew-drop, and in the all of material things; operating, also, by contingent forces in the soul of a little girl, or in the great aggregate of spirit which we call the world of man; operating so perfectly as Cause and so perfectly as Providence that he is Father and Mother to every soul. I say this Idea of God is infinitely lovely, and awakens in the heart of a man, who draws near thereto, the deepest and tenderest love. There is no doubt, no fear.

With this Idea of God, and this Love of Him, there comes a Perfect Trust in God, as Cause and Providence: — not only a trust in the daylight of science, where we see, but in the twilight, even in the darkness of ignorance, where we see not: — an absolute trust in his motive, his purpose, and his means; so that we shall not desire any other motive but the motive of God, nor any other purpose but the purpose of God, nor any other means but the means he has provided thereto.

With that trust there must come a perpetual Hope, for yourself, for all mankind; for as dark as the world may be, dark as my own condition may be, my outward lot, my inward state, still I know assuredly that God foresaw it all, provided for it all, and that he cannot fail in motive, in purpose, or means thereto; and thus light will spring out of darkness and bliss come forth out of bale.

With this there will come Tranquillity and Rest for the soul; that Peace spoken of in the fourth canonical Gospel, which the world cannot give nor take away.

Then there will come a real Joy in God. I mean the happiness which the Mystics call the "sense of sweetness" that comes when the conditions of the soul are completely met; when the true Idea of God and the appropriate Feeling towards him furnish the personal, human, inward condition of religious delight, and there is nothing between us and the Infinite Father. That is the highest joy and the highest delight of human consciousness. The natural desires of the body may fail of satisfaction, — their hunger shortening my days on earth, — and I may be poor and cold and naked; I may be a prisoner in a dungeon of Austria, or a slave on a plantation of Carolina; I may be sick and feeble, and the conditions of domestic and of social welfare may not be complied with; — but if the soul's conditions are fairly met within on the side that is turned towards the Infinite, then through the clouds the Beauty of God shines on me and I am at peace.

So there will come a Beauty of Soul, I mean a harmonious spiritual whole of well-proportioned spiritual parts, and there will be a continual and constant growth in all the noble qualities of man. God will not be thought afar off, separated from Nature, separated from man, but dwelling therein, immanent in each, though yet transcending all. Nature will be seen as a revelation of God; and the march of man will reveal also the same Providence, as the world of matter — human consciousness disclosing higher characteristics of the Infinite God. Communion with him will be direct, my spirit meeting his, with nothing betwixt me and the Godhead of God. I shall not pray by attorney, but face to face. Inspiration will be a fact now, not merely a history of times gone by. Worship, the subjective service of God, will be not by conventional forms of belief, of speech, or of posture; not by a sacramental addition of an excrescence where nature suffered no lack, nor by mutilation of the body, or mutilation of the spirit, the sacramental cutting off where God made nothing redundant: but by conscious noble emotions shall I subjectively worship God; by gratitude for my right to the Father, and in his universe the thanksgiving of an upright heart; by aspiration after a higher ideal of my own daily life; by the sense of Duty to be done, which comes with the sense of Right to be enjoyed; by penitence where I fall short; by resolutions, that in my "proper motion," I may ascend, and not by adverse fall come down; by the calm joy of the soul, its delight in Nature, in Man, and in God; by the hope, the faith, and the love, which the large soul sends out of itself in its religious life; and by the growing beauty of character, which constantly increases in love of wisdom, in love of justice, in love of benevolence — in love of Man, in love of God. That will be the real worship, the internal service of the Father.

So much for the subjective part of this form of religion.

Of the Objective Part also a word. God, who is thus subjectively served in the natural forms of Piety, must be objectively served or worshipped in the natural forms of Morality; that is, by keeping all the laws of God. In Nature, the material world, the law of God is the actual constant mode of operation of the forces thereof, — the way it does not act. There all is necessitated, and we know of the law by seeing the fact that it is always kept; for the ideal law of matter is the actual fact of matter, learned by observation, not by consciousness. So the material universe and God, in every point of space and time are continually at one. If law is a constant of God, obedience thereto is a constant of matter. But in man, the law of God for man is the ideal constant mode of operation of the human force, — the way it should act. This is not always a fact in any man; and we learn it not merely by observation of our history, but by consciousness of our nature. Morality is the making of the ideal of human nature into the actual of human history. Herein the ideal of God's purpose becomes the actual of man's achievement; and so far man and God are at one, as everywhere God and matter are at one. Then for every point of Right we seek to enjoy, there is a point of Duty which we will to do.

Thus in general, morality will be the objective service of God, as piety is the subjective worship of God. These two make up the whole of Religion. They are the only "divine service:" Piety is the great inward sacrament and act of worship; Morality the great outward sacrament and act of service — other things are but helps. Piety will be free piety, such as the spirit of man demands: Morality will be free morality, such as the spirit of man demands; both perfectly conformable to the nature which God put into man, to the body and the spirit, — the mind and conscience, heart and soul.

This morality will consist partly in keeping the Law of the Body; in giving it its due use, development, enjoyment, and discipline, in the world of matter.

The popular theology, in its ascetic rules, goes to an extreme, and does great injustice. It counts the body mean, calls it vile, says that therein dwells no good thing. It mortifies the flesh, crucifies the affections thereof. But the body is not vile. Did not the infinite Father make it, — not a limb too much, not a passion too many? God make any thing vile! and least of all this, which is the consummation of his outward workmanship, — the frame of man! Far from us be the thought.

The Atheistic philosophy goes to the other extreme, and clamors for the "rehabilitation of the flesh," and would have a paradise of the senses, as the sole and earthly heaven of man. Theology turns the flesh out of doors, and the soul has cold housekeeping, living alone; Atheism turns the soul out of doors, and the flesh has no better time of it; no, has a worse time, with its scarlet women "tinging the pavement with proud wine too good for the tables of pontiffs." Absolute Religion demands the use of every limb of the body, every faculty of the soul, all after their own kind, each performing its proper function in the housekeeping of man. Then there will be freedom of the body, freedom for every limb to perform its function, and to perform no more. That is the morality of the body.

This morality will consist also in keeping the Law of the Spirit; that is, in giving the spirit its natural empire over the material part of us, and in giving each spiritual faculty its natural place in the housekeeping of the spirit; so that each, the intellectual, the moral, the affectional, and the purely religious faculty, shall have its due development, use, enjoyment, and discipline in life. Then there will be spiritual freedom; that is, the liberty of every spiritual faculty to perform its own work, and no more. This is the morality of the spirit.

The popular Theology restrains each spiritual faculty. It hedges you in with the limitation of some great or little man; it calls a man's fence the limit to God's revelation: it does not give the mind room, nor conscience room, nor the affections room, nor yet the soul sufficient space to serve God, each by its natural function.

One of the good things of Atheism has been this: it offers freedom to the human spirit. That is its only good, and its only charm. In a Church of the Popular Theology the great mind cannot draw a long breath, lest it should wake up the "wrath of God,"—which, we are told, never sleeps very sound, nor long at a time. In the free air of Atheism the largest mind is told to breathe as deep as he can, and make as much noise as he will; there is no God to molest and make him afraid. That is the only charm which Atheism ever had to any man. It raises men from fear, and it bids them be true to that part of their nature which they know.

Well, such will be the form of Religion coming from Theism; such its Piety and Morality. You see it will be a form of religion which fits well upon the finite side,—on man; for it is derived from his nature, and represents all parts thereof, doing justice to the body, to its every limb, to all its senses, functions, passions; doing justice to the spirit, every faculty thereof, intellectual, moral, affectional, and religious. It fits just as well on the infinite side—on God; for it is drawn from human nature on the supposition that God made human nature from perfect motives, of perfect material, for a perfect purpose, and as a perfect means thereto. This form of religion, then, is the application of God's means to the purpose of God.

As "Christian" Theology professes to be derived from a verbal revelation of God,—represented by the Church, as the Catholics say, by the Scriptures as the Protestants teach,—so the Absolute Religion is derived from the real revelation of God, which is contained in the universe; this outward universe of matter, this inward universe of man; and I take it we do not require the learned and conscientious labors of a Lardner, a Paley, or a Norton, to convince us that the universe is genuine and authentic, and is the work of God without interpolation; we all know that. I call this the Absolute Religion, because it is drawn from the absolute and ultimate source; because it gives us the absolute Idea of God,—God as Infinite; and because it guarantees to man his natural rights, and demands the performance of the absolute duties of human nature.

So much for this Form of Religion in itself.

II. Now see how this Form of Religion will appear in the Actual Life of Man, and the subjective religious thought become an objective religious thing.

See it first in the form of Individual Human Life; in a Person.

He will be the most religious man who most conforms to his nature; who has most of this natural piety and of this natural morality. There will be various degrees thereof, only one kind. He will worship God the best, or subjectively serve him, who has the most love of truth, the most love of justice, of benevolence, of holiness; the greatest love of Man, and the greatest love of God; who most desires and strongest wills to possess these great qualities; in short, he who has the most natural piety.

He will serve God the best, objectively worship him, who has the most of truth, of righteousness, of friendship, of philanthropy, of holiness — fidelity to himself; he who best uses the great or the little talent and opportunity which God has given; in a word, he who has the most Morality. He will be the most completely religious man who most keeps the law of God, for his body and for his soul; and of course who coördinates the flesh and the spirit, and duly subordinates the low qualities of the spirit to the higher; — for a very little activity of the higher faculties of man is worth a great deal of activity of the lower; even as an ounce of gold can any day purchase some tons of sand.

This it seems to me, is the true scale of man's spiritual faculties: — Intellect is the lowest of them, dealing with truth, use, and beauty in their abstract and concrete forms; next comes Conscience, aiming at justice and eternal right; next the Affections, loving persons, and sacrificing my personal joy to the delight of another person; and highest of all comes the religious faculty, which I call the Soul, that seeks the infinite Being, Father and Mother of the Universe, and loves him with perfect love and serves him with perfect trust. So in the individual the soul, taking cognizance of the infinite being, and his Relation to us, is thereby our natural master. Is not this true which I state? It is not merely my psychological knowledge of man which tells me this; it is the world's history which tells it; it is the consciousness of your heart, and my heart, which cry out for the living God, and assure us that we must subordinate every thing to him.

What a difference there will be between the saint of Absolute Religion and the saint of the popular Theology. The real saint is a man who aims to have a whole body, and a whole mind, and a whole conscience, and a whole heart, and a whole soul; and to live a whole, brave, manly life, at work in the daily calling of grocer, or mason, or legislator, or cabinet-maker, or historian, or seamstress, or preacher, or farmer, or king, or whatsoever it may be: that will be the aim of the saint of natural religion. But the popular saint is an exceedingly different thing; a meagre, church-rid mope, "a-dust and thin," a ghost of humanity that haunts the aisles of the church; for the popular saint is dyspeptic in body, dyspeptic in mind and conscience, in heart and soul: you see by his face that his spiritual digestion is poor, his stomach is weak, and his religion does not agree with him. He must send off to the Jordan to get water to christen his baby, before that baby is thought safe from the damnation of hell; baptism with the spirit of God and the spirit of Man is not enough. But the real saint of absolute religion must be a free spiritual individual. His Piety must represent him, and his Morality must represent him, and he will carry them both into all his work. Knowing that God gave him faculties as God meant him to have them, each containing its law in itself; knowing that God provided them as a perfect means for a perfect purpose, and that that purpose is one which cannot fail, — he will use these faculties in the true service of God; and he will work as no other man, — with a strength, and a vigor, and a perseverance; ay, and a beauty of character too, which nothing but Absolute Religion can ever give. So there will be the greatest strength to do, to be, and to suffer, sure to conquer at the last. He will sail the more carefully, for he knows that careful sailing is the service which God requires of him; he will sail the more confident, because he knows that his voyage is laid out, and his craft is insured by the Power who holds the waters in the hollow of his hand; yes, that it is insured against ultimate shipwreck at the great office of the infinite God. Will he not work therefore with greater earnestness and zeal because he knows that God gave him these talents as perfect means for a perfect end; with more confidence because he knows the end is made sure of; and with more caution, because he knows that the true use of the means is the only service God asks of him?

See this same thing in its Domestic Form, — that of Human Life in the Family. The family must represent the free spiritual individuality of man and woman, regarded as equal, and equally joining by connubial love — passion and affection — for mutual self-denial and mutual delight; — for there is no marriage without mutual self-denial as means, for mutual delight as end. Marriage between a perfect man and a perfect woman, would be mutual surrender and mutual sacrifice.

In all forms of religion that I know, from the book of Moses to the book of Mormon, from Confucius to Calvin, woman is degraded before man; for in all forms of religion hitherto Force has been preferred above all things, and the great quality which has been ascribed to God is an Omnipotence of Force. That is the thing which Christendom has worshipped these many hundred years, not love; a mighty head, a mighty arm, not a mighty heart. As force is preferred before all things in God, so in man; hence in religion; thence in all human affairs. And as woman has less force than man, less force of muscle, less force of mind, has more fineness of body, superior fineness of intellect, has eminence of conscience, eminence of affection, eminence of the religious power, eminence of soul; as she is inferior to man in his lower elements, and superior in his higher, — so she has been prostrated before him. Her Right of nature has been trodden underfoot by his Might of nature. This degradation of woman is obvious in all forms of religion; it is terribly apparent in the Christian Church. The first three Gospels, — the last is an exception — the writings of Paul and Peter, the book of Revelation, have small respect for woman, little regard for marriage. The Bible makes woman the inferior of man; his instrument of comfort, his medium of posterity; created as an after-thought, for an "helpmeet" to man, because "it was not good for man to be alone." Marriage in the New Testament — in the first three Gospels at least — is only for time: "in the kingdom of Heaven they neither marry nor are given in marriage." It is a low condition here; celibacy is the better of the two; "it is not good to marry;" — only "all men cannot receive this saying." The Christ was represented as born with no human father, — his very birth a fling at wedlock.

The Christian Church has long taught that marriage was a little unholy; and woman was bid to be ashamed of that part of her nature which made her a daughter first, and afterwards a wife and mother. What do Jerome, Augustine, and Aquinas, and the Popes say of connubial love? They have Paul as warrant for their unnatural creed. All this depreciation of woman comes from the idea of a God with whom might is more than right; the idea of a God that is mighty in his head, in his outstretched arm, but is feeble in his conscience, and feeble in his heart; a most unmotherly God.

But the Absolute Religion will give woman her true place in the family, as the equivalent of man; and when the family is of two free spiritual individualities, grouped together by mutual love, for mutual self-denial and mutual delight, then we shall have a family religion such as the world never saw before. And that will not be deemed the most religious family, which has the most of psalm-singing and of prayers, — excellent things, I deny not, — but that wherein every law of the body and every law of the spirit are most completely kept; where man is joined to woman, and woman joined to man in passional and affectional love, with mutual sacrifice and mutual surrender; the wedlock of equals, not the huddling together of a superior and an inferior.

See this in its Social Form, — that of Human Life in Communities. All men will be regarded as equal in nature, equal in rights, equally entitled to take a just and natural delight in the world of matter, on the same just and natural conditions which God has laid down. The Absolute Religion of the individual must be "professed" in the institutions of society, and be made life in the world of men. Then Morality will take the form of Industry in all its million modes; of Natural Enjoyment of the products of industry; of Justice, regulating the intercourse of men by the golden rule, which is alike the standard measure in the mind of Man and in the mind of God; the form of Friendship with a few, from whom we ask delight in return for the joy we give; the form of Philanthropy to all, asking no return. Industry will be deemed a divine service; and a man's shop, library, bank, office, warehouse, farm, his station in church or state, — all will be deemed the special temple wherein he is to worship the Father by natural Morality, — service with every limb of his body, every faculty of his spirit, every power over matter or man which he has gained. Friendship, with its mutual triumph and reciprocal surrender, Philanthropy, which comes as charity to palliate the effects of ill, or as justice to remove the cause of ill, — these will be deemed the noble factors in the religion of society, to work out "a far more exceeding, even an eternal weight of glory." Then the tools of a man's work, the farmer's plough, the mason's trowel, the griddle of the cook, the needle of the seamstress, and the scholar's pen, will be reckoned the consecrated vessels of our divine service, and of man's daily communion with man.

There will be a Church, doubtless, for gathering the multitudes from the cold air, to warm their faces where one great man lights the fire with sentiments and ideas which he has caught from God. There will be a Sabbath for rest, for thought, for ideas, for sentiments; hours of self-communion, of penitence, of weeping; aspirations, hours of highest communion and life with God; but the whole world will be a temple, every spot holy ground, every bush burning with the Infinite, all time the Lord's day, and every moral act worship and a sacrament. Then men will see that voluntary idleness is a sin; that profligacy is a sin; that deceit is a sin; that fraud in work and in trade is a sin; that no orthodoxy of belief, no multitude of prayers, no bodily presence in a meeting-house, no acceptance of an artificial sacrament, can ever atone for neglect of the great natural sacrament which God demands of every man.

Will not that be a change in society? Now, the man of the popular theology sneaks into Church on the first day of the week, and hopes thereby to atone for an abnegation of God on the other six; communes with God through bread and wine, and refuses to commune with him in buying and selling; is a liar, a usurer, a kidnapper before men, while he professes to be a saint before God. What is taught to him as "revealed religion," does not rebuke his pride, nor correct his conduct.

Then, with the teaching of the true Absolute Religion, it will be seen that the great man is only the great Servant of Mankind. He that is powerful by money, office, culture, genius, owes mankind an eminence of industry, justice, and love, as pay to God for the opportunities, the station, the strength, which he has received. God gave him greatness by nature; society gave him greatness of culture, of wealth, of station; — Why? That he might do the more service, not take the more ease. The man of genius is born to be eyes for the public. If he looks out only for himself he has denied the faith, and is an Infidel.

Then it will be seen that the true function of the powerful class, — men strong by Money, wherein New England is so rich, men strong by Culture, whereof New England is even now so poor — is to do mankind an eminent service; to protect the needy, the defenceless, the ignorant, and the wretched. Riches are valuable as they fertilize the soil for human excellence to grow on, not for some lazy weed to rise and rot. If wealth impoverish him that gets, or those from whom it was won, there is a twofold curse, blasting him that takes, and those who aid therein. If superior culture only shuts out the scholar from common men, he had better have spent his years in a coal pit than a college. True religion, true manhood, teaches that if you receive genius and talent from God, or culture at the cost of men — you owe the use of all to men, to the poor, the ignorant, the feeble-minded. Science is moral when it opens the eyes of the blind, and teaches the foolish to understand wisdom; Wealth is pious when it helps Charity palliate the ills she cannot cure, and aids Justice to extirpate the wrongs which curse mankind; Strength is religious when it bears the burdens of the weak.

When the knowledge of the infinite God is spread abroad in Society, social honors will not be given to a man for the accident of famous birth, or merely for gathered gold; not for the station to which some human chance has blown the man; not for his culture of intellect alone, nor for the dear gift of genius which God gave him at his birth; but for the use he makes of his native gifts or labored acquisitions; for his faithfulness to himself, to man, and God; for his justice, his love, and his piety, shown by the use of one talent or ten.

There will always be diversities in natural powers and in the use thereof, and so diversities of culture, of property, of social station and social power. God is democratic and loves all, but the odds between the natural gifts of John and James may be greater than the difference betwixt the plains of Lombardy and the Alps which look down thereon. Men may try to forget this fact; America may put little, mean men with mediocrity of intellect, into her president's chair; may put little mean men with ordinary mind and with feeble conscience, with inferior affections and a paltry soul, into their pulpits; but God still goes on creating his great masterly men, with immense intellect and commensurate moral, affectional, and religious powers, who while they come to bless, perforce, must overawe and terrify the littleness which burrows in state and church; men who receive the earliest salutation of new-rising truth, and shed it down, reflecting from far up the Higher Law's intolerable day on president and priest. Alas, great minds have hitherto been commonly the tyrants of the times, oppressors in the state, and worse oppressors in the church: and humble men believed that God was only Might, not also Right and Love; so they paid a base and servile homage to the great oppressor, and trod down justice, mercy, love, in their haste to kneel before a Pope or King: Jesus of Nazareth is still exceptional in the world's long life; Napoleon is instantial. But if selfish popes and kings are common history, the self-denying Christ is prophecy of what one day shall be. For as God made the mountains stony, huge, and tall, that they, screening the vale below, might wrestle with the storm, and clothe their shoulders with ice and snow — garments woven for them and carefully put on by each wayfaring cloud, — and therewith robe the plains beneath in green and vari-colored dress; so has he made great, mountainous-minded men as forts of defence for all the rest, and treasuries of help. Great men shall not always misuse their five talents, nor little men hide their one piece of the Lord's small money in the ground; mankind long stumbling will one day learn to walk.

Then men will see that that is the most religious community where, proportionately, the most pains is taken to secure the welfare of all, to speed Genius on its triumphant way, to help the poor, the feeble, men of imperfect body and imperfect brain, and those sad wrecks of circumstance we now pile up in jails to moulder and to rot. A Steeple and a Gallows will not always be the signs significant of a Christian land. Men will not measure the religion of society by the number of the temples and priests, but by the colleges and school-houses, the hospitals, the asylums for the old, the sick, the deaf, the blind, the foolish, the crazy, and the criminal; nay, they will measure it by the honest Industry in business; by Truth in science; by Beauty in literature; by Justice in the state; by the Comfort, the Health, the Manhood of the men.

Look at this in its Ecclesiastical form, that of Human Life in Churches. Men will combine about some able man for these three purposes — to kindle their religious Feelings by social communion; to learn the true Idea of God, of Man, and of the Relation between the two, the idea of duty to be done and rights to be possessed; to make the idea a Fact, so that what at first was but subjective feeling, then a thought, shall next be translated into deed, done into Men, Families, Communities, States, and a World, and so the Ideal of God become the Achievement of Mankind.

Then the function of the Church will be to keep all the old which is good, and get all possible good which is new. No creed, no history, or Bible shall interpose a cloud betwixt Man and God; reverence for Moses, Jesus, or Mohammed shall be no more a stone between our eyes and truth, but a glass telescopic, microscopic, to bring the thought of God yet nearer to our heart. The Bible's letter shall no longer kill; but the spirit which "touched Isaiah's hallowed lips with fire," and flamed in the life of a Nazarene Carpenter till its light shone round the world, will dwell also in many a new-born soul. No man shall be master, to rule with authority over our necks; but whoso can teach shall be our friend and guide to help us on the heavenly road.

Then the minister must be a man selected for his human power, — for his power of mind, of conscience, and of heart and soul; with well-born genius if we can find it, with well-developed talents at the least. His function will be to help awaken the feeling of Piety in all men's hearts; to bring to light the ideas of Absolute Religion which human nature travails with, longing to bear; and to make the inward worship, also, outward act. He must help apply this idea to life. Negatively — this will be criticism, exposure of the false, the ugly, and the wrong, the painful part of preaching, the surgery of the church. Positively — it will be creation, making application of religion to the individual, the family, community, state, and world. So the minister will not aim to appease an offended God, grim, revengeful, and full of paltry resentment; nor to communicate a purchased salvation from the fabled torments of hell; nor to add the imputed righteousness of a good man to help us to an unreal heaven. But with the consciousness of God in his heart, with the certain knowledge of God's infinite perfection, sure of the perfect motive, purpose, means of God and conscious of eternal life, he is to preach the natural laws of man. He is to lead in science, if it be possible, — in physics, ethics, metaphysics; to lead in justice, applying its abstract laws to concrete life — not to hinder them by institutions, or by books, by the Vedas, the Koran, or the Testament; to lead in love, connubial, friendly, philanthropic; ay, to lead in holiness, — the subjective service of God which is worship in spirit and in truth, the objective worship, which is service by the normal use, development, and enjoyment of every limb of the body, every faculty of the spirit, every power acquired over matter or man. He will be more anxious to understand truth, beauty, and justice, to have love and faith; more anxious to communicate these to man, and organize them into individual, domestic, social, national, human life, than to baptize men in water from the Jordan, the Ganges, or the Irrawaddy. He will be accounted the most valuable minister who most helps forward the highest development of mankind; and that will be held as the most religious Church whose members live the manliest life of the body and the spirit — with the most of normal use, development, and enjoyment of all their nature, — do the most of human duty, enjoy the most of human rights, and so have the most and the manliest delight in themselves, in Nature, in Man and God.

See this religion in the Political Form, that of Human Life in Nations. Here the aim will be to take the Constitution of the Universe for the foundation of political institutions, making absolute Justice the standard measure in all political affairs, and reënacting the Higher Law of God into all the statutes of the people's code. Men of Genius, in all its many modes, will be the nation's telescopic eye to discover the Eternal Right. The highest thought of the most gifted and best cultured men will become the ideal which the nation seeks to incorporate in its code, to administer in its courts, and revive in its daily life. That will be thought the most religious nation whose institutions, constitutions, statutes, and decisions, conform the most to abstract right, applying this to its action abroad and at home; where the whole people are the best and the best off; and the higher law of God is carried out in the action of the nation with other states, of the government with the people, of class with class, and of man with man. As proofs of the national religion you will bring forward the character of the people — their conduct abroad and at home, their institutions and their men.

This religion must take a Cosmic, or General Human Form, in the Life of Mankind. It will unite all nations into one great bond of brotherhood. As the members and various faculties of Thomas or Edward are conjoined in a man, with personal unity for all, but individual freedom for each; as several persons are joined together in a family, with domestic unity for all, but individual freedom for each; as the families form a community, and the communities a state, with social and national unity of action, but yet with domestic and social individuality of action; so the nations of the world will join together, all working with cosmic human unity of action, but each having its own national individuality of action. This would realize the dim ideal of Pagan Zeno — who counted men, "not as Athenians and Persians, but as joint-tenants of a common field to be tilled for the advantage of all and each," — and ot Christian Paul — who taught that the God whom the Athenians ignorantly worshipped "made of one blood all nations of men."

Then law would be justice, loyalty righteousness, and

patriotism humanity. Men conscious of the same human nature, and consciously serving the infinite God, must needs find their religion transcending the bounds of their Family, Community, Church and Nation, and reaching out to every human soul. But hitherto forms of religion have been a wedge to sever men, and not a tie to bind. The popular theologies of the world in this life aim to separate the "Christian" from the "Heathen," the Protestant from the Catholic, the Unitarian from the Trinitarian, the new school from the old school; and in the next life, the "reprobate" from the "elect," the sinner from the saint.

On the last five Sundays, I have spoken of Atheism and of the Popular Theology. I hope I did no injustice to Atheism, none to the Atheist. It is a sad thought, his world without a God; his here, but no Hereafter; his body, and no Soul. I hope I did him no injustice. One thing he surely has that the popular theologian has not: he has Freedom; freedom from fear, freedom to use his faculties. This freedom will last forever. But the theory of the atheist abuts in selfishness, and in darkness his little light goes out.

I hope I did no injustice to the Popular Theology. It is grim, it is awful. It bears great truths in its bosom, and those truths will last forever; but the popular theology as a system must fall. It rests on two columns.

One is the Idea of an Angry God, imperfect in wisdom, in power, in justice, love, and holiness; a finite, and jealous, and revengeful God; creating man from mean motives, for a mean purpose, and of a mean material,— God with a hell under his feet, "paved with skulls of infants not a span long," and swarming full of horrid, writhing life, that chokes it to the brim.

The other pillar is the Idea of a Supernatural Christ, a *God and* yet a man, with a supernatural birth, supernatural works, resurrection, and ascension — a supernatural atoning sacrifice to take away the sins of the world. These are the Jachin and Boaz of this theology.

Philosophy strikes down the first column, and there is no angry God, no infinite hell "paved with skulls of infants not a span long," and full of horrid, writhing life; and so Theology swings in the air at one end.

Criticism strikes away the other pillar, the supernatural Christ: there is no supernatural Christ, a God and yet a man, with a supernatural birth, supernatural works, resurrection, ascension, — an atoning sacrifice to take away the sins of the world. And so Theology swings in the air at the other end. It lacks a philosophical basis and historical foundation; false in its idea, and false also in its historic fact.

The scientific atheist mocks at the God of the popular theology. Lalande says, I have looked far off through my telescope, and there is no God betwixt me and the furthest star, for I have seen all the way through. Ehrenberg, with his microscope, finds a million million of creatures in a single cubic inch of polishing slate from Germany; but he finds no theological God therein. The chemist analyzes the materials of the world into their elements, and he finds oxygen, carbon, and the rest, but he finds no theologic God therein. The scientific atheist mocks at the Church's God.

The popular idea of God is inadequate for Science; ay, yet worse, it is inadequate for Philanthropy; for the philanthropist loves the poor, the beggar, loves the

Indian, the slave, the outcast, the atheist, and the criminal; and Theology says "The slave is the posterity of Ham, whom God cursed by Noah and spurned from his feet; and sinners are to have an everlasting hell in the world to come." The atheists turn off with scorn from the theologic idea of a God who knows less than Alphonso of Castile; and the philanthropist, with a tear, turns from the damning deity of the popular Church.

Hence comes the position of Religion to-day. Look at Boston: how small is the Church and how poor; how big is the tavern and how rich! Why, the keeper of the tavern in Boston is more influential than "the minister of Christ:" the consecrated preacher in his pulpit trembles before Felix in his bar. The Holy Ghost of the Church, with the other two persons of the Trinity, yields to the Spirit of the Tavern; there is "no room for them in the inn;" happy if they can find a manger with the oxen, and a swaddling garment for their new-born piety in the cattle's crib. Look at Boston, with its hundred clergymen, — religion is no restraint in business, no restraint in politics; not at all; and in our literature of mediocrity, — that is the only literature which America yet possesses — religion is a force infinitesimally small, and not felt. It dares not speak against drunkenness and prostitution; it is dumb religion, and dares not even oppose the stealing of men out of their houses in this town. The minister's "kingdom is not of this world;" no, verily, it belongs to a world that is dead and gone. Respectable gentlemen do not ask Morality in a lawyer; they expect it not in a politician; they ask it of the minister. God be thanked, they do ask some little of it there. But it is only moral decency, — compliance with easy-mannered virtue, not the morality of a Paul whose spirit was stirred in him when he saw the city wholly given to idolatry; no, it is only the Ephesian morality of Demetrius! But a lawyer whose life is corrupt, who is unscrupulous and unprincipled, or a politician who is rotten, will not find that he is less trusted by the great cities of this country. Tell men that slavery is wicked; that to play the pirate in Cuba is sin, — what do they say? They quote the constitution. "Politics is national housekeeping, not national morality," say they. "Talk of the Higher Law, do you? You are a fanatic! We disposed of that long ago."

I say the Popular Theology is not a "finality," — to use the language of the day. It is doomed to perish. Let me do it no injustice. Mankind is very serious; a very honest mankind; and its great works are done with sweat and watching and sore travail. Down on its knees went mankind to pray for this theology; and we have it. With many faults it has great truths. The truths will never perish; they will last while God is God. Even its faults have done mankind no small service. War has taught us activity, and discipline of body and mind; has helped the organization of men; shown the power of thousands when molten to a single mass, and wielded by a single will. But the popular theology has taught greater things than that: it has shown the omnipotent obligation of Duty; to sacrifice every thing for God — the body and the spirit, the intellect, with its pride of reasoning, the conscience with its righteousness; the affections, with their love of father and mother and wife and child. The warrior all stained with blood and sweating with his lust, it taught to subordinate the flesh to the spirit, to scorn the joys of the sense, to practise self-denial of ease and honor and health and riches and life, for the good that is purely spiritual. This is the lesson which ascetic Protestantism has so grimly taught to you and me, and ascetic Catholicism to the Christian world. The monks and nuns, the martyrs of the Inquisition, the saints who went hungry and naked and cold; the infidels and atheists who turned off from all religion frighted by this bugbear of the Church; the dreadful doubts and fears and madness and despair of the world, — these are the tuition fees which mankind has paid for this great lesson.

Let this theology pass. Science hates it. Every Cyrena from the London clay — a leaf gathered from the Book of God now newly unfolded from the flinty keeping of a pebble on a subterranean beach, myriads of years older than Moses — confutes Moses and turns the popular Theology upside down. Philanthropy hates it; hates its jealous God, its narrow love, its pitiless torment, and its bottomless and hopeless hell. Let it pass. It can do little for us now; little for the mind and the conscience of the world; nothing for the affections, nothing for the soul. It can only drive men by fear, not charm by love. Let it pass; and its ministers tremble before the bank, the shop, and the tavern. Let the churchling crouch down before the worldling if he will.

But will Atheism aid us any more? It will do nothing, cheer nothing. It has only this to perform, — to rid men of fear and bondage to ancient creeds. It never was a spring of action, and never can be. No! We must root into the soil of God, else we perish for lack of earth. An earth without a Heaven, a here with no Hereafter, a body without a Soul, and a world without a God — will that content the science and satisfy the philosophy of these times? Fill your mouth with the east wind! Atheism can never teach man that solemn, beautiful word,—*I ought;* only *I must*, which is Fatalism; or *I will*, which is Libertinism; never *I ought*, which is the mark of perfect obedience, and perfect freedom too. Atheism knows not the word Duty which marries Might with Right.

Well, shall we be without religion,—this Caucasian race, which has outgrown the worship of Nature, Polytheism, the Hebrew form of faith, classic Deism, and is fast outgrowing this popular Theology? I smile at the dreadful thought. Shall the great forces of modern civilization be wielded only for material ends? Here is America, a young nation, yet giant strong, with twenty million souls all cradled in her lap; and three million souls spurned as dust beneath her cruel feet. She has set her heart on this continent, "I will have all this goodly land," quoth she. She has set her affections on money, vulgar fame, and power. Every mountain gives us coal, iron, lead, water for our mill; California delights to tempt us with her gold. And America, speaking with the new and brazen trumpet of the State, says, "There is no Higher Law forbidding me to plunder Spain and Mexico, or crush the Black as I slew the Red." Says America, through the other trumpet, the old and brazen trumpet of the Church, "There is no Higher Law! Plunder and crush!"

Is that to be so? Is modern civilization, with science that formulates the heavens and reads the hieroglyphics of the sky, with mechanical skill which surpasses all the dreams of faery,—modern civilization, with such riches, such material power, such science, such physics, ethics, metaphysics, with Berlins of scientific lore, with London, Paris, and New York, affluent with energy — is this to be an irreligious civilization; genius without justice, riches without love, organization for the strong, the rich, and the noble-born, an organization to oppress, a civilization without God? No! You say no, and I say no; human history says no; human nature says no!

What shall hinder? The popular Theology? The usurer, the politician, the kidnapper, in their selfishness, laugh at your Old and New Testament, and spurn at your hell. The Christian churches are on the side of sin; oppression is favored by them the old world through, and oppression is favored by them the new world through. "Renounce the world!" says the priest, and means "Renounce the Higher Law of God." Soon as sin is popular the church christens it, and re-annexes the sin to itself. Did the American Church do aught against the Mexican war? Will it do aught against the Cuban war? It will put Cuban gold into its treasury to evangelize the heathen. What does it do against the awful sin of America at this day? It has strengthened the arm of the oppressor; it has riveted chains on the bondman's neck. But just now — thanks to the Almighty God! — the churches of New England and the West, met in solemn convocation at Albany, have protested against this mighty sin; and have charged their clergymen who went to those corners of the land where the sin is practised, to bear their testimony against it; and if men would not hear them, then to depart out of their city. This is the first time; and it marks the turning of the tide which ere-long will leave this old theology all high and dry upon the sand, a Tadmor in the desert.

The religion which we want must be of another stamp. It must recognize the Infinite God, who is not to be feared, but loved; not God who thunders out of Sinai in miraculous wrath, but who shines out of the sun on evil and on good, in never-ending love. It must respect the universe, matter, and man; and worship God by natural Piety and serve Him with the Morality of nature.

Then what a force Religion will be! There will be a religion for the body, to serve God with every limb thereof; a religion for the intellect, and we shall hear no more of "atheistic science," but Lalande shall find God all the world through, in every scintillation of the furthest star he looks at, and Ehrenberg confront the Infinite in each animated dot or cell of life his glass brings out to light; yea, the chemist will meet the Omnipresent in every atom of every gas. Then there shall be a religion for Conscience, the great Justice; a religion for the Affections, the great Love; a religion for the Soul, perfect Absolute Trust in God, Joy in God, Delight in this Father and Mother too.

Then what Men shall we have! not dwarfed and crippled, but giant men, Christlike as Christ. What Families! woman emancipated and lifted up. What Communities! a society without a slave, without a pauper; society without ignorance, wealth without crime. What Churches! Think of the eight and twenty thousand Protestant churches of America, with their eight and twenty thousand Protestant ministers, with a free press, and a free pulpit, and think of their influence if every man of them believed in the Infinite God, and taught that the service of God was by natural Piety within and natural Morality without; that there was no such thing as imputed righteousness, or salvation by Christ; but that real righteousness was honored before God, and salvation by character, by effort, by prayer, and by toil, was the work! Then what a nation should we have! ay, what a world!

We shall have it; it is in your heart and in my heart; for God, when he put this idea into human nature, meant that it should only go before the fact, — the John the Baptist that heralds the coming of the great Messiah.

"Eternal Truth shines on o'er errors' cloud,
Which from our darkness hides the living light;
Wherefore, when the true Bard hath sung aloud
His soul-song to the unreceptive night,
His words, like fiery arrows must alight,
Or soon, or late, and kindle through the earth,
Till Falsehood from his lair be frighted forth.

"Work on, oh fainting Heart, speak out thy Truth;
Somewhere thy winged heart-seeds will be blown,
And be a grove of Pines; from mouth to mouth,
O'er oceans, into speech and lands unknown,
E'en till the long-foreseen result be grown
To ripeness, filled like fruit, with other seed,
Which Time shall plant anew, and gather when men need."

SERMON VII.

OF IMMORTAL LIFE.

1 CORINTHIANS XV. 49

WE SHALL ALSO BEAR THE IMAGE OF THE HEAVENLY.

VII.

OF THE FUNCTION AND INFLUENCE OF THE IDEA OF IMMORTAL LIFE.

I ASK your attention this morning to a sermon of the true Function and legitimate Influence of the Idea of Immortality. The subject is most intimately connected with the Theism lately spoken of.

The boy stolen from his mother by wolves in Hindostan, and brought up by them with their own young, becomes like a wolf. He seems to have no thought except for the day; his motives are gathered only from his present wants; no more. He satisfies his animal appetites, and then sleeps. Behold the sum of his consciousness! He knows no past, cares for no future, and has nothing within him which checks any instinctive desire. There is man reduced to his lowest terms, living from the lowest motives, animal selfishness; for the lowest ends, animal existence, brute enjoyment; by the lowest means, the instinct of brute desire. In that case human nature is as poor as it can live.

The cultivated citizen of Boston extends his thought in the present, to all the corners of the earth, takes in all the countries of the globe; the doings in Europe and in Asia affect his daily consciousness. He embraces the stars of heaven; his telescopic thought sweeps the horizon of the universe. The discovery of a new planet is a joy to him, though his eye shall never taste its light. He connects himself with the past; he remembers his father and his mother, loving to trace his branch of the family-tree far down, — now to a New England sachem, now to a Norman king, or till it touches the ground in some Teutonic savage three thousand years ago. He loves to follow its roots underground to Noah, or Adam, or Deucalion, or Thoth, or some other imaginary character in the Heathen or Hebrew mythology. Thus he enlarges his present consciousness by recollecting or imagining the past, and is richer for every step he takes in history or fantasy. Not satisfied with this, he reaches forth to the future, with one hand building genealogies and tombs for his grandsires, and with the other houses for his grandchildren.

Thus our cultivated man enlarges his consciousness by the thought of men that are about him, behind him, and before him; all of these lay their hands, as it were, upon his shoulders, to magnetize him with their manhood, present, past, or to come; for as there is a long train of men, our brothers, reaching out from you and me to the furthest verge of the green earth, so there is another long train, six hundred or six thousand generations deep, standing behind us, each laying its hands on its forerunner's shoulders, and all communicating their blood and their civilization unto us who inherit the result of their bodily and spiritual toil.

It is a delight thus to extend our personality in Space, by knowledge of matter and man, and control over both; and in Time, by our connection with the family, reaching both ways, by our relation to the human race, in its indefinite extent backwards and around us on either hand. Human motives are gathered from the whole range of human consciousness and human knowledge, and our inward life is enlarged and enriched by the sweep of our intellect.

So the daily life of a civilized man in Boston comes to be consciously influenced by his wider knowledge of the present, by his acquaintance with the past, by his anticipations of the future. This man is checked from wrong and encouraged to good, by the character of his acquaintances about him; some men by recollecting their father and their mother, whose names we would not sully with our daily sin. Almost every parent is animated by the desire to bless his children in generations that are to come. Thus the generations are bound together, and the personality of John and Jane in actual history is carried back to the first man, and in fancy is carried forward to the last. A grandfather in the house, a baby in the cradle, a mother at hand or afar off in the hills of Berkshire, remembering us in her evening prayer, — each of these is a hostage for the good conduct of mortal men. This young man will not dice or drink lest he wound the bosom which bore him. That young woman denies herself for her child, forbears the enormities of life lest she should poison the blood in the veins of one not yet born, or now drinking life from her breast. The wider is the circle of human observation, without or within, the more plenteous is the harvest of motive and delight gleaned up therefrom.

But men go further than that, and extend their individuality beyond the grave. The belief in the future life is at first a dim sentiment, an instinctive feeling, then a conscious desire, a dreaming of immortality;

then the hope and fear thereof; and at last it is a certain confidence in eternal life, an absolute delight in immortality.

Thus successively the human landscape widens out from the wolf's den of that savage boy till it takes in family, neighborhood, nation, mankind, all ages past on earth, all generations yet to come; yes, till our horizon of consciousness in its sweep includes God and Eternity.

There is a God of Infinite Perfection: the Soul of each man is destined to Eternal Life. These are the two greatest truths which human consciousness as yet has ever entertained. They are the most important; and if the human treasures of thought were to go to the ground and perish, all save what some few men grasped in their hands and fled off with, escaping from a new deluge, should clutch these two truths as the most priceless treasure which the human race had won, and journey off with them to pitch my tent anew, and with these treasures build up a fresh and glorious civilization. When a man is influenced by hope and fear for the Future World, he is a higher being, much higher, than when this life was the limit to his thought.

But the influence of the Idea of Immortality has by no means proved an unmixed good. It has brought much evil on the world. It has been connected with the idea that God was malignant; and then the prospect of future life has been the culprit's anticipation of trial, torture, and damnation without end. Men have believed that the other side of the grave the Devil waited, armed with his torments, to seize poor Dives, who had his "good things in this life," and in the next stage make him smart for the purple and fine linen he wore in this. So the consciousness of immortality has often clouded over the future life with fear. Thus there is a popular ballad of the Middle Ages which describes a boy suffering bereavement, disease, poverty, and many a grief; and he says,

> "I would fain lie down and die,
> But for the curse of immortality."

I have heard ministers preach whose notions of the future life were of the grimmest sort, — so that with their belief, I would not have sent a rat or a mouse beyond the grave; nor wished my worst enemy to cross over, — and yet they said the common notion of immortal life was "too good to be true!" It was too bad to be true. I knew it was so bad that God would blot it out as a contradiction which could not be, and would never allow it to be a divine fact, only a human folly, which those men dreamed of.

In virtue of this fear, the belief in immortality has secured to the priesthood an immense amount of power, and excessive dominion over mankind; an authority wellnigh irresponsible, and which has led to great cruelty on their part. The priest taught men, "It is a terrible thing to fall into the hands of the living God. He is angry with the wicked every day, and keeps his anger forever." "Alas," groaned the believer, "what shall I do to be saved?" Then the priest replied, "*I*, and I alone, can appease the wrath of God. O selfish Baron Rackrent, full of sin, and waiting to die, give me thy money, give the Church thy broad lands, or else forever suffer and rot in hell!" And the Baron, extending his selfishness beyond the tomb, frightened at the picture of the "Last Judgment" painted on the walls of the Church, or the "Dance of Death" sculptured in the graveyard, where Death and the Devil waltz and saraband mankind to Hell, gave to the priests the riches which they set their celibate hearts upon, and robbed his own heirs of many a fair rood of upland and of meadow under the influence of this fear and of the priesthood who fanned its dreadful flame.

The thought of immortality has turned men away from natural Piety and natural Morality. The priest declared, " That will do very well to live with, it is good for nothing to die by." So this belief, thus distorted, has led to unnatural modes of life; has crushed the delight out of many a heart, and has hindered the human race in their progress. Even now the fear of death and of torment sicklies over the countenance of men when their mortal hour draws nigh; tears, alarm, and whimpering and snivelling on a death-bed, are commonly thought by ecclesiastical persons to be better evidence of religion in the heart than a life forty or fifty years long, adorned every day by the beauty of holiness within and the beauty of righteousness without.

All these evils come from the idea that God is malignant and loves to torture the children of men; and that idea itself has come from the infancy of mankind, and like other poor follies is one day to be outgrown and left behind us with the childish things of our boyhood.

These evils continue at the present day; for God, though called a Father, is commonly thought a tyrant. So his government of this world is represented as a tyrannical despotism, and his Heavenly Kingdom is commonly painted so that it is the last thing which one would think of with pleasure. I never saw a picture of the "Last Judgment," which did not make me shiver with horror at the thought that any man could be so savage as to paint it. I never read a "Judgment Hymn" in a Psalmbook, from Origen of Alexandria to Lyman Beecher of Boston,—even Luther's, modified by three hundred years of civilization since his death—which was not fit to make a man's blood curdle in his veins. Only one sect has taught the doctrine of immortality in such a guise that any man need wish it to be true—the Universalists; and that sect is only a small fraction of the Christian world. If the common notions of eternal life were true, then we ought to call it Eternal Death; immortality would be the greatest curse God could inflict upon mankind. It is too bad to be true. Annihilation would be better:—

> "Feelingly sweet were stillness after storm,
> Though under covert of the wormy ground."

In the popular mythology, God is represented as turning Adam and Eve out of Paradise, with bitter execrations,—"Cursed is the ground for thy sake; in sorrow shalt thou eat of it all the days of thy life; thorns also and thistles shall it bring forth to thee." Fortunately that part of the popular mythology was writ by a man who makes no mention of immortality. Probably he had never heard of it. If he had he might have added that God knit his brows at mankind, baring his red right arm, and then said, "Eat also of the tree of life and live forever, and I will torture you for all eternity." The Hebrew writer probably had not heard of immortality; he did not add that; he left it for Christian doctors to do. So in the popular theology the Fall was the first misfortune of mankind, and Immortality the last. To die bodily was looked upon as the first curse, but to be unable to die in the soul is looked upon as the last curse. Read sermons—and they are of the commonest—on the fate of the wicked in the next life, and they shall tell you, almost all of them, that the wicked, the reprobate, the damned, will call out for the hills to fall on us, on the mountains to cover us; and the remorseless hills will not stir; the unpitying mountains will not start an inch; man shall ask for annihilation and have Hell for answer.

Yet spite of this horrible doom prepared for mankind, as it is alleged, which makes immortality a curse and the thought of it a mildew, — the doctrine is so dear to the human heart, to the reflective head of mankind, that it is clung to, loved, believed in, and cherished by the mass of men all over the world. Even the Churches' fabled hell cannot frighten mankind out of their love for eternal life, " This longing after immortality."

> ——— " For who would lose
> Though full of pain, this intellectual being,
> These thoughts that wander through eternity ? "

The doctrine of eternal life is always popular. If you were to poll the world to-day and get the ayes and noes of all mankind, nine hundred and ninety-nine out of every thousand would give their vote for immortality. Yet few have ever reasoned about it much, and demonstrated their immortality. Most men think that they take it on trust from the mouth of their priest, or from "revelation," — the Christians from the Bible, the Mahometans from the Koran. But it is not so; we do not take it on trust from a man. Like what else comes from the primitive instincts of the human heart, we take it on trust from the Father; from no less authority.

I mention these things to show first, how deep is the instinct of immortality in our heart, for all nations above the nakedness of the most savage have fastened their hopes on this; they have dug down to this primitive rock, never very far from the surface; and next to show how strong it is, which even the fear of the future eternal torment cannot annihilate. For sixteen or eighteen hundred years the Christian Church has preached the docrine of immortality in such a form that it is only another name for the wrath of God and eternal torment to the mass of men; but with all this preaching it has not scared the belief thereof out of the heart of man, and it cannot.

And yet dear as this doctrine is to the heart of mankind, for many hundred years you find powerful men of great ability aiming to destroy the belief in it. These philosophers have had a bad name in human history because they denied what the heart of man loved to believe, what the analogy of Nature plainly taught, and what also the noblest philosophy proves as its very highest affirmation. It is a strange thing that men who have preached eternal damnation for the vast majority of mankind, have a good name in every Church, — St. Augustine, Gregory, — half a dozen of that name; — St. Bernard, a mighty preacher of eternal ruin; and in our own country, Edwards, Hopkins, and Emmons, among the most venerable names of our American Church. But on the other hand, men who have declared that God was too good to persecute his children beyond the tomb, — they have everywhere received a bad name.

If a man denies the immortality of the soul, his oath is not allowed in the courts of Christendom. Even in Massachusetts he is an "outlaw," and can prove nothing in a Court of "Justice," except by the testimony of some "believer." His account-books are no "evidence" in court, his testimony of no value. But a man who teaches that the God of the Christians is a thousand times more cruel than any idol-deity of Scandinavia or Hindostan, who will "torture with fire and redhot plates of iron," all but ten in the million, has his oath allowed him in every court!

But we ought to look at the reason which has led the philosophers to deny the doctrine. Some of them have doubtless been low and vulgar men, — as mean as their theological opponents, — and from lowness and vulgarity denied what their lowness and vulgarity hindered them from comprehending. But that is a very small class amongst philosophic men; and it is a rare thing to find a low and vulgar man flying in the face of popular opinion for the sake of an idea. Such men preach the popular doctrine, not the opposite. But it is a fact of history that in old time, from Epicurus to Seneca, some of the ablest heads and best hearts of Greece and Rome sought to destroy the idea of immortality. This was the reason: they saw it was a torment to mankind, that the popular notion thereof was too bad to be true; and so they took pains to break down the Heathen mythology, though with it they destroyed the notion of immortal life. They did a great service to mankind in ridding us from this yoke of fear. The Pagan philosopher and scoffer was a "forerunner" of Jesus, — quite as much so as John the Baptist. Be assured of this; — it is a great thing to destroy an organized tyranny, even if at first you set up no government in its place; for such is the creative power of the human spirit that, if it have a free chance to work, it will soon raise up new Romes out of the dust, and leaving the monarchies of the old continent will build up republics in the new. After you have hewn down the forest and driven off the catamount and the wolf, it is not a hard thing to raise corn and sheep in the new soil.

But soon as Christianity became established in the State, the old tyranny of fear got set up anew; and as the doctrine of immortality appeared in a more distinct form and became more apparent in the Christian than in the Hebrew or Heathen Church, so this fear of future torment became more distinct and more powerful; yes, it became absolute. It was connected with the doctrine of the Fall; with "foreordination by the divine decrees," which is the Fatalism of the Christian Church,—the same thing which had taken a form slightly different in the Greek and Roman theologies, and was again to appear, modified a little further, in the Mahometan theology;—with the idea of "total depravity," and the "infinite evil" of sin; and in such bad company, what wonder is it that the doctrine of immortality became what it did become? It was fear of God, not love of him. It was fear of future torment which brought down the knee and the neck of Christian Europe under its priestly tyrants. It was not love of God which built the costly domes of Italy, and the cathedrals of the North. No, it was fear of hell. An atheistic pope wished to build up a costly church in Rome. He wanted money,—he had rack-rented all Italy,—and so he sent round his apostles, first to preach the wrath of God, the torments of the future world; next that the priesthood had power to appease that wrath and abate those torments; then, as a third thing, that they would do all this for money. Monk Tetzel went about to sell his indulgences,—pardons for sins past, present, and to come. He offered to ticket men all the way through to Heaven; and they might take any quantity of luggage of sin with them, by paying a small additional fare. He had a drum beat; and when men assembled he mounted his stand, opened his ticket-office and began hawking and peddling his ecclesiastical wares. Luther said, "I will make a hole in Tetzel's drum!" — So he did. "The pope," said Luther, "cannot save men from Purgatory; his tickets will not be taken anywhere on the road. Keep your money and renounce your sin!" The sale of indulgences went down all at once; the market stopped.

But the tyranny of fear was not broken: there was only one mode less of escaping it. You could no longer buy off the wrath of God. There lay the bottomless pit, and there was none to ticket men across. Other men undertook to make a larger hole in that same drum; to smite in both heads of it. They said, "The soul is not immortal: death is the end of you!" These men labored to destroy the Christian mythology, just as the old scoffers and philosophers had sought to make way with the Heathen mythology. Did that denial satisfy the world? Quite far from it.

The Human Race is under great obligation to these deniers. These "atheists" have done mankind great service. Epicurus, Pyrrho, Lucretius, Bruno, Voltaire, Paine, Hume, are among the benefactors of the race. It is a great thing to destroy a superstition which rides men as a nightmare. But some of them were among the most miserable of all this earth's martyrs that I have ever read of. There they sat, surrounded by jollity and elegance, wine and scarlet women, the victims of circumstances which they could not control. Their fate was far more pitiful than that of St. Sebastian or St. Catharine. Who would not rather be shot through and through with arrows, or broken for once on a wheel of iron and wood, than be shot at with doubts of immortality and broken constantly with dread of annihilation? Believing men who build up a new religion are always harshly treated, scourged in the market, beaten, let down out of windows in the wall of the city, shipwrecked, persecuted, leaving their heads in a charger, or their bodies on a cross. They have our sympathy, and deserve it, — brave souls in hardy iron flesh. But the unbelieving men who broke down the old religions, and saw no other light in the dusky ruin they made, — they are sadder martyrs in the world's great story! Drop a tear then on the grave of Voltaire, on the tomb of Pomponatius, and on the fires which consumed Jordano Bruno. You and I are made free by their sufferings; by their sorrows are our joys made more certain. In a better age Voltaire might have been as devout and religious as Gerson or Luther, and Bruno have been burned not as a heretic, but as a Christian.

The work of theological destruction is not yet over; far enough from it. The popular mythology must go the same way with the old Greek and Roman mythology, and other martyrs are doubtless demanded for that. No Emperor Julian, apostatizing from the progress of mankind, can save what is false, or destroy the true.

The leading philosophers of Europe seem to have small faith in immortality; some positively deny it; a few mock at it. Many of the enlightened Germans, whom oppression drives to America, deny the immortality of the soul, some openly scoff at the hope of eternal life; and say all belief therein is a misfortune, for it clouds over men's happiness now with fear of future torment, hinders their progress, and makes them believe that Virtue and Justice are not good for their own sake, but only as means to another end. There is a good deal of truth in their objections no doubt; but they all apply only to a false idea of immortality and a wrong use of it; not at all against the true doctrine itself. It seems to me these philosophers wholly overlook the deep desire of mankind for personal immortality; — the natural belief which is so general that it is universal, except in those who have cultivated their intellect at the expense of the conscience, the affections, or the soul; or in whom, in early life, some prejudice has hindered the natural instincts of mankind. They forget what a powerful motive to good it is, what a present enjoyment it affords to the human race; and their denial, it seems to me, is most unphilosophic. And yet they are doing the same service now that Zeno and Lucretius and Lucian did for Christianity. They are the forerunners of some better "dispensation" that is to come.

I know some men fear that these bold deniers of immortal life will destroy the belief of mankind therein. I have no fear of that. Spite of the Catholic Church, for sixteen hundred years preaching immortality as a curse, and the Protestant Church for three hundred years proclaiming it as a mildew and blight, — men have still entertained the belief; and if all the learned clergy of the Protestant world, if all the Catholic clergy of the dark ages, could not make any considerable number of men doubt of immortality, I do not believe that a handful of philosophers speaking in the name of philosophy or mockery, can ever put down that which has held mankind so strongly for two or three thousand years. Immortality has kept the field against Augustine and Jerome, the Basils, the Gregories, and Bernard; has held its own spite of Aquinas and Calvin and Edwards and Hopkins and Emmons, and I think it can laugh at Strauss and Comte and Feuerbach. Has it not in its time heard devils roar, and yet held its own against the Hell of the Church? Do you think, then, it has any thing to fear from the Earth of the material philosophers?

We know little of the next life; nothing of the details thereof. In all the accounts of the future world which are commonly thought by Christians and Mahometans to come from miraculous revelation, you see how poor is the invention of mankind: the basis of the future heaven is always human, earthly. The Mahometan heaven is only what the Mahometan wishes to make earth, a paradise of the senses; all the passions, littleness, and vulgarity of the Mussulman are carried thither and repeated on a great scale. It was so in the Greek heaven; in the heaven of the ancient Germans. The Book of Revelation in our Bible is the work of some bigoted Jew, apparently not at all improved by the Christianity of his time; and its heaven is only a New Jerusalem, a most uncomfortable place for anybody but male and unmarried Jews. With the Puritans, Heaven was a New Plymouth or a New Boston, where the "Elect" had the monopoly which they wanted to get in the old Plymouth or old Boston, but could not quite accomplish; where all the time was Sunday, and the chief business was going to meeting; the chief joy was psalm-singing and listening to Calvinistic explanations of the Scripture, now and then delighting their eyes with the sight of their former opponents writhing in the pains of damnation. It was the Puritans' earthly life, idealized a little, and made eternal; they hoped to see their enemy tortured in hell whom they could not whip at the tail of a cart on earth. The ancient ghosts, who used to be seen, and the modern ghosts, who are now only heard, in their "News from Heaven" only reveal things taken from our daily life. The theological details of the future life are chiefly imaginary, and drawn from our daily intercourse with common things.

It seems to me, however, that we may for a certainty know this,—that man is immortal; that I consider as fixed as the proposition that one and one make two. Then that God is infinitely perfect, a perfect Cause and a perfect Providence; that I consider equally certain as that one and one make two. Of course his infinite care must extend over the whole existence of mankind; must make the future life an infinite blessing for mankind on the whole, an infinite blessing for every human soul. This follows from what has already been said of the nature of God; for the infinite God must create his work from perfect motives and for a perfect purpose, form it of perfect material and provide it with perfect means to attain the perfect end he has proposed. Accordingly, his scheme of things must be so contrived as at last to achieve perfect welfare for the whole of mankind, and for each particular person.

The Form of the future life we know nothing of—whether man shall have a body or no body; and if a body, what shape of body; whether it shall resemble the human shape or any other shape that we can imagine. Man can know nothing of that; no more than the unborn babe can dream of the exploits which it shall perform in after years, in science, art, and daily life.

I am glad that we do not and cannot know this, I do not wish to know; and if it were possible for me to receive a "miraculous" knowledge of what should take place the other side of the grave, I would say to the being who brought the tidings, "Stand back! I do not wish to know." Time is the best fortune-teller. What God has put out of man's power to reach, it is not man's need to have, and it is not his wisdom to grasp after.

The notion of eternal misery, of punishment for the sake of punishment, the doctrine that God exploiters the human race and that men are "tortured for the glory of God,"—that notion deserves all the scorn, all the hate, all the ribaldry, all the mockery which it ever met with from Lucian and Lucretius, from Pomponatius and Voltaire, from Thomas Paine and Richter and Feuerbach: their hammer is not at all too heavy for their hard work.

But the idea of immortality as it belongs to the Absolute Religion, consistent with the Infinite Perfection of God, the philosopher need not hate that; for the belief therein is true to the spontaneous consciousness of human nature, to the reflective consciousness of philosophy, and it is of the greatest value to man as a hope, encouragement, and reward. Let me be sure of two things,—first, of Thine Infinite Perfection, O Father in Heaven! then of my own Immortality,—and I am safe, I fear nothing; I am not a transient bubble on the sea of Time, I shall outlast the "everlasting hills," I am immortal as the monads of matter, immortal as its laws! I may rely on myself, respect myself, feel within me the yearnings after immortality, and I know there is an Infinite Heart which yearns infinitely for me and will take me to itself and bless me at the last.

Then I can rely on something better than I see with my eyes—on the Ideal Excellence which I think in my heart. I can make a sacrifice for it; I can postpone my Now for an immortal Then; I can labor for noble things which it will take a thousand years to accomplish. Things about me may fail, the mountain may fall and come to nought and the rock be removed out of its place, be exhaled a vapor to the sky — I shall not fail. I see

> "The Soul is builded far from accident:
> It suffers not in smiling pomps, nor falls
> Under the brow of thralling discontent;
> It fears not Policy, — that heretic
> That works on leases of short-numbered hours,
> But all alone stands hugely politic."

If to-morrow I am to perish utterly, then I shall only take counsel for to-day, and ask for qualities which last no longer. My fathers will be to me only as the ground out of which my bread-corn is grown; dead, they are like the rotten mould of earth, their memory of small concern to me. Posterity, — I shall care nothing for the future generations of mankind. I am one atom in the trunk of a tree, and care nothing for the roots below, or the branch above. I shall sow such seed as will bear harvest at once. I shall know no Higher Law: Passion enacts my statutes to-day; to-morrow Ambition revises the statutes, and these are my sole legislators. Morality will vanish, Expediency take its place. Heroism will be gone, and instead of it there will be the brute valor of the he-wolf, the brute cunning of the she-fox, the rapacity of the vulture, and the headlong daring of the wild bull; — but the cool, calm courage which, for truth's sake, and for love's sake, looks death firmly in the face and then wheels into line ready to be slain, that will be a thing no longer heard of. Affection will be a momentary delight in other men. The friendship which lays down its life for father, mother, wife, or child, for dear ones tenderly beloved, which sucks the poison from their wounds, — the philanthropy which toils and provides for the friendless, the loveless, the unlovely, and the wicked, — that will only be a story of old time, to be laughed at as men laugh at the tale of the Grecian boy who loved the New Moon as his heavenly bride.

But if I know that I am to live forever, and when yonder sun has seen the whole host of heaven circle about the centre of the universe a million million times, that I still live on, making a greater progress in every forty years than what I have grown to since first I left my mother's arms; — if I know that Mankind will still survive with ever-greatening faculties in some other life, directed by the same Infinite Mind and Conscience, and Heart and Soul that made us first, and guides us in our heavenward march; if I know that each beggar in the street, that every culprit in the jail, or out of it, or haling men thither, has an immortal soul, and will go on greatening and beautifying more and more, — then I shall take the highest qualities which I know, or feel, and work with them; and I shall feel that my personality is one of the permanent forces of the universe, and shall toil with conscious dignity and loving awe. I shall respect myself, and so respect each brother man.

In a hostile country the enemy builds his house of tent-poles and cloth, to last a single night; pillages the neighborhood, hews down the tree to eat its half-ripe fruit, careless of the toil which planted and the hope that waits therefor; and to-morrow he marches away, his city of a night reduced to tent-poles and canvas, packed up in his cart: a bit of vari-colored bunting on a stick, is the symbol of his nomadic havoc. But the resident farmer carefully gathers and providentially plants the seed, and painstakingly rears up the tree, prunes it, grafts it, waits his score of years, and then, apple by apple, he gathers its fruit, the soft for present use, the sound for future store; and his broad barn of limestone, his house of brick, and his marble church, — these are the symbols of the resident. So, under the stimulus of immortality, we shall cultivate those plants of the soul which take deep root, which require years, even ages, to grow, and slowly bear their fruit, a blessing for generations yet to come.

If I know that I am to live forever, in the heat of sensual passion, I shall not set my heart on lust and mere bodily delight; I know something more delightful. In the period of ambition, I shall not set my heart on gold only, or the praise of men; I know what is richer, I know a fame better than fame. I shall remember that I am more than passion's slave, or the madman of ambition; I shall give both their due, — passion its own, and ambition what belongs thereto. Riches and honor, — I shall give them both their own. Then I shall go deeper down, and bring to light the brighter diamonds which I quarry in the human mine.

Consciousness of immortality will not lead to contempt of this life, to weariness of it, to neglect of its duties. Looking up, I shall wish to set my foot on every round of the human ladder. In the dark places of the earth the candle of the Infinite will shine on the habitations of cruelty; and I shall see the way to stave them to the ground, and in their place build up fair-faced dwellings for the sons of men.

To the mortal eye this is a sad world. What a history it is before me, — looking out of these four or five thousand eyes! What daydreams of yours and mine have broke into nothing! What toils unrequited, what sorrows which the world did not know, — all laid away in our consciousness, stratum over stratum, deposited under tranquil or troubled seas!

Look at the world; — at Boston, with all the sorrow which festers in her heart; at happy America, with her dreadful evils; at Europe, with her France, so high, and then so low; with her Germany, full of contemplation, — and a chain on her neck; with Italy and Spain ground under a tyrant's foot; look at Asia, "the cradle of the human race," the cradle turned over and the child spilled out; — at Africa, the nursery of the slaves of the world; — at the Islands of the Sea; — and consider that man is only mortal, and what a spectacle it is! I should die outright at the thought of that! But as I know that I shall live forever, and that the Infinite God loves you and me, each man that walks the ground, — I can look on these evils of the world, on America, Europe, with her France, Germany, Italy, Spain; — I can look on Asia, Africa, and the Islands of the Sea; — and it is all only the hour before sunrise, the light is coming; yes, I am also to light a little torch to illuminate the darkness, while it lasts, and help until the dayspring come.

How heavy are the griefs of personal mortal life! Health decays into sickness, hope into disappointment; death draws near to our little troop of pilgrims, and when we pitch our tent he takes away some beloved head, — a baby now, then an old man, then a father or a mother, a husband or a wife, a relative or a friend, — and at last we sit there, near the end of our pilgrimage, solitary, over our night fire, a few embers only left, and they burning low, while the enemy draws near to quench them, then clutches us and we vanish also into night.

> "Alas for love, if this were all,
> And nought beyond the earth!"

The Atheist sits down beside the coffin of his only child — a rose-bud daughter whose heart death slowly eat away; the pale lilies of the valley which droop with fragrance above that lifeless heart, are flowers of mockery to him; their beauty is a cheat. They give not back his child for whom the sepulchral monster opens its remorseless jaws. The hopeless father looks down on the face of his girl, silent, not sleeping, cold, dead. The "effacing fingers" have put out the eye, yet marble beauty still lingers there, and love, a father's love, continually haunts the disenchanted house. Atheism cannot speed it away; affection has its law, which no impiety of thought annuls. He looks beyond, — the poor sad man, — it is only solid darkness he stares upon. No rainbow beautifies that cloud; there is thunder in it, not light. Night is behind — without a star. His dear one has vanished, her light put out by thunderous death, not a sparklet left. There is no daughter for him — but alas, he is a father still; yet no father to her. For her whose life the blameless baby took, long years gone by, there is no mortal husband, no immortal mother. Child and mother are equal now; each is nothing, both nothing. "I also shall soon vanish," exclaims the man, "blotted out by darkness, and become nothing — my bubble broke, my life all gone, with its bitter tears for the child and the mother who bore her, its bridal and birthday joys, which glittered a moment — how bright they were, then slipped away, — my sorrows all unrequited, my hopes a cruel cheat. Ah me! the stars slowly gathering into one flock, are a sorry sight — each a sphere tenanted perhaps by the same bubbles, the same cheats, the same despair — for it is a here with no Hereafter, a body with no Soul, a world without a God!"

Hard by in the same village, the selfsame night, a thoughtful man, born, baptized, and bred a theological Christian, full of faith in the popular mythology of the churches, accepting its grimmest ghastliness, sits down by the bedside of his prodigal son, his only child, — life's substance squandered on harlots, wasted in riotous living. Death knocks at the profligate's oft battered door: no syren shakes the wanton windows now. The last hour of the impenitent has come. The father looks on that face so like its mortal mother once, now stained by riot, and scarred by lust, the mother's image broke and crushed: so in the sack of a city, a statue of Mary is whelmed over a church portal, and thrown down, and the fragments of shattered loveliness are crunched to dust beneath the lumbering cannon wheels and vulgar drays, while from the street the artist eyes the shards of beauty wrought from his dreams and prayers. The father feels the breath of the vampyre of the tomb as it slowly numbs the youthful limbs, — joint by joint, finger by finger, hand by hand: he sees the mist cloud over the inanimate and soulless eye. Life slowly ripples out from that once manly heart. Telescopic memory sweeps the horizon of the father's consciousness. He remembers the cradle, — bought with such triumph; the birth-night; the little garments previously made ready for the expected guest; the prayer of gratitude for the given and the spared when first he saw his first-born son; he recalls the day of his marriage, when he stood on the world's top and Heaven gave him that angel — it seemed so then — to be loved, a real angel now, long since gone home to Heaven, her heart broken by the son's precocious waywardness. The father watches the ebb of mortal life, it is the flood of hell, bitter, remorseless, endless hell; his son sinks into damnation — joint by joint, and limb by limb. Now he has sunk all over! The mortal father turns to religion for comfort. Theology tells him of the fire that is never quenched, of the worm which dieth not, the torments of his child — the smoke ascending up forever and ever, and bidding him be glad at the eternal anguish of his only son. His Bible becomes a torment; — in the "many mansions" of its Heaven he knows none for the impenitent prodigal whom Death drives from husks and swine. He looks up after God; a grisly King makes the earth tremble at his frown — angry with the wicked every day, and keeping anger forever; there is no Father. He turns to the "Man of Sorrows and acquainted with grief," asking "will not Mary's Son help me in peril for mine? for a sword pierces through my own soul also." But the Crucified thunders "Depart from me ye cursed, into everlasting fire prepared for the devil and his angels;" and all the host of theological "Christians" respond — "He shall go into everlasting punishment! Amen!" For him there is no Christ — nor never shall be one. Religion is a torment, immortality a Curse, and God a Devil! "Is there no Mother for my son?" he cries. The finger of Theology, hiding the morning star, points down to Hell, and the voice of Night with cold breath whispers "Forever."

At the grave the "Atheist" and the theological "Christian" look each other in the face; one has laid away his daughter for annihilation — he is the father of nothing; the other has buried his son in eternal torment, the father of a devil's victim, of a soul forever damned! What comfort has the one from Nothing, the other from Hell? Human Nature tells both, "it is a lie. Atheism is here a lie; the popular theology is there another lie."

Yes, it is a lie. Eternal morning follows the night; a rainbow scarfs the shoulders of every cloud weeping its rain away to become flowers on land and pearls at sea; Life rises out of the grave, the Soul cannot be held by festering flesh. Absolute Religion puts this ghastly theology to everlasting rest; the Infinite Mother will mercifully chasten, heal, and bless even the prodigal whom death surprised impenitent; Love shall cast out fear.

But conscious of the infinite perfection of God, with the consciousness of immortality in my heart, all this time I smile through my tears, as Death conveys in his arms, one by one, the dear ones from my side. I see them go up like fabled Elijah in his car of flame. I see their track of light across the sky, and I am contented; I am glad; I also shall presently journey in the same chariot of fire, and sit down again beside the dear ones who have gone before; —

> "Nightly I pitch my moving tent
> A day's march nearer home." —

I smile on it all, and am a conqueror over Death.

My friends, I look at things as they are, at least strive to do so, and if I had come to the conclusion that man was mortal only, I should proclaim my conscientious conclusion, strongly, and clearly, and right out. If I thought in my heart that there was no God, why, then I should proclaim that odious conviction. Nay, if I believed in the God of the popular theology, the God who retails agony and damns babies, paving his spacious hell with "skulls of infants not a span long," — that he made religion a torment, immortality a curse, and was himself a devil, why I should tell that too, — and would never hold back from mortal men what I thought Truth, howsoever much it might tear my own heart to get it, or my lip to proclaim it. But, looking with what philosophy I have, with what nature God has given me, I come to the other conclusion, and wish only that I had poetic eloquence to set it forth till it went into every man's heart, and drove fear out therefrom, and planted everlasting life therein.

I see not how any man can be content with blank annihilation, to have no consciousness of immortality, no consciousness of God. — Chance! Fate! Annihilation!

"Are these the pompous tidings ye proclaim,
Lights of the world, and demi-gods of fame?
Is this your triumph — this your proud applause,
Children of Truth, and champions of her cause?
For this hath Science searched, on weary wing,
By shore and sea — each mute and living thing?
Launched with Iberia's pilot from the steep,
To worlds unknown, and isles beyond the deep;
Or round the cope her living chariot driven,
And wheeled in triumph through the signs of heaven?
Oh! star-eyed Science, hast thou wandered there
To waft us home the message of despair? —
Then bind the palm, thy sage's brow to suit
Of blasted leaf and death-distilling fruit!"

"What is the bigot's torch, the tyrant's chain?
I smile on Death, if heavenward Hope remain!
But if the warring winds of Nature's strife
Be all the faithless charter of my life;
If Chance awaked, — inexorable power! —
This frail and feverish being of an hour;
Doomed o'er the world's precarious scene to sweep,
Swift as the tempest travels on the deep;
To know Delight but by her parting smile,
And toil, and wish, and weep, a little while; —
Then melt, ye elements, that formed in vain
This troubled pulse and visionary brain!
Fade, ye wild flowers, memorials of my doom!
And sink, ye stars, that light me to the tomb!"

But with the consciousness of immortality, with a certain knowledge of the Infinite Perfection of God, the perfect Cause, the perfect Providence, I can do all things: no doom is hopeless; disaster is the threshold of delight.

"Nearer, my God, to Thee!
E'en though it be a cross
That raiseth me,
Still all my song shall be, —
Nearer, my God, to Thee,
Nearer to Thee!"

SERMON VIII.

OF PROVIDENCE IN GENERAL.

GENESIS XXII. 8.

GOD WILL PROVIDE.

VIII.

A SERMON OF PROVIDENCE.

IN a previous sermon I have already spoken of the Infinite God as Cause, and as Providence. But the constant Relation of God to the world which He creates and animates, is a theme too important to be left with the merely general treatment I have bestowed upon it. Atheism and the Popular Theology are both so unphilosophical in their Theory of the Universe; the function ascribed to finite Chance, the Supreme of the Atheist, in the one case, and to the Finite God, the Supreme of the theologian, in the other, is so at variance with the primitive spiritual instincts of human nature, and so unsatisfactory to the enlightened consciousness of cultivated and religious men, that the subject demands a distinct and detailed investigation by itself. It will require three sermons: — the first going over the matter very much at large and treating of Providence in its universal forms, the others relating to the application thereof to the various Phenomena of Evil — to Pain and Sin. I shall not hesitate to repeat the same thoughts and even the same forms of expression, previously made use of in these sermons. I do this purposely, both to avoid the needless multiplication of terms, and the better to connect this whole series of discourses together.

The notion that God continually watches over the world and all of its contents is one very dear to mankind. It appears in all forms of conscious religion. The worshipper of a fetiche regards his bit of wood, or amulet, as a special Providence working magically and exceptionally for his good alone. Polytheism is only the splitting up of the idea of God into a multitude of special Providences — each one a sliver of deity. Thus man has

> "Parcelled out the glorious name."

The Catholic invokes his Patron Saint, who is only a rude symbol and mind-mark of that Providence which is always at hand. Pantheism puts a Providence in every blade of grass, in each atom of matter. The Epicureans of old time denied the Providence of God and dreamed of lazy deities all heedless of the Universe. But their theory is eminently exceptional in the theological world, yet performing a service and correcting the extravagance of men who run too far, in devout exaggeration attributing all to God's act.

In virtue of the functions of Providence ascribed to God, he is called by various names: Lord, or King, means providential Master ruling the world and exploitering its inhabitants for his good, not theirs. That is the favorite Old Testament notion and title of God: he is King, men are subjects, or even slaves. Yet other names therein appear, for the Old Testament is not unitary. In the New Testament, from his providential function God is often called Father, indicating the affection which controls his power: he is not merely King over subjects, and Lord over slaves, but a Father who rules his children for their good, restrains that he may develop, and seemingly hinders that he may really help. Hence in the Old Testament, slaves are bid to fear God; in the New Testament, children are told to love him. However, the New Testament is not more unitary in this respect than the Old, and the cruel God appears often in the Gospels, the Epistles, and the Apocalypse, not a Father but only a Lord and King, exploitering a portion of the human race with merciless rapacity.

A King is bound politically to provide for his subjects, inasmuch as he is king; political providence is the royal function. A father is affectionally and paternally bound to provide for his children, inasmuch as he is father; affectional providence is the paternal function. But as the father, or the king, is limited in his powers, so the paternal or political function is limited; for duty does not transcend the power to do. Their providence is necessarily imperfect, not reaching to all persons in the kingdom, or to all actions of their subject. A good king and a good father, both, wish to do more for their charge than their ability can reach. Their desirable is limited by their possible.

The Infinite God is infinitely bound to provide for his creatures, inasmuch as he is infinite God; Infinite Providence is the divine function, his function as God.

A Duty involves reciprocal obligation; a Right is the correlative of a Duty. There is a human Duty to obey, reverence, and love God, with our finite nature; but also, and just as much, is there a human Right to the protection of God. So there is a divine Duty on God's part, of Providence toward man, as well as a divine Right of obedience from man. I mean to say, as it belongs to the finite constitution of man to obey, reverence, and love God — the duty of the finite toward the Infinite; so it belongs to the Infinite constitution of God to provide for man — the duty of the Infinite toward the finite. Obedience belongs to man's nature, Providence to God's nature. We have an unalienable lien upon his Infinite Perfection.

I know men often talk as if God were not amenable to his own Justice, and could with equal right care for his creatures or neglect them; that his Almighty power makes him capable of immeasurable caprice and liberates him from all relation to Eternal Right. Hence it is often taught that God may consistently make a vessel of honor or of dishonor out of this human clay, as the potter does; or may consistently jest with his material, waste it, throw it away, destroy it, as the potter's apprentice does for sport in some moment of caprice; or may break the finished vessels as the potter himself does when drunk, or angry. In virtue of this general notion, it is popularly taught in all Christendom that God will thus waste some of his human clay, casting human souls into endless misery; and in the greater part of Christendom it is taught that he will destroy the majority of mankind in this way; that he has a natural Right to do so, and man has no Right to any thing but the caprice of God.

This doctrine is odious to me; and I see not how men can entertain such an idea of God, and still call him good. This doctrine is equally detestable whether you consider it in relation to the condition of men consequent thereon, or to the character of God which causes that condition. This false idea tends to unsettle men's moral convictions. The consequence appears in various forms. The State teaches in practice that national Might is national right; that so far as the state is concerned there is no right and no wrong; whatever it may will is justice, the nation not amenable to moral law. The Church theoretically teaches that Infinite Might is infinite right; that God repudiates his own Justice; that so far as God is concerned there is no right, no wrong; with him caprice stands for reason. The atheist agrees with the theologians in this, only he rejects the ecclesiastical phraseology, knowing no God.

I will not speak of Mercy, commonly conceived of as the limitation of Right, strong manly Justice obstructed by womanly sentiment and weakness. But speaking of bare Justice I say, that from the idea of God as Infinite it follows that he has no right to call into being a single soul and make that soul miserable for its whole life; or to inflict upon it any absolute and unrecompensed evil; no right to call into life a single worm and make that worm's life a curse to itself. It is irreverent and impious to teach that he could do this. It is a plain contradiction to the idea of God. It is as impossible for him to create any thing from an imperfect motive, for an imperfect purpose, of imperfect material, or as imperfect means, as it would be for him to make Right, wrong, the same thing to be and not to be, or one and one, not two, but two thousand. I as finite man am amenable to the laws of my finite, human nature; he as Infinite God to the laws of his infinite, divine nature. To say that God has a right, or a desire, to repudiate his Infinite Justice, that he will do it, or that as God he can, is as absurd as to say that he will and can make one and one two thousand and not two. And to me it seems as impious as to say there is no

God. Indeed it is a denial of God, not merely a negation of his phenomenal existence, but of the very Substance of his Being.

Now from the Infinite Perfection of God it follows that his Providence is Infinite, that is, completely perfect and perfectly complete; that as Cause and Providence he works continually to bless his creatures, and only to bless them.

This must be so: for the opposite could only come from a defect of Wisdom — he did not know how to bring about their welfare; from a defect of Justice — he did not will their welfare; from a defect of Love — he did not desire it; from a defect of Power — he could not bring it to pass; or a defect of Holiness — he would not use the power, love, justice, and wisdom for his creatures' sake. This might be said of conceptions of God as finite, — of Baal, Melkarth, Jupiter, Odin, Jehovah; never of the Infinite God; he, inasmuch as he is God, must exercise an infinite Providence over each and all his works. The universe, that is, the sum total of created matter and created mind, must be perfectly fitted to achieve the purpose which God designs; that must be a benevolent purpose, involving the greatest possible bliss for each and all, for the Infinite God could desire no other end.

From this it follows that the material part of the universe, and its spiritual part also, must be perfectly adapted to this end. A perfect whole, material or spiritual, consists of perfect parts, each answering its several purpose, and so the whole fulfilling the purpose of the whole. No part must be lost; no part absolutely sacrificed to the good of another, or of all others, and to its own harm and ruin.

All this follows unavoidably from the idea of God as

infinitely perfect. Starting from this point all is plain. But concrete things often seem imperfect because they do not completely serve our transient purpose, while we know not the eternal purposes of God. We look at the immediate and transient result, not at the ultimate and permanent. Thus the mariner cannot come to port by reason of the storm and rocks which obstruct his course; he thinks the weather imperfect, the world not well made, and you often hear men say, "How beautiful the world would be if there were no storms, no hurricanes, no thunder and lightning." While if we could overlook the cosmic forces which make up the material world, we should see that every actual storm and every rock was needful; and the world would not be perfect and accomplish its function had not each been put there in its proper time and place.

An oak-tree in the woods appears quite imperfect. The leaves are coiled up and spoiled by the leaf-roller; cut to pieces by the tailor-beetle; devoured by the hag-moth and the polyphemus, the slug caterpillar and her numerous kindred; the twigs are sucked by the white-lined tree-hopper, or cut off by the oak-pruner; large limbs are broken down by the seventeen-year-locust; the horn-bug, the curculio, and the timber-beetle eat up its wood; the gad-fly punctures leaf and bark, converting the forces of the tree to that insect's use; the grub lives in the young acorn; fly-catchers are on its leaves; a spider weaves its web from twig to twig; caterpillars of various denominations gnaw its tender shoots; the creeper and the woodpecker bore through the bark; squirrels — striped, flying, red, and gray — have gnawed into its limbs and made their nests; the toad has a hole in a flaw of its base; the fox has cut asunder its fibrous roots in digging his burrow; the bear dwells in its trunk which worms, emmets, bees, and countless insects have helped to hollow; ice and the winds of winter have broken off full many a bough. How imperfect and incomplete the oak-tree looks, so broken, crooked, cragged, gnarled, and grim! The carpenter cannot get a beam, the millwright a shaft, or the ship-builder a solid knee for his purpose; even the common woodman spares that tree as not worth felling; it only cumbers the ground. But it has served its complicated purpose; given board and lodging to all these creatures, from the ephemeral fly, joying in his transient summer, to the brawny bear for many a winter hibernating in its trunk. It has been a great woodland caravansary, even a tavern and chateau, to all that heterogeneous swarm; and though no man but a painter thinks it a perfect tree, — and he only because the picturesque thing serves his special purpose, — no doubt the good God is quite contented with his oak, and says, "Well done, good and faithful servant." He designed it to serve these manifold uses, and also to furnish beauty for the painter's picture and meaning for the preacher's speech. Doubtless it enters into the joy of its Lord, having completely served his purpose; he wanted a caravansary and chateau for these uncounted citizens. To judge of it we must look at all these ends, and also at the condition of the soil that had a superabundance of the matter whereof oak-trees are made.

We commonly look on the world as the carpenter and millwright on that crooked oak, and because it does not serve our turn completely we think it an imperfect world. Thus men grumble at the rocky shores of New England, its sterile soil, its winters long and hard, its cold and biting spring, its summers brief and burning, and seem to think the world is badly put together. They complain of wild beasts in the forests, of monsters in the sea, of toads and snakes, vipers and many a loathsome thing — hideous to our imperfect eye. How little do we know! a world without an alligator, or a rattlesnake, a hyæna, or a shark, would doubtless be a very imperfect world. The good God has something for each of these to do; a place for them all at his table, and a pillow for every one of them in Nature's bed.

Though Theologians talk of the infinite goodness of God and the perfection of his Providence, they have yet a certain belief in a Devil; even if it is not always a personal devil, at any rate it is a Principle of Absolute Evil, which they fear will, somehow, outwit and override God, getting possession of the world; will throw sand into the delicate watch-work of the Universe and completely thwart the Providence of the Eternal.

This comes from that dark notion of God which haunts the theology of Christendom; yea, of the Hebrew, the Mahometan, and Hindoo world. It is painful to see how this notion prevails amongst intelligent and religious men. They tell you of the greater activity of the Evil Principle; they see it in the insects which infect the grain and fruit-trees of New England, forgetting that God takes care of these insects as well as of man. When we study deeper, we see that there is no evil principle, but a good principle, so often misunderstood by men. If we start with the idea of the infinite God we know the purpose is good before we comprehend the means thereto.

There are two ways in which men assert the doctrine

of God's Providence, two philosophical and antagonistic doctrines thereof.

I. One makes God the only Will in creation; animals are mere machines, wholly subordinate to their organization; man is also a mere machine, wholly subordinate to his organization. Thus all the action in the world, material and spiritual, is the action of God. The universe consists of two parts, one real, the other phenomenal. First, there is God the Actor; next, a parcel of Tools or Puppets, wholly passive, having no will or life of their own; and with these God works, or plays. On this supposition his Providence has a clean sweep of the universe; every sentiment, good or bad; every thought, true or false; every deed, blessing or baneful, is his work. The sun is an unconscious instrument of God; I am a conscious instrument, but still a bare tool in God's hand, not a free agent.

This comprehensive scheme, reducing life to mechanism, appears in many forms. It belongs to the gross philosophy of the materialist; it is the cardinal doctrine of the pantheist, material or spiritual, the most offensive and dangerous of his doctrines. It is the great idea with the fatalists of all Classes. But it appears in the theological sects also, as well as in philosophic parties; for man cannot escape from his first principle, neither in philosophy nor in theology. It lies at the basis of the Catholic and Protestant theology. Calvin and d'Holbach agree in this. The contradiction it leads to is plain in the preaching and writings of almost every Calvinistic or Catholic Theologian who tries to reconcile his theology with the common facts of consciousness. Now he says you must do for yourself and then God will help you; but adds you can do nothing till God begins it for you. The popular hymn contains the same contradiction,

"Bound on a voyage of awful length,
Through dangers little known,
A stranger to superior strength,
Man vainly trusts his own.

"But oars alone will not prevail
To reach the distant coast;
The breath of Heaven must swell the sail,
Or all the work is lost."

But in Dr. Hopkins and Dr. Emmons and their followers and predecessors, as well Protestant as Catholic, this doctrine is logically carried out to its natural results: in defiance of consciousness; they boldly and simply declare that God is the direct author of every thought and feeling, will and deed. It is curious to see how men reach the same result, starting from opposite points; curious to see how Antinomianism — Catholic or Protestant — arrives at the most objectionable characteristic of Pantheism, which it yet so abhors.

On this hypothesis the function of Providence appears quite simple: all action is God's action. The phenomenal actor may be human, but the only real agent is God. For example: Cain kills Abel with a club, the spite of his heart flashing from his angry eye. That is the phenomenon. But the fact is, God killed Abel with Cain's arm; Cain and the club were equally passive instruments in the hand of God. Here the intervention of Cain, with his malicious feeling and flashing eye, is only a part of the stage machinery, for theatrical effect, but the contriver and worker of it all is God.

His ways are simple: matter and man have really nought to do. This doctrine shocks common sense and is at war with the consciousness of every man. It is eminently at war with religious feeling; for on this supposition actual suffering and sin are of no human value; they lead to nothing; it is in vain for the grass to grow, the human hay is cut and dried by foreordination.

II. The other doctrine of Providence makes man s will free, absolutely free, not at all conditioned by circumstances, bodily organization, and the like. The philosophical question of freedom and necessity I do not design to enter upon. It is one of the most difficult questions in metaphysics, and I certainly am not able to solve the riddle. There are difficulties in either hypothesis, and I have not psychological science enough to explain them in the court of intellect. Philosophy is intellect working in the mode of art; Common Sense is intellect working after its natural instinct, not in the technical mode of art. Philosophy demonstrates; common sense convinces without demonstration. In default of philosophy, we must follow common sense; that does not settle the matter scientifically and ultimately, but practically and provisionally, subject to revision in another court. But common sense decides in favor of Freedom. Every man acts on that supposition; and supposes that other men are likewise free. Courts of law proceed on this hypothesis; public opinion distributes praise or blame; my own conscience commends, or else cries out against me. I am conscious of freedom.

But a little experience shows that this freedom has its limitations and is not absolute. It is conditioned on every side, — by my outward circumstances, the events of my history, the accidents of education, the character of my parents and daily associates; by the constitution of my body — its varying health, hunger and thirst, youth, manhood, and old age. In comparison with a shad-fish, or a blackbird, Socrates has a good deal of freedom, and is not so much subordinate to his organization, or his circumstances, as they; but in comparison with the infinite freedom of God his volitiveness is little. To speak figuratively, it seems as if man was tied by two tethers — the one of historic circumstance, the other of his physical organization — fastened at opposite points, but the cord is elastic and may be lengthened by use, or shortened by abuse and neglect; and within the variable limit of his tether man has freedom, but cannot go beyond it. Still further, to carry out the figure, one man gets entangled in his confining line and does not use half the freedom he might have; another continually extends it and becomes more free.

It is plain that however these circumstances may or may not limit our ideas, or will, they must determine the form of our conceptions and our power to execute them in works.

On the hypothesis that man is absolutely, or partially free, the function of Providence is much more complicated. There are primary and secondary powers; there are other agents beside God, using the power derived from him to work with after their own caprice: so God acts in part by means of the freewill of men. This theory seems to me conformable to common sense and common consciousness, and is perhaps the most philosophic of any that has yet been arrived at.

So much for these two theories of Providence.

There are two modes in which God's providence is commonly supposed to act, namely, the General and the Special.

God's general providence, it is said, takes in the greater part of cases in the material and spiritual world, and provides for them. In this way he is thought to accomplish his function by general laws, which are a constant mode of operation, representing the continual and inferior activity of God; but this does not extend to all cases. God's special providence attends to particular cases, not otherwise provided for, and disposes of them. One is a court of common or statute law, the other a court of equity. In special providence God is supposed not to act by general laws, but without them, or against them. All normal action in Nature comes from general providence; all Miracles from special providence. Thus a freshet in the Connecticut, and the annual rising of the Nile, belong under the general providence of God and come by the action of steadfast laws; but the miraculous Flood in the time of Noah came of God's special providence, having no cause in Nature, only in the caprice of God. This form of special providence in Nature is known only to the theologian, not to the man of science.

To take examples from human affairs, it is maintained that God's general providence waited on the whole human race, but the Hebrews were under his special providence, and he went so far in their case as to make a contract with Abraham, which St. Paul thought God was under an obligation to keep, and could not invalidate.

All men in general are under the general providence, but Christians enjoy the special providence of God, or as Dr. Watts has it,

> "The whole creation is thy charge,
> But Saints are thy peculiar care."

It is said that the forms of religion in China, India, Egypt, Greece, and Mexico, came by the general providence of God, growing out of the nature of man, or coming at the instigation of the devil, having their root in the human or the infernal nature; while the Hebrew and the Christian forms of religion came by his special providence, started in God, and were miraculously transplanted to human soil.

Certain Christians are thought still more eminently under God's special providence. They are the "elect," and the world was made for them. The Mahometan thinks the same of his form of religion and of the elect Mussulmans. Christian theologians say that saints, the elect, share the "covenanted mercies" of God and are favorites, enjoying his special providence, while the rest of men are left to his "uncovenanted mercies," and have need to tremble. The governor of Massachusetts a few years ago, in his proclamation for a day of fasting, invited men to pray God to bless the whole United States in general, but to have "a special care of the good State of Massachusetts." The Hebrews, thinking God cared nothing for the Gentiles, praised him saying, "Thou didst march through the land in indignation. Thou didst thrash the heathen in anger; thou wentest forth for the salvation of thy people;" "Thou didst drive out the heathen with thine hand."

So Christians think God has his favorites amongst men, and, like a partial father, takes better care of some of his children than of the rest: you and I share his common concern and are under his general laws; Jesus of Nazareth had his special care and was under special laws. It would be thought a great impiety to suppose that God felt as much concern for Judas as for Jesus, and would no more suffer the son of Simon to be ultimately lost, than the son of Mary. Yet if you think twice you will see that the impiety is on the other side; for if God does not care as much for Iscariot as for Christ, as much desiring and insuring the ultimate triumph of the one as the other, then he is not the Infinite Father whose ways are equal to all his children, but partial, unjust, cruel, wicked, and oppressive. You do not think so well of the British government because it neglects its feeblest subjects, the laboring millions, making England the paradise of the rich and strong, the purgatory of the wise and good, and the hell of the poor and weak. You condemn the government of the United States because it has its favorites, and oppresses and enslaves the feeblest of its citizens to increase the riches of indolent and cruel men. You would not employ a schoolmaster who turned off the dull boys and beat the bad ones, disposed to truancy and mischief, driving them out into the streets to swelter in crime, to fester in jail, or rot on the gallows. What indignation would suffice towards a mother who neglects a backward boy, takes no pains with the girl that is a cripple, or with a son who has an organic and hereditary tendency to dissipation and licentiousness? I do not like to say a man is impious without proof that he means it; but to attribute so base a character and such unjust conduct to God as you would not respect in a government, allow in a schoolmaster, or endure in a mother, is thoughtless, to say the least of it. But that is the common idea of God in the Christian churches, and the common idea of his providence.

The modern notion of a special providence, wherein God acts without law or against law, is the most spiritual and attenuated form of the doctrine of miracles, the last glimmering of the candle before it goes out. Men who give up the miraculous birth of Jesus still claim that he was under the special providence of God. As the State has general laws which apply well enough to the majority of cases, but has special legislation for the exceptional cases which were not provided for by the general statutes; and as it has a jury whose function is to determine if the law shall punish this or the other man who has violated it, so the popular theology teaches that God's providence has its general legislation, which applies well enough to the majority of cases, and its special legislation, which applies only to the exceptional cases, with its particular mercy, which like the jury refuses to execute the law when it seems too hard. For it is tacitly taken for granted by the popular theology that God did not foresee and provide for all the wants of the Universe, material or spiritual, but is sometimes taken by surprise, things not turning out as he designed or expected, and so he must interfere by special miracles, mend his work, set up makeshifts and provisional expedients. Thus it is represented that the loneliness of Adam in Paradise, his seduction and fall, the subsequent wickedness of his descendants, the transgressions of the Hebrews, and the general sinfulness of mankind at a later day, were all a surprise to the Creator, things not turning out according to his thought. New expedients must accordingly be devised to meet the unexpected emergency.

In like manner it is taught that Jesus of Nazareth

was under the special providence of God; that all history prepared for him and pointed to him; that he had a special mission; while you and I are only under the general providence, history has not prepared for us, does not point to us, and we have no special mission; — in short, that Jesus is a providential man, with a providential function and history, while you and I are not providential men and have no providential history or function.

This common theological notion of the limited general providence and limited special providence of God belongs to the very substance of the popular theology, and springs from its idea of God as finite in power, in wisdom, in justice, and in love. Some ancient and some modern philosophers, seeing the change and progress in manifestation, believe there is a corresponding change in the manifestor, and declare that God is not a Being but a Becoming. The popular theology has the same vice, — though the theologians are not conscious thereof, and denounce it, believing that God grows wiser by experiment, and must alter his plans. Yet in contradiction of their own statements, they declare him without variableness and shadow of turning; while according to the popular theology the history of God is a history of revolutions, even in his dealing with his chosen people, the revelation through the Messiah being flat opposite to the revelation through Moses which it annuls. Pantheism and the popular theology, hostile as they are, agree in this strange conclusion — the negation of the Infinite, and the affirmation of a variable God. The pantheist consciously denies the one and affirms the other, in laying down his premises; the theologian does it unconsciously, in developing his conclusion.

From the Nature of God as Infinite, from the relation he sustains to the creation, as perfect and perpetual Cause thereof, it follows that his Providence must be not barely special — eminently providing for certain things, — or general — taking care of the great mass but letting exceptional particulars slip through his fingers; — it must be universal. It must extend to each thing he has created, to all parts of its existence and to every action thereof. If it be not so, then either some parts of creation are entirely derelict of God, destitute of his Providence, without his care, neglected by him and outlaws from God, put to the ban of the Universe; or else destitute of his Providence during some portions of their existence, or in some acts of their lives. Either case is at variance with the Infinite nature and function of God. For when the Infinite God created the universe, it must have been from a perfect motive, of a perfect material, for a perfect purpose, and as a perfect means thereto; and he must therefore have understood it all completely — in each of its parts, and perfectly — in all the details of each part; and, knowing all the powers, he foreknows all the actions, necessitated or contingent, and provides for each. This must be true of the Universe as a whole; and of each part thereof. All its actions must be thus provided for. The laws of the Universe, the constant modes of operation of the material or human forces, must be founded on this complete and perfect knowledge, and coextensive therewith, and be exponents of that motive and servants of that purpose. This is what is meant, when it is said the laws of matter and of mind, belong to the nature and constitution of matter and of mind. These laws are formed after a complete knowledge of all the properties, functions, and consequences of matter and mind. Before there were two particles of matter in existence, the Infinite God must have understood the law of attraction, in its larger form as gravitation, its smaller as cohesion, and have known that thereby the tower of Siloam would one day fall and slay eighteen men; that many a beetling crag would tumble to the ground, and Alpine landslips bring thousands of men to premature destruction. But all those laws, thus made, must coincide with the motive of God and be means for his purpose; they must suit the welfare of the whole creation and of each part thereof. This must be true of the material world which is unconscious and not free; of the animal world which is not free yet partially conscious; of the human world which is conscious and partially free; and of all superhuman worlds with higher degrees of consciousness and freedom.

To this universal extent must all things be under the Providence of God; to this extent his constant modes of operation must needs reach out.

Then if you look at the relation of God to any one thing, say the grub of a Buprestian beetle boring into the bough of the oak I just now spoke of, it seems as if God made the bough of the tree expressly for that little incipient insect; and the oak for the bough; and the soil for the oak: the globe, with all its ups and downs, which Geology relates, seems made for the soil; and the Universe for the globe. So it appears that that little larva of a beetle is the end, or final cause, of the universe, stands on the top of the world, and has all creation to wait on him, with the God thereof as providential overseer. Then regarding this grub as the one thing the Universe was designed to serve, theologians might say, "Behold God's providence is special; He has special legislation to suit this Buprestian grub, and has aimed the whole world at this mark. See how all things prepare for that; the sun and moon are only its forerunners, and in the fulness of time behold a grub!"

But when the theologian studies the condition of the next grub in an oak-apple, or a gall-nut, or in the nearest bough, he finds them all as well conditioned, and sees that God takes care of the Lymexylon, the Hylecætus, and the Brenthus as well as of the Buprestian; that each of them stands just as much on the top of the world, with the universe to wait thereon and God as overseer. You may study all the inhabitants of the oak-tree — the toad, the squirrel, the fox, the bear, it is true of them all. Yes, it is true of every special thing in the world, when you fully understand that special thing in all its existence, in each act of its life. We cannot by experiment and observation prove this so clearly in every instance as in some special case, but starting with the Idea of God as infinite, the conclusion follows at once, — that his Providence in reference to each particular thing is a perfect Providence.

Then if you look at the relation of God to the Universe, you see that, as far as you understand it, the whole is as well taken care of and provided for as the most contented grub who lives on the bounty of the oak; and you say, "Here is general providence, God acting by general laws for general purposes; things work well on the whole, and 'if now a bubble bursts, and now a world,' it is only a small exception. The attraction of gravitation is a good thing, it keeps the world together; and if the tower of Siloam, thereby falling to the ground, slays eighteen men of Jerusalem, that number is too small to think of, considering the myriad millions who are upheld by this same law."

A law that is perfectly special, providing for each, is also completely general, providing for all. In other words, it is universal. God's Providence must be infinite, like his nature. Special and general are only forms in which we conceive of that providence; — in its relation to a single thing men name it special, to many things, general, while it extends to all and is universal. Accordingly it neither requires nor admits of miraculous makeshifts and provisional expedients, which theologians think indispensable to their finite God.

When God created mankind he must have given thereto the powers which are requisite to accomplish all his purpose. This must be true of mankind as a whole, and of Amos and Habakkuk, of each man, as a part thereof; of each man considered individually as an integer, and considered socially, or humanly as a fraction of the community, or race, and so a factor in the social, or general human result of the life of mankind. Of course God must foreknow what use or abuse would be made of these powers, given in their present proportion, just as well as he knows it now, after all the experience of centuries. Knowing human nature, he must foreknow human history. For example, God must have foreknown that young children would stumble bodily in getting command of their limbs, in learning to walk, and suffer pain in consequence thereof; that older children would stumble spiritually in getting command of their spirits, in learning to think and to will, and suffer in consequence of that; that mankind as a whole would stumble in getting command of the material world, and the development of their human powers; and accordingly there would be suffering from that cause.

Now God, inasmuch as he is God, acts providentially in Nature not by miraculous and spasmodic fits and starts, but by regular and universal laws, by constant modes of operation; and so takes care of material things without violating their constitution, acting always according to the nature of the things which he has made. It is a fact of observation that in the material and unconscious world he works by its materiality and unconsciousness, not against them; in the animal world by its animality and partial consciousness, not against them. Judging from the nature of God and of man, it must be concluded that in the providential government of the human world, he acts also by regular and universal laws, by constant modes of operation; and so takes care of human things without violating their constitution, acting always according to the human nature of man, not against it, working in the human world by means of man's consciousness and partial freedom, not against them.

Here in the human world God's providence must be as complete and as perfect as there in the material or animal world, in each department acting by the natural laws thereof, not without or against them. As by the very constitution of material or animal things God's providence acts by the natural laws thereof — statical, dynamical, and vital laws — so from the very constitution of man it appears that his perfect Providence must work according to the spiritual laws thereof; for it is not conceivable either that God should devise laws not adequate for his purpose, or capriciously depart from them if made adequate. Call this Providence special as it applies to Hophni and Phineas, or general as it applies to all the children of Jacob, it is plain that it must be universal, applying to all material, animal, and human things.

If these things are so, if God be Infinite, then the Hebrew nation is under his universal Providence; but the Amalekites whom the Hebrews overthrew, and the Romans who captured the conquerors, and the Goths who vanquished the Romans, are all and equally under the universal Providence of God who cares equally for them all. Not only are the nations under his Providence in their great acts, but in their little every-day transactions. Theologians love to think that God was present with the Hebrews in their march out of Egypt, at Mount Sinai; that their exodus and legislation were providential. It is all true; but the same Providence watched equally over the English Pilgrims in their exodus; over the British Parliament making laws at Westminster, the American Congress at Philadelphia and Washington. It is well to see this fact in Hebrew history; well also to go further forward and see it in all human history, and to know that human nature is divine Providence.

The common theological notion of a special Providence, with its special favorites, is full of mischief. Some intensely national writer in the Hebrew Old Testament tells us that Noah cursed the descendants of Ham for their father's folly; theologians inform us that in consequence thereof his descendants are cast-off, outlaws from God. But there are no outlaws from the Infinite Father: to say he casts off any child of his,

Hebrew or Canaanite, is as absurd as to say he alters the axioms of mathematics, or the truths of the multiplication table. It is inconsistent with the nature and constitution of the Infinite God; it is as impossible as that one and one should be two thousand, and not two. The African nations, whom the Caucasians enslave, must be as dear to God as the pale tyrants who exploiter them, just as much under his infinite Providence, which will not suffer any ultimate and unrecompensed evil to befall the black or white.

All individuals then must be equally under the same providential care of the Infinite God; not merely great men, the Charlemagnes, the Cromwells, the Napoleons, "men of destiny" as they are called, but the little men; not merely the good men, the heroes of religion, the Moseses and the Jesuses, but the ordinary men, and wicked men, not barely in their great moments, when they feel conscious of God, but in their daily work and humble consciousness. Then it is plain that not only Moses and Jesus are providential men intrusted with a special mission, but you and I and each man are just as much providential men, equally intrusted with a mission, not the less special because it is humble and and our powers are weak. The unnatural Spartan father rejects and disdains his idiot girl, leaving her to perish on Mount Taygetus; the theologian casts off his son, grown up wicked and a public criminal, leaving him to perish unpitied in his jail. But the loving-kindness of the Infinite Father watches over the fool; the tender mercy of the Infinite Mother takes up the criminal when mortal parents let him fall. There is no child of perdition before the Infinite God.

Now God, as the infinitely perfect, must accomplish

his providential function by the laws which belong to the nature and constitution of things; that is, by the normal and constant mode of operation of the natural powers resident in those things themselves; in material and animal nature by the forces and laws thereof; in human nature by its forces and its laws. For as Providence is the divine execution in time of the eternal divine purpose, it is absurd to say that God supersedes or annuls the means which he primarily designed for that purpose. The classic deist supposed the material world was the work of one God; and the arrangement of human affairs the work of another. Between the two there was a collision and a quarrel, the world-governor must interfere with the work of the world-maker; Causality and Providence were antagonistic. But with the idea of the Infinite God this antithetic dualism vanishes at once away.

The creative Causality of the Infinite God is likewise conservative and administrative Providence.

So from the nature of the infinitely perfect God and the consequent perfection of his motive, material, purpose, and means thereto, it follows that he will not destroy as infinite Providence what he created as infinite Cause; that He will not violate the laws and break the constitution which he himself has made. Accordingly, in the midst of God's Providence working from a perfect motive, for a perfect purpose, and by means of the constitution and nature of man, a Providence extending to all men and to their every act, it is plain that Human Freedom is safe, and the Ultimate Welfare of each man is made sure of, as certain as the existence of God, or of man.

Atheism tells you of a world without a God, a great going, but a going with none to direct: the popular

Theology declares that this going is directed by a finite and changeable God, jealous, revengeful, loving Jacob and hating Esau, working by fits and starts, even in wrath destroying what he made imperfect, beginning anew and designing to torment the great mass of mankind in everlasting woe — "miserable to have eternal being."

But with the absolute Religion, a knowledge of God as Infinite how different do all things appear! We have confidence, absolute trust in the motive and Purpose of God, absolute trust also in the Means which he has provided in the nature and constitution of things. The human faculties become then the instruments of Providence. Every man is under the protection of God — and all fear of the final result for you, or me, or for mankind, quite vanishes away. The details we know not; experience reveals them a day-full at a time; the result we are sure of.

Timid men who think that God is miserly and the great Hunker of the Universe, sometimes fear the material world will not hold out; some little "perturbations" are discovered, now the Earth approaches the Sun for many years, perhaps never twice has described exactly the same track; so they fear the earth will fall into the fire and the world be burned up. But by and by we find that these "perturbations" only disturbed the astronomer, doubtful of God; that to the Cause and Providence of the world they were eternally known, fore-cared for; that they are normal acts of faithful matter, and so all undisturbed the world rolls on. Constant is balanced by constant. Variable holds variable in check. In her cyclic rotation round the earth the Moon nods; the Earth oscillates in her rythmic round, while the Sun nods also, as the centre of gravity of the solar system shifts now a little this way, then a little that; nay the whole Solar System, it is likely, swings a little from side to side: but all this has been foreseen, provided for, balanced by forces which never sleep, and one thing set over against another in such a sort that all work together for good, and the great Chariot of Matter sweeps on through starry space keeping its God-appointed track. Such is the Providence of God in the Universe, not an atom of star-dust is lost out of the sky, not an atom of flower-dust is lost from off this dirty globe; such are the laws by which God works his functions out in Nature. Ignorance is full of dread and starts at terrors in the dark, trembles at the earthquake and the storm. But science justifies the ways of God to matter, knowing all and loving all, discloses everywhere the immanent and ever active force. Where Science does not understand the mode of action, nor read the details of perfection clearly in the Work — it points to Infinite Perfection in the Author, and we fear no more.

SERMON IX.

OF PROVIDENCE — THE ECONOMY OF PAIN.

ECCLESIASTICUS XLII. 24.

HE HATH MADE NOTHING IMPERFECT

IX.

OF THE ECONOMY OF PAIN AND MISERY UNDER THE UNIVERSAL PROVIDENCE OF GOD.

LAST Sunday I spoke of Providence in its most general form, as the universal execution of the perfect purposes of God by the perfect means He had originally devised. Closely connected with this are two things which demand attention, namely, the phenomena which are called Evil and Sin, and the relation thereof to the causal and providential function of the Infinite God.

To understand this matter of Evil, to know its mode of origin and of operation, and the purpose it serves, considerable nicety of thought is necessary; and of course considerable precision in the terms which express and define thought.

The word Evil is ambiguous in its meaning, and has both a wide and a narrow signification. Sometimes it means something painful for which there is no adequate compensation to the sufferer. Sometimes it means something painful for which there is an adequate compensation to the sufferer. In this Sermon I will use the word Evil in its general and ambiguous sense, while the two special forms thereof, — the uncompensated and the compensated, — I will call Absolute Evil and Partial Evil.

So much for the definition of these terms.

The phenomena called Evil may for convenience, be distributed into two general forms, or modes: —

I. Evil which does not come from a conscious and voluntary transgression of a natural law of the Body or the Spirit; that is, Pain and Misery. This may be more minutely designated and distinguished by reference to the part through which we suffer — as physical pain, suffering by the body; spiritual pain, suffering by what is not body.

II. Evil which comes from a conscious and voluntary transgression of a natural law of the body or the spirit; that is Sin, meaning thereby the transgression with all its subjective and objective consequences.

So much also for the definition of these terms.

To-day I shall speak only of Pain and Misery; and of them chiefly in the form of Physical Evil.

In the world of mere Matter, there is no consciousness, no freedom, no will. It is subject wholly to statical and dynamical laws in their various forms; and there is therefore no Pleasure and no Pain. That department of creation seems designed merely for a theatre on which animated beings are to find scope for action, and whence they may obtain their means of livelihood. I think no man pretends to find any evil there.

But there is the world of Animals and of Man conscious in higher or lower degrees, and with more or less of freedom, gifted with partial power of will. Here is the field for Pleasure and Pain — the elements of Happiness and of Misery, the two poles of life. Here occur the phenomena of Evil.

By Pleasure I mean the state which comes from the fulfilment of the natural conditions of animate existence; from the normal satisfaction of natural desires. By Pain I mean the state which comes from non-fulfilment of those natural conditions; from the absence of the normal satisfaction of those desires. Of course I include in that state not only the negative form of evil — lack of the desirable, but the positive form of evil — presence of the hateful. Happiness is prolonged pleasure; Misery is prolonged pain.

Happiness is great in proportion to the greatness of the faculties which seek their natural satisfaction; and in proportion likewise to the completeness of the satisfaction itself. So there is a qualitative distinction, of the specific modes of Happiness — as it comes from satisfying high or low desires; and a quantitative distinction of the particular degrees thereof — the satisfaction being partial or total. On the other hand Misery is great or little in proportion to the faculties and their satisfaction; and there is the same qualitative and quantitative distinction — of modes and degrees thereof.

Let us now look at some of the phenomena of Physical Evil. And for clearness' sake let us attend first to the simplest forms thereof, and thence ascend up to the more complex and difficult.

In the Animal world happiness usually preponderates over misery. The two most powerful groups of instincts in the animal world are those which relate to the preservation of the individual and the perpetuation of the race. Those instincts are commonly satisfied. Hence comes the general aspect of happiness throughout this department of the universe. Not one mosquito in a million, it is probable, ever tastes of blood; and not one in a million ever suffers from hunger. You never saw a melancholy fly, or a wild squirrel that was unhappy; the elephant, the lion, the monkey, and the crocodile seem to have a good time in the world. Happiness is obvious in the young of animals; but it is just as actual in the old, only it assumes a graver form, and so is not so apparent to the careless, or inexperienced eye:

> "Thy creatures leap not, but express a feast,
> Where all the guests sit close, and nothing wants."

Still some animals, it is obvious, suffer pain; all are capable of it; perhaps all the higher animals, some time in their lives, are made to suffer. It may be asked, "Is it possible that there shall be pain in the animal world which the Infinite God has created from perfect motives, of perfect material, for a perfect purpose, and as a perfect means thereto?" I answer, Yes.

I do not pretend that I can clear up all the difficulties in this matter by the inductive mode — of studying the details, and thereby learning their law and showing how each particular form of evil turns into good; — I shall be obliged to refer to the idea of God as Infinite, and from that deduce the value of the function of the special forms of pain and misery. This will often happen. The wisest man is only a child as yet. Philosophy has read but few pages of this great book of Nature, whereof all must be known fully to understand a part. When I know there is an Infinite God, I am sure that his purpose is good and his means adequate

I spontaneously trust therein. This instinctive trust outruns the reflective demonstration of science. Still it is both pleasant and satisfactory to learn the use and function of things by themselves, by an inductive study of the facts, and not be constrained to deduce the conclusion merely from the idea of God. In some instances this is not difficult; nay, in the present condition of science, it is not hard to learn the general tendency of things in Nature, and thence get the analogy of the whole to help explain particular parts. But no man I think as yet has been able to explain all these cases by the purely inductive process. To do that he must know all the powers and consequent actions and history of each thing in the universe.

All finite things must needs be conditioned; the Infinite alone is absolutely self-conditioned. Thus the bodies of animals must needs depend on the world about them; wherein are things helpful — meant for the animals they serve, and things harmful — not meant for the animals they hurt. Continued use of the harmful things would destroy the individual and so the race.

Accordingly the animal frame is made susceptible of Pain from the use of the harmful Substances, and of Delight from the use of the helpful.

Sometimes this pain comes before the consummation of the use: thus poisonous plants are commonly odious to the eye, or nauseous to the smell, or hateful to the taste of the creature they would injure. Here the momentary pain, the transient disgust, comes as a forewarning against a foe. Poisonous plants, it is said, have somewhat in their structure which warns off the animals they would else destroy, some special ugliness telegraphing to the senses, the unfitness of the thing for use. "The Devil," says a chemist, "is always chained." If not he is painted black, to scare away the creatures he would molest. How nicely the sheep and horses avoid all noxious things. Lobelia would kill horses; the pungent plant reads the riot-act of Nature as soon as it is tasted and warns the offenders of their transgression. The benevolent motive and purpose of this form of pain is obvious at once.

Then there are Modes of Action which are possible to an animal, but which would be fatal if persisted in: these also are attended by pain. A young rabbit heedlessly running through briars tears his tender skin and smarts; and so avoids this rending of his coat. If the pain did not warn him, he would tear his skin to pieces and lose his life in seeking to save it. A dog running over sharp stones would soon wear out his feet; the pain warns him of the peril before it is too late. If he were to lose a limb he must go limp and lame all his life, for another leg will not shoot out to take the place of the one he has wasted and used up. The suffering makes him careful; he keeps his feet, and goes four-legged all his days.

The lobster and the crab have a thick and nearly insensible shell, for protection against ravenous enemies; but such is the nature of their covering that their limbs are brittle and easily rent off, another soon taking the place of that which is lost. The animal suffers but little pain from that injury. With him it is no great hardship to lose a limb which is so easily supplied anew. But the lobster cannot bear any great change of temperature, such is his constitution; it would destroy his life. So his shell is a good conductor of heat, and he is keenly sensitive to the alternations of heat and cold.

This sensitiveness and the pain it brings if he goes out of his proper temperature, keep him always in such places as suit his organization, in a temperature congenial to his nature, in waters which also supply his food. The dog can bear a great range of temperature, clad in his non-conducting coat, which also accommodates itself to the changes of climate. Variations of heat and cold are not painful to him. The dog's sensitiveness of touch, and the lobster's sensitiveness to heat and cold bring pain to both; but the suffering keeps the lobster in his place, and preserves the limbs of the dog safe and sound. Give the dog the lobster's insensibility to pain from the sense of touch, he would run, or fight till he wore his legs off of his body; give the lobster the dog's sensitiveness to this form of pain, and living as he does in the ceaseless wash of the waters, with brittle limbs, his life would be a torment while it lasted, and in torment would it soon end. Give the dog the lobster's sensitiveness to heat and cold, he would be miserable most of the time and soon die; give the lobster the dog's indifference to temperature, the currents of the sea would soon sweep him away from his food, from his natural position, and he and his race would speedily perish. The pain of both is only adequate to keep each in his proper place: it is the tether by which they are bound out and kept from harm.

Such is the general use of this form of pain in the animal world; it is a natural warning against ruin, a sentinel for ever mounting guard over the natives of the earth, the sea, and air, giving early admonition when danger draws nigh.

If you look widely and carefully, you will find there is always the most nice and cunning adaptation of the pain to the end it is to answer. Is a condition of existence neglected, an instinct left without its satisfaction; is a wrong mode of action resorted to, or improper food eaten, uneasiness and pain warn the offender of his mistake, and drive him from it. This pain is so effectual that the master-instincts of an animal become irresistible: only external violence can check the rush of Nature, and if driven out she soon comes back. How uneasy are the birds of passage at the time of their annual migrations! Their pain warns them against the ruin which a northern winter, or a southern summer, would bring upon the Swallow, or the Stork.

The pain which comes from Fear is of the same remedial character. The Hare has a feeble body; a rude touch drives her life out of the thin walls of its habitation. She is the natural prey of the hawk, the fox, and the wild-cat; even the mink and the weasel easily master her. See how she is furnished with quick, capacious, and variable ears, with prominent and ready eyes; nimble to start and swift to run. She is cautious, timid, and fearful to a remarkable degree; she runs from any danger, facing nothing that is formidable. She has no power to resist any of her natural enemies. Fear is her sentinel. When her last hour comes, she dies almost at a touch from her enemy, apparently with little pain. Her chief suffering is from fear, and that is only adequate to attach her life to her.

So far as I have seen, or read, this is true in all departments of animal life — the ordinary mode of death, though often a violent one, is attended with very little pain; and the suffering from fear is only sufficient to keep the creatures on their guard. The bull is strong and tough, able to endure a severe contest with a powerful enemy. He is constitutionally courageous, and marches forth to meet the danger which threatens him. The timidity of the hare would be ridiculous in the bull, and his fearlessness fatal to her.

Then there is the pain which animals suffer at the Loss of their Mates, or their Young. You see examples of this in all animals that match in pairs, and guard and protect their little ones. The monogamous robin mourns at the loss of his mate, or at the plunder of his nest. The ferocious white bear, it is said, moans like a human mother at the loss of her cubs. The suffering of sheep and cows when their children are torn from them, is too well known and very sad. But this pain, with the attendant fear of the loss, is only sufficient to lead the mates to protect each other, the parents to watch over and defend their child. This fear often creates a certain heroism in the bosoms of animals which are otherwise cowardly. The hen is commonly a garrulous and restless busybody, bustling about all day, a weak and timid animal, fleeing from every trifling danger. When the maternal instinct moves her to brood over the eggs which contain her unseen progeny, how all is changed! The restless busybody sits silent and patient as a stone, all day incumbent on her nest. An extraordinary amount of heat is developed in her body. Her timidity vanishes; she becomes courageous, and rushes out to defend her nest, and still more to protect her new-born brood. She defies danger, and will sacrifice her life rather than desert her little flock. If the brood is lost, her torment is exceeding great. After her fledglings are grown up they become strangers to her; her anxiety and her courage vanish out of sight, or sleep as a reserved power, till another occasion calls them forth. Here pain is the ally of affection, the family girdle to keep her little household together. In animals which require no parental care, there is no fear of this sort, no affection for it to guard. The salmon and the herring drop their embryo in the appropriate spot, leaving it to the care of Nature. After the young calf has outgrown the need of its mother's care, to her it is but one of the common herd; the feeling of kindred is extinct.

In all these cases the conservative function of these four forms of pain is evident at once, as soon as the facts are made known. And the balance between the provisional pain and the final purpose it is to serve is so exactly sustained, that it is a delight to the thinking man to see the ways of Providence with these little children of the common Father.

> "Each creature hath a wisdom for his good:
> The pigeons feed their tender offspring, crying,
> When they are callow; but withdraw their food
> When they are fledge, that Need may teach them flying."

Still there are sufferings in the animal world for which I can see no present recompense. Some lose a limb in youth and suffer all their life; others are scantily fed. Those in the hands of man are often maimed, ill-treated, and hindered from developing their nature as animals, and so made to suffer. Man "improves" the breeds of cattle. He does not always improve them as horses, cows, or swine, but only as animated tools for his service. Sometimes he only exploiters them. His "racers" and "draft horses," his "Ayrshires," and "North-Devons," his "Merinoes" and "Saxonies," are as much works of human invention as the spinning-jenny and the printing-press. Very useful contrivances for man's purpose, they are less horses, oxen, and sheep, it seems to me, than were their savage progenitors thousands of years ago. They have suffered a change. They cannot defend themselves if turned out in the forests, nor find their food in the wild where the Aurochs rejoices to live. But I doubt that this change is attended with any necessary unhappiness. The domestic dog seems to me quite as happy an animal as the wild dog. If we take into the account all the animals connected with man, with or without his consent, they have far more happiness than misery. The horse and the cow seem in part designed for the use and service of man, and may perform that service with no unnatural harm to themselves. Their nature is exceeding pliant under the plastic hand of man; the artificial forms of the cow-kind seem to me as happy as the wild forms.

But still there is pain and misery in the animal world. Now howsoever Paul may interpret the Hebrew Bible, it is plain the Infinite God "doth take care for oxen." The injuries of a whale that in his childhood gets his jaw broken, and goes all his life with a twisted mouth, a deformed and most unlucky whale; the misfortunes of a horse owned by some master more beastly than the brute, must have all been known by God at the creation, provided for and compensated in some way. The use of animal pain in the majority of cases, it is easy to discern, and to see that it has a benevolent function to accomplish. The general analogy of Nature leads to the inference — it is no more, — that it must likewise be so in these exceptional cases. But from the Idea of the Infinite God we know it must be so; that this exceptional pain must not be absolute evil to the individual sufferer, but disciplinary — leading to some good else not attainable; and so compensated by the ultimate welfare which it helps attain. I do not pretend to know how this is brought about; I know not the middle terms which intermediate between the misery I see and the blessedness I imagine. I only know that the ultimate welfare must come to the mutilated beast overtasked by some brutal man. If it be not so then the universe is not a perfect world; it is imperfect in this particular, that it does not serve the natural purpose of these creatures, who go incomplete and suffering. If God be Infinite then he must make and administer the world from perfect motives, for a perfect purpose, and as a perfect means, — all tending to the ultimate and absolute blessedness of each thing he directly or mediately creates; the world must be administered so as to achieve that purpose for each thing. Else God has made some things from a motive and for a purpose not benevolent, or as a means not adequate to the benevolent purpose. These suppositions are at variance with the nature of the Infinite God.

I do not see how this benevolent purpose can be accomplished unless all animals are immortal and find retribution in another life. I know many will think it foolish, and some impious, to speak of the Immortality of Animals. But without this supposition I cannot "vindicate the ways of God" to the horse and the ox. To me the immortality of all animals appears in harmony with the analogy of Nature, rational, benevolent, and beautiful. Many of the arguments for human immortality apply as well to the case of the bee and the elephant as to John and Paul. The argument from consciousness is here out of place — as man knows nothing of the consciousness of the sheep and swine.

There are but two arguments which I have ever heard brought against the immortality of animals — one is drawn from the selfishness of man, who wants a monopoly of all desirable things, and so would shut beast and bird out of heaven; the other comes from the common notion of the Deity, that he is a mean and stingy God, making heaven little and hell large. Let both pass for what they are worth. If the Spanish Inquisitor and the American Kidnapper can be thought immortal and capable of eternal happiness, I see not how we can deny eternal life to any Abyssinian Hyæna, or to a Rattlesnake from Kentucky, far less ugly and venomous. It seems to me that philosophical theology confirms the instinctive nature of the "poor Indian,"

> "Who thinks, admitted to that equal sky,
> His faithful dog shall bear him company."

If this be so, then pain or misery in the animal world is not an Absolute Evil; in the majority of cases it is a beneficent sentinel to warn creation of the approach of ruin, and in the exceptional cases is a servant that by some unknown way conducts to bliss,

> "Making a chiming of a passing-bell."

In the World of Man the affair is much more complicated; but if the animal world be rightly understood, this other is not difficult to comprehend. The amount of individual freedom is so much greater with men than with animals, that we commonly say, man is free — self-ruled, — while beasts are bound, ruled wholly by some objective force, tools and not agents. Man's tether is indeed much longer than theirs; and his margin of possible oscillation is much greater. For man having powers so much more various, and consequently an immediate destination so much nobler, stands, in general, in more complicated relations with Nature, and the individual with his species, and is subject to a greater variety of conditions. Accordingly there is with him so much the more room for generic and individual caprice, for violating the conditions of welfare and of material existence; so much more room for pain and misery. This is so with mankind, and with each man, at every particular stage of his conscious existence.

But in addition to this statical complication of his nature, man has other dynamical complications which take place in his historical development. Man is progressive; each man advancing not only from babyhood to manhood, — for that is so with the lion and the lobster, — but also from manhood till death. Not only is each man thus progressive as an individual, but each nation as a people, and mankind as a race. Amid the fluctuations of individuals the nation rolls on from its babyhood to its manhood; and amid the fluctuations of states and families, of nations, the mighty Stream of Humanity sweeps on to its destination, bearing in its eternal bosom every human excellence which any individual or any people, has developed and brought to light.

At every step the individual, the nation, and the race are subject to the natural conditions of personal, social, and general human welfare; conditions which are rigorous and unavoidable. All this development of the individual and the race is progress by experiment; for while the crystal is formed, and the tree grows, by processes which have their origin solely in the Infinite Cause; while each individual lion and the whole lion-kind grow up with little conscious thought, or personal will, the individual man, and the man-kind do to a considerable extent shape their own forms of being. This progression by experiment involves both experiments that fail and experiments that succeed. The failure brings pain; if long continued, misery. This is so with the merely speculative experiment, with thought: the faulty demonstration, "the sum which will not come out right," pains the boy at school; the halting tragedy racks the feeble-minded poet; nay the imperfections in the works of Homer and Æschylus, of Dante and Shakspeare, tortured those mighty bards. Still more is this the case with practical experiments, with deeds: the little girl, learning the limits between the Me and Not-me, mistakes and burns her fingers in the candle's flame; the great nation learning the limits between the Just and the Unjust, or the Expedient and Unprofitable, mistakes and loses millions of men Necessity confines the beasts within a narrow road where instinct impels them on; they cannot wander much. Freedom opens for us a long and wide field, with opportunity for pain and misery. The child makes unsuccessful experiments in becoming a man; the man in reaching after more manhood; mankind, in all our history makes experiments that fail; all are painful. Such are the conditions of our human lot, conditions which to the nature of a finite, progressive, and free being seem as much indispensable as gravitation to atoms of matter representing the primary law.

The actual amount of pain and misery is far greater in the human world than in the animal world. It seems to me greater in proportion to their respective quantity of being. The Caucasian baby is a grief to her mother before she rejoices that a child is born; he is a torment to himself before he has his first teeth; a trouble to his father in growing up. Man has all the animal sources of pain, and many more peculiar to himself, springing from his more mountainous quantity of being, its nicer quality, and the greater complication thereof. The grown animal is not capable of progressive development; has no experiments to make, no failures to mourn over, nor suffer from. The race of animals makes no failures, no progress, no experiment. No lion in Africa weeps for his prodigal son. The tigress is not crossed in love. No patrician game-laws hinder the fox from "free warren" everywhere. The hippopotamus has no feudal superior; the wild-cat has eminent domain in the woods, "free fishing and fowling." There is no despotic Nicholas or Ferdinand to torture the race of wild swine, with unreasonable institutes hedging in the liberty of Nature. No revolutionists, no red-republicans jostle the rulers of the woods and seas; no progressive Kossuths and Mazzinis overturn the oligarchy of white or black elephants, and form a democracy among the cattle. There is no pain from bad institutions,—no failure to have good ones. No timid owl or monkey is ever alarmed at the "Spread of Infidelity." The ravens that wander crying for lack of meat and finding it as they fly, have no fear of eternal damnation, no "Adam's fall" to make their faces gather blackness; the "federal head" of the crows never "fell." There is no popular theology, no atheism, with the pigeons and blackbirds.

The aspect of the world of animals is one of happiness. What a contrast between that and the condition of man! The bob-o'-link in the grass under my window seeking food for her little nest-full of promises, is happy as a bird can be; her joy runs over in delightful song. Her beauty of sound meets the morning beauty of light, and what a psalm they sing, the sunrise and the bird, to eye and ear! Compare her with the mothers in the houses all about me, and in the great cities of the world, the mothers who groan in labor — of beggary, of prostitution, of drunkenness, of many-liveried sin! Not one mosquito in a million suffers from hunger; of the thousand million men how many will die outright of starvation; how many go stooping and feeble for want, and will at last be thereby shuffled off the stage of life! How contentedly this caterpillar makes ready for her transfiguration, one day to come out fair as the light with more than mythical resplendence. How sadly the seamstresses of Boston, New York, and London, prepare their garments of transfiguration — the shroud which painful fingers are so long in making ready for death, who is always in sight, yet so slow in coming! What an odds between the Song of a Cocoon and "the Song of a Shirt!" This grasshopper,

> "Green little loiterer in the sunny grass,
> Catching his heart up at the feel of June,"

is never to seek for his daily bread. Yonder cow takes no thought for raiment; the beaver is not afraid of being warned out of his lodgings and turned upon the world, his wife and children brought to the side-walk; the pains of parturition and dentition, with that troop of diseases which crowd about the cradle of human infancy, are all unknown to the wild camel, the bear, and the elephant. The buffalo is never concerned for the raiment of his sons and daughters, clad and shod in Nature's best. No wild-cat has any difficulty in training up her sons; the horse-leech has no concern for the marriage of his two proverbial daughters. Every oyster is contented with his own "bank." There are no changes of tariff to perplex the free-traders of sea, and land, and sky. No protective system is repealed to the damage of the insect-manufacturers — of the bee, or the spider, or the silk-worm. The Providence of God is the great Protective-system for all these children of the world. The universal laws — they never change. The aristocracy of the ant-hill does not exploiter the common people; not a queen bee feared a crisis in "the year of revolutions." Compare a hive of bees — in woods or garden, — or a family of beavers, with Boston or Lowell, with Paris or Lyons; and what an odds betwixt the welfare of the two! Consider the poverty, the want, the ignorance, the disease, the drunkenness, and vice, and crime, and shortened life, which make up the misery of the poor; consider the anxiety and servility, the disappointed ambition and defeated affections, which so mar the welfare of the thriving and the rich; and what a difference there is between this human misery and the contentment of the beast; — a difference which, at first sight, seems out of proportion to the different degrees of power and of freedom — misery increasing as the square of the amount of freedom! The whole world of Nature does not furnish a St. Giles parish for the beasts; not a human city is without one!

Still omitting nothing and extenuating nothing, it seems to me the proportion of misery in the world is overrated by benevolent men. Happiness, contentment of the actual wants, surpasses unhappiness, that discontented hunger after what cannot be reached. It is so in convents and asylums, with the poor in large towns like London and New York, — such is the human power of accommodation to circumstances. Plastic man is pliant also. Take any settlement of men, Esquimaux, Pawnees, Turks, Chinese, Gaboons, Bushmans, Britons, happiness far surpasses misery. Go into the lowest parts of Boston, or London, to the abodes of want and crime, it is so there. True it is a low form of happiness, and you mourn at so much contentment with so little welfare.

Yet there is pain and misery of the saddest sort. It comes from non-fulfilment of the conditions of animal life — from want of food, of fire, air, and water, of shelter and raiment; from sickness, fear, grief; from the lack, or the loss, of objects of passion and affection; from defeated ambition, defeated love; from want of culture — of one or all the faculties.

All this must have been foreseen; it is a part of the scheme of things — the calculated consequence of man's ignorance, or want of self-adaptation to the world of matter. It can be no astonishment to God. Yet at first sight it appears as if there was an imperfection in God's work. This misery, which haunts mankind, seems a disgrace to the world and a standing impeachment of the Providence of God. "Call this a perfect world," says some kind-hearted man, "a perfect means for a perfect purpose? Under the Providence of the Infinite God is it! — Then whence this vermin pain which bores into every house and every heart? The world is full of Evil, Absolute Evil; this toad, ugly and venomous, squats, full of poison, in every garden which man plants. Could not God make a world without Misery?"

Well, the finite must needs be conditioned — its existence one of limitation. The question is whether the *present* condition contains any absolute, or any needless partial Evil. As it was shown before, pain is incidental to the development of a finite being with even a small amount of freedom. But as man is more free, and individually and generically progressive, a larger amount of pain is incidental to his existence. But look at some conjectural schemes of human life.

Suppose man had been made with no capability of progress either of the individual, from manhood to old age, or of the race, from the beginning to the end; and put in the rudest condition of the lowest tribe of men — of the Bushmans, or the Patagonians; but had all his wants as completely and as easily met as the oysters in the waters of Virginia, so that the whole world was a perpetual Point Comfort to each man; that there was no pain, no possibility of suffering; so that he had no desire which could lead him astray at all, no freedom to go astray, but by his organization was bound fast to the actual, — would be a better state of things? Nobody thinks so.

Suppose this unprogressive and painless creature elevated to the highest degree of our present civilization — to the intellectual condition of the philosophers who make up the Academies of Paris, of Berlin, and of London; surrounded with all the circumstances which suit that stage of development; as fully satisfied as the oyster, and as incapable of any progress — individual or generic; — incapable of pain; without freedom of further development; by his organization bound fast to the actual, no ideal beauty — intellectual, moral, affectional, or religious, — hovering about his head; and that an undisturbed satisfaction filled up the consciousness of man. Would that be a better state of things than the present condition of Germany, France, and England — better as a finality than the present as a stage of progress in the ever unfolding growth of man? No thinker will think so. For those philosophers are as far from a full enjoyment of all the powers of their human nature almost as the Bushmans.

We are made with a nature which demands continual progress; the instinct of development is amazingly powerful in the race. Mankind is not content to stand still, stopping at the Bushman's elevation, or at the stage where the modern philosopher gathers into his comprehensive mind the riches of present human consciousness. The Ideal haunts the human race and through eminent tongues calls out to man continually, "Onward, onward." All advance is progression by experiment; many an attempt fails of its end — the human child is borne with pain. But who is there that does not see that man has a higher, nobler destiny than the creatures which have no freedom, — bound to the present?

Suppose man made capable of progress, and — as finite — of experiments that fail, and yet incapable of pain. Would that be a good exchange? Look at some examples. A man will not eat when he is hungry: suppose God by a transient miracle, or a permanent law forbid the pain which now comes from lack of food; the man would die of inanition, die without warning. Suppose he would eat when not hungry, or in excessive quantity, and no pain followed this violation of the natural rule of temperance; he would die of repletion, die unwarned of his peril. Suppose he would eat what was harmful, things not meant for human food; would it be well if there were no disgust of any sense, to notify the man before the mistake, no torture in any member to warn him of the error? Would it be well to have an amount of pain not adequate to remind him of the peril?

What if a man would not work even for the most needful things; and God, like a foolish mother, to spare him the present consequences of laziness, either by special fleeting miracles, or by general and permanent law, gave him all the desirable outward things which now come from the long-continued toil of men. What if all things came at his desire; he

> "— need but wish and instantly obeyed,
> Fair ranged the dishes rose and thick the glasses played!"

Why what a world it would be, where "wishes were horses and beggars might ride;" a universal lubberland, peopled by beggars on horseback riding after their proverbial wont! If man lived he would be a suckling for ever, never attaining the dignity of stripling. But he would not live, thus conditioned only by his wishes. This suckling of caprice, like a kite without a string, would soon come to the ground, unwarned by any pain till death finished him. A child not conditioned by its parents, is a spoiled child, father and mother only special providences of ruin. A school of children with no schoolmaster to regulate them with "Thou shalt," and "Thou shalt not," what a hurly-burly is it of most unprofitable going which yet goes nowhere! A young man suddenly made master of an unexpected fortune, and so presented with the freedom of riches he had never won, is always brought thereby in great peril, and commonly finds the excessive fortune a misfortune.

Imagine men so active that they will toil all the

time, and neither rest nor sleep; would it be wise and well to leave them with no possibility of pain to warn them before the frame lay there worn out and dead? Suppose they wrought by night and not by day, would it be an improvement on the present state of things if no inconvenience and no pain attended the capricious violation of Nature's law, until death ended the mistake?

Suppose a man worked at the right time and in the right proportion, but worked wrong, against the nature of things; that he planted his pear-trees with the roots up and the branches down; or set the roots in husks of corn, in straw, in dried moss, in the feathers of birds, or the hair of beasts; and made his own bed out of moist rich earth, every night covering up his limbs in that. Suppose God should alter the constitution of things to suit our man, so that his accommodating pear-tree grew and bore fruit, the roots up, the branches down, or grew out of husks and hay, hair and feathers; and that his body did not suffer from sleeping wrapped up in garden mould; that the pear and the man changed beds capriciously and God made the world accommodate the silly whim: would that be an improvement, better than the present rule — "as you make your bed so you must lie?"

What if a man put things to the wrong use — making wheaten bricks of the corn he grew, piling them into walls for his house, and roofing over this pasteboard palace with tiles of bread; would it be a misfortune if the next storm soaked through his roof and walls, and brought this whole mass of unleavened bread upon the head of its maker?

What if he made his bread of wood and sand and clay, not of corn, and God interfered with our booby and allowed him to suffer no pain for his stupidity?

Would that be a good plan? What a school the world would be with no regulation but the finite caprice of each John and Jane!

If a man provides the proper articles for food and shelter, but gets them in insufficient quantity, or of a quality which will soon perish, or lives in a spot which is unhealthy; would it be well for God to twist the material world so as to accommodate the human folly and let him off with a whole skin? Should you think the world well made if it altered to suit the caprice of each man in it; and if every whimsey had a universal right of way over all the world — Nature a "servitude" to nonsense! If a man makes a cart to carry himself and his chattels from place to place, and makes it ill, or drives it badly, if it breaks down when overloaded, or turns over when one wheel is driven into a ditch and the other into the air, and if the man be hurt and his goods spilled out, is there a flaw in the world, think you, because he suffers chagrin at the failure, and pain by the bruise? When his carriage, ill made, overladen, driven badly, was about to overturn, suppose its owner prayed to all the saints in heaven, you would not think it a kindness in the Infinite God to alter the laws of Nature to suit this ill conduct of a cart. Would you have the man turn out for gravitation, or have God push the planet to the wall to let our lubber's cart go by?

A boy makes a kite with a frame of iron, and planks it over with live-oak. The thing would sink in water; shall God alter the constitution of the world and make it float in air? or leave the boy to profit by his chagrin, and try till he learns the laws of Nature and makes a kite to correspond? If a man gets displeased with this planet and wishes to ride round the sun in his own gig, is God to pave the road and furnish him a horse? Shall God give the new moon to every baby who cries for it? The girl pricks her fingers in learning to sew—shall God make the hand as senseless as the needle to spare little miss the use of her wits?

A man sails the sea, he gets a poor and leaky ship, ill moulded, ill built, ill rigged, and overloaded too, manned and mastered badly; he takes no pains to learn the coast he sails from, or to; little care to look out for rocks, or shoals, but drives up towards land, all heedless, in a storm; then, when his crazy hulk is in imminent peril, he and his miserable crew—all ignorant and half drunk—for safety pray lustily to God. Is it a hard thing that he gets the ocean for answer; that his planks go to pieces and he is strangled in the deep; or if with much ado he treads the waters under him and comes alive to land, has he a right to complain of hard usage because the fatherly Providence did not empty the waters out of the sea to save a foolish man the trouble of thinking?

In making the world, what if God had fashioned it so that shipwreck was impossible; that when a vessel approached a rock, of her own accord she wore off, or tacked and stood away; that it was needless for the mariner to study navigation, or seamanship, or the art of building ships, but every tub would sail perfectly, with any requisite speed and burthen, and find its own way to any destined haven; so that you need only write thereon, "Bound for London," and put off from land, and the craft found its way there as surely as a stone to the bottom of a well when dropped in at the top; that a mariner need take no thought at all, for God tempered the wind to the sailor self-shorn of his wits! Would that be so good a scheme as the present one which demands stout ships — built with all the art of human science to correspond with the Nature which God has made, — prudent masters, careful men, a compass in the binnacle, a chart and chronometer in the cabin, light-houses along the coast, scrutinizing surveyors to scan the heavens, to search the bosom of the sea and learn to trace the footsteps of the storm and so be served by wind and tide, by star and sea and land? The shipwreck brings loss of goods and loss of life, pain to full many a heart; but you see what all this suffering means. If I, standing on the shore, saw a vessel about to go to pieces in a storm, dashed on a rock, had I the power, doubtless in my human weakness and ignorance, I should rend the rock in sunder, or should chide the sea, and hold it back e'er it should swallow down the ship, strangling such hopeful life. But at the creation the Infinite God knew all the powers of the sea, the storm, the future ship, the men therein; foreknew their history, and doubtless arranged all well. For answer to our special prayers comes the eternal action of the universal law. Thus we learn by the elements; the winds are our ministers, the sea not only a constant ferryman, that huge St. Christopher, fetching and carrying from land to land, but a teacher also. Yea all Nature is a "Schoolmaster to bring us to Christ."

What sufferings have we seen of late years on emigrant ships, crowded with passengers without fire, water, or even air, heedless, ill-fed, unclean? What if God "interposed" at the prayer of some mortal and allowed no man to suffer from cold, hunger, or ship-fever! Would that be better than to leave man to suffer till the nations learned the laws of Nature, and enforced them by statutes of their own, and then came safe across the sea, not sick, not cold, not wet? God makes the elements as perfect Cause, administers them as perfect Providence, and made the mind of man one element whereby to work out human welfare. Shall not that factor perform its function?

Men build iron roads, and put thereon a train of iron cars, drawn by the iron horse. The axles are iron, the wheels iron; the friction is great, the draught is difficult, the metal wears out. What chagrin of engineers, what complaint of shareholders! Shall God, by permanent law, or fleeting miracle, alter the constitution of things to abate the friction; or leave men to study the structure of their own limbs, and make an artificial cartilage of compounded metals, and moisten it with such synovial liquor as science can devise, and so save the wear and tear of their machine? If a stone gets in the boy's shoe, shall God all at once soften the stone, or harden the foot; or shall he leave the boy to suffer till he shakes the annoyance from his own shoe and walks off erect and easy? If God give adequate intellect at first, is he to supersede the necessity of using it? What a Providence that would be, at cross purposes with itself!

Here is a lazy young man, yet very exorbitant; he wants the power of riches, the honor of office, the enjoyment of high culture — the distinction of all the three; but he devotes himself only to his moustache, his cigar, and his dress. Is it the fault of Providence that he continues a most uncomfortable dunce, neither respected nor respectable; that he is full of pain and chagrin, and walks the street with the air of a dyspeptic pirate, complaining of "the ingratitude of republics" and talking of suicide? Would it be a good thing if God made money to drop miraculously into his idle hands, crowned him with office, and gave him the culture which earnest men elaborate so slow by painful thought! Would it be kind in fact to the grumbler himself? A foolish mother would give him all these things, unconditioned; the dear God says, "What would you have? Pay for it and take it." No spoiled children with the Infinite Mother! If Themistocles feels chagrin, and cannot sleep a-nights for thinking of the trophies of Miltiades, shall God come and rock the cradle of this great Athenian baby; or let him lie awake till he grows up a great Athenian man!

Some men add to their family more than they can feed, shall God turn stones to bread to stop their mouths? It rains pottage; Esau will not hold up his dish. Shall God make rain come the other way, to please the lout? What a world it would soon be, each hairy Esau turning out a whining clown, not a valiant hunter, the world a fool's paradise, where betwixt man and God it was always "Hail fellow! well met."

If a nation does not work, or works wrong, — brewing its corn into beer, not baking it into bread, producing rum and tobacco, not houses and cloth; if it applies to a wrong purpose its sea-chariots, or land-chariots; will build forts and not cities, breed soldiers and "nobles," not farmers and mechanics, — loaf-consumers, or destroyers of loaves, not loaf-makers — has the nation a right to complain against God for its want of bread? Or when complaining with many prayers, shall God send a miracle to feed the men, not leave them to hunger till their own hands stop their mouth? If half the people are left uncared for by the powerful class and turn out badly, steal, rob, and murder, knowing no better, have the men who have been careless a right to complain at the result? Nay when all African Hayti rises "in blackest insurrection," what right has the master to complain?

Not long ago there was a famine in Ireland. It was thought a most hideous famine even in that land where hunger is the constant condition. England kept a day of fasting and prayer, asking God to "interpose, and withdraw his hand!" Ah me! The prayer was sadly unwise and sounded irreverent. Had the Father meddled unwisely with his world? The good God had done no wrong; his hand is never out of place. The famine came in mercy to man; England had oppressed Ireland, pushed the Irish to the brink of ruin, and did not seem to care much how soon they went over. The Irish had not planted corn, nothing but the potatoe. And that would decay; not all at once, but little by little. Long years ago the potatoe prophesied, rising early and warning men whether they would hear or forbear: "I am not fit to be a nation's bread. If you do not learn the lesson, why I shall rot in the ground, and you will starve above it!" That was the word of the Lord by the mouth of his servant Potatoe. No prophet ever spoke plainer, neither Trojan Cassandra, nor Elias the Tishbite. He spoke to deaf ears. The many were too ignorant, or feeble; the few too idle, or selfish, to heed the word. So after the oracle came the history, and then the lamentation, the fasting and the prayer. In other lands, here in America, the potato also failed, but men died not in consequence; they had bread to eat and lived on. What did the famine mean? It spoke plainly as tongue could tell, "Grow more and better food; eat and live, Oh ye Irishmen! for why will ye die?"

Not many centuries ago there was a famine every ten or twenty years in the most refined nation of Europe, — there were ten dreadful famines in France in a single century. The priests prayed, and said "the world is coming to an end. God is angry because you do not come to mass, you unbelievers, you! He will starve you to death; and then torture you in hell." But the prayer brought no bread. Shall the prophet wait for the crow to feed him? The feeding will be of ravens, not prophets. Whence came the famine? Men had fought each other instead of conquering the forces of Nature; had raised soldiers, not farmers and clothiers. The famine warned them of their error, — a painful warning, but the misery not excessive. It sowed wheat.

A little while ago there came the cholera, scaring the world. Men attributed it to the "wrath of God;" begged that dear Father "to withdraw his hand," thinking him meddlesome and ill-tempered! Men had been ignorantly violating some of the natural conditions of bodily well-being, nay of bodily existence. If we went on so we should all perish and the race die out. The disease brought pain and death, plainly telling us of our mistake and our consequent danger; bidding us avoid the special cause of that mischief. Would it have been well for the Infinite Providence to alter for our caprice the Constitution of the Universe and the preëstablished harmony between Nature and the frame of man? The public prayers changed not the purposes of God, nor his motive, nor his means. But the board of health swept the cholera out of many a town.

Man is sick, he prays for health. Shall God abolish the pain, or leave man to find out and remove the causes of his body's grief and seek medicine to palliate the disorder — while

> "In every path
> He treads down that which doth befriend him
> When sickness makes him pale and wan!"

All these forms of pain and misery are clearly of a remedial character, and come to warn us of a mistake, to drive us from error before we are ruined. Without the pain, we should have been yet more pained. If our request could be granted without the fulfilment of the natural condition thereof, it would send leanness into our souls.

> "To have my aim; and yet, to be
> Further from it, than when I bent my bow—
> To make my hopes, my torture; and the fee
> Of all my woes another woe—
> Is in the midst of delicates to need,
> And e'en in Paradise to be a weed."

The pain we feel at the premature death of our associates is of the same character. Old age, I take it, is the only natural death for man. That we never mourn at, nor regard as evil. My father, a hale man of threescore, laid in the ground his own mother, fourscore and twelve years old. She went thither gladly, with no anguish, no fear, with little pain; went as a tall pine tree in the woods comes to the ground at the touch of a winter wind, its branches heavy with snow, its trunk feeble, its root sapless, worn-out, and old. He shed no tears, he was not sorry that the shock of corn fully ripened on earth was, in due time, gathered to Heaven. He need not mourn; he should not mourn. It was the course of Nature; and the child piously buried the venerable, hoary head of his mother, long knocking at the gate, and asking to be let through. But if he lost a child it was a sad day, a dark year; for the child perished immature. Sadly in June or July the gardener sees his unripe apples scattered on the ground, disappointing his hopes of harvest. But when

> "An apple, waxing over mellow,
> Drops in some autumn night,"

he only rejoices that Nature's ways come rounding to their appropriate end. When the father buries the child, the mourning Rachel, refusing to be comforted, shows there is a mistake somewhere; the pain warns us thereof before we all perish.

This seems to be the meaning and the merciful use of the grief we feel at laying down our dear ones immature, when these leaves of our tree are shattered "before the mellowing year." At the present day such is the state of medical science that the Doctors of Medicine know almost as little of man's body as the Doctors of Divinity know of his spirit. Between disease and the doctor there is a wall, thick and high, with here and there a loophole which some scientific man has made. Men look through and see dimly in spots; and pass through some medicines and advice, to palliate the mischief a little. The pain we feel when our friends die an unnatural death; our own reluctance to depart — life's duties not half done, nor half its joys possessed; — the sympathy which all men feel with those that suffer thus, making another's misery our own, — these drive us to break down that wall, to cure the disease, to learn the law of health, that all may ride in sound bodies the stage of mortal life, check the steeds at the proper bound, dismount from the flesh, and continue our journey in such other chariot as God provides for the ascension.

A child plays on the edge of a rock; the mother

creeps up stealthily, and suddenly plucks away the romantic boy loving to look down into the deep darkness. Pain comes on the same motherly errand. Shall God let us fall in, not warned of the pit?

The terrible diseases which sweep off half the human race before they count three summers and those which decimate the ranks of adult men, are a warning to mankind showing that we live unwisely yet. The result of the pain we suffer is a continual effort to live wiser, better, longer, and so the term of human life continually grows more and more.

All the pain and misery of the character thus far spoken of, are plainly medical and benevolent. If it did not hurt the hands to burn, or freeze them, who of us would grow up with a finger? If feet did not smart with abuse, they would be treated as shoes, worn out in childhood, and no hardy boy would have a foot left. If broken teeth did not ache, so long as walnuts have a shell, no child would be safe; the world would be full of toothless striplings. The pain of poverty and want, of ignorance, of disappointed ambition, of affections bereaved or disappointed in a sadder sort; of the accidents to individuals by flood and field, to nations by war; of the diseases which prey upon mankind — the rats and mice of the world's housekeeping, — it all has this meaning and this use. See with what scorpion whips Poverty drives the Irishmen out of Ireland; and pursues them in America, forcing them to work and think. The American beggar hears the lash which once he felt, and avoids the blow. In half a century we shall see the result — the Irishmen will be also industrious, thoughtful, well-fed, well-clad. Men run trains of railroad cars together, or attempt to pass a river when the drawbridge is up; and there is the wreck of matter and the crush of men. The remedy for the pain is at hand. The great annual destruction of human life in America, by the carelessness of men who control the land and water carriages wherein the public ride, is a warning against our folly; the evil perfectly within our own control. All these things must needs have been foreseen. The attendant pain is the perpetual check on human caprice, the constant of Nature which controls our variable whim.

See how pain occasioned by loss of friends, with the wide sympathy it calls out, forces us to study the laws of health, to cure the sick, to keep men sound. Famine makes men creative to produce, and prudent to spare. The cholera teaches temperance and cleanliness, which once the plague bid mankind learn. Every case of typhoid warns us of broken law; a shipwreck rings the bell to notify us to have stouter vessels, or have them better sailed, with fitter apparatus on board, and better beacons on the coast. If men are too indolent, and will not rule themselves, the tyrant binds on his burdens, which grow more and more difficult to be borne. The suffering from bad political institutions in Naples, Spain, Hungary, and all the world, is not more than sufficient to warn mankind, to make them seek out and avoid the cause of smart. A nation like a man, shivers long at night, before it gets courage to rise, to hew wood, to build a fire and so be warm again. Is the pain of Europe at this day too great for this end? The frost does not yet bite sharp enough to wake mankind from savage sleep. Before us Pain, a flitting messenger, hurries to warn us; behind stands Misery to drive. But the one warms us from our bale; the other drives us to our bliss.

If we pursue the inductive course as far as we can see, and then follow the way of deduction from the Idea of the Infinite God, to this conclusion must we come at last — that the present physical pain and misery in the world of animals and men is not an Absolute Evil; quite far from it, it is a partial Good; that it is disciplinary, preparing us for the Ultimate and Absolute Good.

But after all this is clearly made out, it must still be confessed that there are millions of men who from no conscious evil of their own suffer a great deal of misery, and pass out of life apparently unrecompensed; — the men who are cut off in early life, tortured by disease, stung by poverty, sacrificed to the purposes of the race, and leave their lesson to others; men disappointed in their tenderest affections; those whose hearts are so sadly bereaved that they go mourning all their days. For the negative, or positive, evil they suffer here, the only adequate compensation must come in another state of being, beyond the grave. I know not the means, no man knows; perhaps no man can ever know in this life. But as God is Infinite; and creates all from a perfect motive, of perfect material, for a perfect purpose, and as a perfect means thereto, it is absolutely certain that the ultimate welfare of each animal or human creature must at last be made sure. This does not follow from any of the finite conceptions of Deity — from Jupiter or Zeus, from the Jehovah of the Old Testament, or the God of the popular theology; but it follows unavoidably from the idea of the Infinite God. As a fluent point generates a line, so the Infinite God generates blessedness, and ever blessedness, and only blessedness. So all the pain and misery God's creatures suffer, must one day be abundantly repaid. It was all foreseen and provided for by him

"Who is of all Creator and Defence,"

as a part of his scheme, here a resultant of necessitated force, there the contingent of individual freedom acting in contact with other forces. But in both cases must it be perfectly provided for. This is as certain as that one and one make two. For as the last conclusion of a geometric demonstration follows unavoidably from the axioms of mathematic science and the data of the problem, so ultimate, complete, and perfect Welfare follows from the Infinite Perfection of God. He has made pain and misery part of the discipline of this life; it must have been in infinite benevolence that he did so. Mankind is doubtless saved by present suffering from suffering worse. Not by the pains of Jesus, but its own is mankind saved. Our own pain and misery are educational discipline; if the roots of culture be bitter, doubtless the blossom will be fair and fragrant, and the final fruit sweet to our soul. The pain and misery which others suffer from ignorance, and causes beyond their own control, help teach us charity; the time, the means, the effort we expend in their behalf is often so much devoted to our highest culture, — the education of Conscience, of the Affections, yea, of the Soul which by nature turns to God.

Now then where is the Absolute Evil of Pain and Misery of this character? There is none such! Two angels, archangels if men will name them such — Gabriel and Michael, — come to warn us; not exceptions to God's Providence, ministers thereof, they come to man and bird and beast, on the same errand of benevolence — to warn us of a mistake; not angels with a flaming sword turning every way to keep us from the Tree of Life; angels they are who walk between us and the Tree of Death to keep man from the Upas of ruin.

If the universe were to end to-day, it would seem a failure, for now only the spring-time of the world's long year is present, and man goes forth, ignorant and weeping, and with pain scatters seeds which one day, all and each, are to bear manifold the bounteous harvest of immortal joy. But all around us seems made for stable duration, and is auspicious of a glorious future for mankind on earth. The coldest of men feel deeply and by instinctive nature, that the misery of the world is only a pain, of growth not of decay.

> "Slight symptoms these; but shepherds know
> How hot the mid-day sun shall glow
> From the mists of morning sky."

I have often asked you to notice how the material forces of Nature work together, how wisely they are distributed; how beautiful are its statical and dynamical laws; how wonderfully Centripetal and Centrifugal, those two strong horses of the Almighty, sweep this earthly chariot through the sky; how chemical and vital forces serve the economy of the Universe, and how the minimum of means produces the maximum of end therein. Yet even there, in Nature, we see but little of the whole, and know but little of what we see. Things yet uncomprehended continually appear. It is but a single page in Nature's book we have learned to read.

So far as human science reaches it is plain that the

sensibility to suffering is distributed with the same wisdom as the organic forces of the world; that Pain and Pleasure have each their calculated work to do, both foreknown at creation, and eternally provided for. In this vast and much entangled labyrinth of living things it is more difficult to see our way than among the material elements,

> " — the eldest birth
> Of Nature's womb, that in quaternion run
> Perpetual circle, multiform, and mix
> And nourish all things."

But when we see the whole we recognize the bountiful benevolence of God. Bacon devised his New Instrument for human thought, the *Novum Organum* of physical science; Newton wrote out in mathematic poetry the Principia of the Universe, the laws that govern quantity in space; La Place yet more magnificently set forth the fair Mechanics of the Sky, the mathematic laws of the heavenly machine, of whose composite forces Beauty and Harmony are the perpetual result; Von Humboldt — laborious still, grown old in being taught and teaching, his mind youthful with all the scientific riches of the world swept into the German Ocean of his long living consciousness, — groups into a harmonious whole this Kosmos of material force, painting in words the Universe, this majestic, Amazonian Flower of God floating upon the sea of space. And what a world of harmonious beauty it is, as seen by the material eye and then reflected in the educated mind of these philosophers!

But when some man, with mind greater than the greatest of these, shall gather into his more affluent consciousness a corresponding knowledge of the world of animals and men; shall devise the New Instrument of a higher science; write in more than mathematic poetry the Principia of this sensitive universe, the Laws that govern Life in time and space, magnificently setting forth the fair Mechanics of the Vital World, its Metaphysic Laws, whose ultimate resultant is lovelier Beauty and Harmony of a yet more sweet accord; and grouping to a harmonious whole this other Kosmos of vital and personal forces, painting in words this white, Amazonian Lily of Human Life floating on the river of God — why, what a wealth of wisdom, of justice, of love and holiness will it not reveal in the Infinite Father and Mother of all that are! Then by the inductive mode alone, without deduction from the idea of God, but only by the study of facts and history, shall men prove, what I can only postulate, the perfect workmanship of God.

In the pain and suffering of mankind, and of our feebler attendants, I see the promise of a glorious future for mankind. I know there is a recompense for every sparrow robbed of her young, or prematurely falling to the ground; that the infinite Herdsman of the universe takes thought for oxen, and is a perfect Providence for the individual and for all mankind. The history of the world is indeed the judgment thereof, but not the final; and what it bears off unrewarded it carries to the great ocean of Eternity, where exact justice shall be done in love to every creature of the dear, eternal God.

SERMON X.

OF PROVIDENCE — THE ECONOMY OF MORAL ERROR.

ECCLESIASTICUS XLII. 24.

HE HATH MADE NOTHING IMPERFECT.

X.

THE ECONOMY OF MORAL ERROR UNDER THE UNIVERSAL PROVIDENCE OF GOD.

LAST Sunday I spoke of one form of Evil, of the physical Pain and Misery in the World of Animals and Men, which come from violating the physical conditions of welfare; designing to show the Function and Economy thereof in the Providence of God. To-day I wish to speak of the other form of Evil, of the Pain and Misery which comes from violating other conditions of welfare; of Moral Error and Sin, with their consequences; designing to show the Function and Economy thereof in the Providence of God. The two departments of inquiry are lands, lying side by side, indistinctly separated, locking into each other by many plies and folds, so that the stream which rises in one runs into the other, and it is difficult, perhaps impossible, in all cases to say where one begins and the other ends, so indistinct are the boundaries. In both these sermons I often cross the lines.

In Theological Ethics there are some broad distinctions of things, marked by corresponding distinctions of language, which ought to be borne in mind. Here are some of the terms I shall use in a technical sense in this sermon.

A mistake is the violation of some Rule of Correctness, or of Expediency. To do inexpediently is a mistake. It produces an experiment which fails, because the calculation on which it is founded is incorrect. Jehu would go from Bethany to Jerusalem; he misconceives the way, takes the wrong road, comes out at Bethlehem instead and loses his journey.

A mistake has its origin in an intellectual deficiency, a lack of knowledge. It may be a lack of knowledge in general — Jehu never knew the way from Bethany to Jerusalem; or a lack of knowledge at that special time — he had forgotten, he had not his wits about him, he did not take heed to his ways, and so he lost his journey. It may come from a lack of general intellectual power. Thus a fool mistakes stones for bread. There are men of weak minds, who do not discern clearly by their intellect; or whose intellectual perceptions do not much influence their will and their conduct, — simpletons, idiots, fools, in respect to power of mind, they often make mistakes through lack of wit.

Mistakes of this sort are often called Errors; and so men speak of "errors of the press," "errors of longitude," "errors of calculation," and the like. In such cases in this sermon, I will use the word Mistake, to reserve the term "Error" for another and strictly technical use.

An Error is the unconscious and involuntary violation of some Rule of Right, of the Moral Law of God. It is to the Conscience what a mistake is to the intellect — it is a moral mistake, as a mistake is an intellectual error. To do unjustly is an Error, as to do inexpediently is a Mistake. One violates the Rule of Right, the other the Rule of Expediency. Every Error is also a mistake, for what is really wrong is always partially and ultimately inexpedient; but every Mistake is not also an Error. Jehu did no moral wrong by mistaking the high road to Bethlehem for that to Jerusalem.

Here is an example of Error: the ill-bred boys steal apples from Ahab's garden; to correct them he shuts the offenders up in jail with old and accomplished rogues, where they grow worse by their confinement; the well-meant correction wrongs and worsens the boys. He has violated a moral law of God, the natural rule of right, seeking to overcome the evil in them by another evil out of them, setting his vengeance against their trespass. But he did this unconsciously and involuntarily: he did not know there was such a natural law; he had no intention of doing wrong; he knew no better way to guard his orchard and correct the young marauders.

Error comes from deficiency of moral power — general, or special, from a lack of moral knowledge: Ahab never knew the Rule of Right which applies to such cases, that justice is the medicine for injustice, love for hate, and good for evil; or he had forgotten, and did not recollect it at the time; or, if he did, his general human conscience was borne down by his special and particular sense of the loss; and for a time it seemed as if he had never known any better. There are men of weak conscience — such as do not discern morally, or whose moral perceptions do not much influence their will, — moral simpletons, moral idiots, moral fools. They often commit Errors, as feeble children stumble, and mouths ill-formed stammer and cannot talk.

A Crime is a Violation of some Human Statute — some positive rule of conduct laid down by the government. To do illegally is a crime. Thus it is a crime in Boston to drive a wagon on the left hand side of the street, in Berlin on the right hand side. In the District of Columbia it is a crime to harbor or conceal a slave who has run away from one of the Barbary States of America; in the District of Tunis it is a crime not to harbor and conceal a slave who has run away from one of the Barbary States of Africa. In Boston it is a crime to take a white dollar which is not yours and appropriate it to your use, and the man who does this is put in jail; while it is no crime, but a legal service, to take this black man, who belongs not to you, but to himself, and appropriate him to your use. The man who does such deeds is held in social and ecclesiastical honor. Christianity is a crime at Constantinople, Mohammedanism at Rome, and effective humanity shown to a black woman escaping from her "owner" in Carolina, is a crime in Boston. To help Shadrach out of the hands of the man-stealers of Boston was the highest crime known to American law; it was "levying war," treason, liable to be punished with death; in Halifax it would be the fulfilment of the golden rule and rendering a service unto Jesus Christ. To protect Ellen Craft while kidnappers were clutching at her life, was a crime in New England; in old England it is an honor. If a man in this city should seize and force into bondage Cuban negroes escaping hither from a monarchic fetter, he would commit a crime: but there are persons here whose official and legal function it is to seize and force into bondage American negroes, escaping hither from a democratic fetter; commissioned for that very purpose.

To kill an unoffending man for your own personal pleasure or profit in Massachusetts, is a crime; in New Zealand it is a matter of common practice. The professional man-butcher has a legal existence in New Zealand, I am told, as much as the professional man-stealer in Boston. It is a crime to resist either in his local function.

A Crime may be a mistake; or it may be an error, for the human statute violated may represent the natural rule of expediency, or of right: or it may be neither an error, nor a mistake; for the human statute violated, may itself be both inexpedient and unjust as in the acts establishing the man-butcher at New Zealand and the man-stealer at Boston. It is no function of the official executors of the statute to inquire whether it corresponds to the Rule of Right. The judge and the hangman are to be just as active in punishing a man for rescuing Shadrach from the kidnappers, as in punishing the worst of pirates, red all over with human blood; for such officers are of law, not Justice, and a crime is an Offence against Law whether just or unjust.

A Sin is a conscious and voluntary or wilful violation of a known law of God. To do wickedly is a Sin. This does not come from lack of intellectual perception, nor from lack of moral perception; but from an unwillingness to do the known Right, and a willingness to do the known Wrong. It comes from some other deficiency, a compound deficiency — from lack of affectional power, or of religious power, or from a perverse will.

Here is an example: Henry honestly owes John a talent of gold, and can pay him, but will not, though

John needs the money. The Non-payment is a negative Sin. William knows it is naturally wrong to steal, he is rich and has no material occasion to make stealing excusable, but he robs Dorcas, a poor unprotected seamstress. The Theft is a positive Sin.

Sin is a violation of the Rule of Right; and so is distinguished from a Mistake. It is conscious and voluntary; and so is distinguished from an Error. It is a violation of a Natural Law of God; and is thus distinguished from a Crime.

I might discriminate a little more nicely and make a distinction between a Subjective Sin — which is a conscious violation of what is thought to be a natural law, but is not; and an Objective Sin, a conscious violation of what is a natural law. In each case the integrity of consciousness is disturbed.

So much for the definition of terms.

There may be various Degrees of Error and of Sin. It is not easy to say where one begins and the other ends; for in ethics as in all science, it is not easy to distinguish things by their circumferences, where they blend, but only by their centres, where the difference is most clearly marked.

It is sometimes said there can be no such Error, or Sin, as I speak of. This is one doctrine of that pantheistic scheme, before mentioned, which appears in so many forms and under such antagonistic names. A natural law of God, it is asserted, can no more be violated, consciously or unconsciously, by man than by matter. A Sin, therefore — in the meaning just affixed to that word — is as impossible as a solar eclipse at the time of full moon; or as a straight line which is not the shortest distance between two points; it is the law of God, and so the will of God that William should rob the seamstress, Henry neglect to pay John, and Ahab clap the boys into jail for pilfering his apples.

The distinction between the normality of matter and the normality of man, if not obvious, is yet clear enough. In physical science we learn the law of matter by seeing what is done; it is derived from facts of observation; by a natural intellectual process, from all the facts we know we gather the Law of the Facts, that is, the Natural Mode of Operation of the material forces we study. Thus we know the law by seeing its observance; know it to be binding by seeing things bound by it, as far as we see at all. It is found solely by the inductive process, by observation and demonstration. It is an Idea which, so to say, rests always on two pillars of fact, — Facts of Observation, Facts of Demonstration. There is no actual exception to the general law; a single contrary fact would show us there was no such law as we supposed. In Nature the ideal and the actual are the same, — the ideal law and the actual fact. This is true in mathematics, true also in physics. Theory and practice are identical.

In ethical science, we learn the law of human nature — that is the Natural Mode of Operation of the human forces in Thomas, or in mankind — not by observation and demonstration, but by an intuition of consciousness. The law is not a fact of observation or demonstration, but of consciousness. It is just as much a law of human nature if Ahab, Henry, and William have violated it all their lives, as if they had consciously complied therewith. If we merely take all the facts of observation made upon man and thence induce a law, we can only see what has worked well hitherto, and get an empirical knowledge of the expedient in time past; the conclusion represents the facts of human history, not the facts of human nature; it applies, at best, only to those faculties already developed and enjoyed, not to those others yet undeveloped. And of course our scheme of ethics will have the imperfections which belong to the persons or actions, who furnish us the facts. The Ideal will not transcend the Actual, but be identical with it. Man has uniformly exploitered woman; the government, the people; the strong, the weak; "it is the natural ethical law of human nature that this should be so." That would be a fair conclusion from this mode of procedure. Indeed the atheist — who studies man in this way, — tells us it is so; the consistent popular theologian, who follows the same course, assures us that we can get nothing better from "the light of Nature;" that all higher ethics come only of "miraculous revelation."

But by attending to the facts of consciousness, to the moral instincts; and by the direct action of the moral faculties which do not follow, but anticipate, experience, we learn from human nature, not merely from human history. Thus we get knowledge of a law of human nature which is an Ideal of Consciousness, though not yet the actual of experience. It is in a great measure a matter of will whether we follow this law and realize this ideal or not. It is our duty to obey this ideal law when we know it; consciously and wilfully to violate it is Sin.

Philosophically to deny the possibility of this kind of Error and of Sin, you must deny either that there is any difference between Right and Wrong; or else that man has any Freedom to choose between them. Some men have denied each; but it appears to me that both are facts of consciousness. I feel conscious of a difference and antagonism between Right and Wrong; that is an ultimate fact of consciousness. The greater part of mankind feel the same thing, and have words to express that fact. I feel conscious of freedom, to a certain extent; that also is an ultimate fact of consciousness. The greater part of mankind feel the same thing. In a matter of this sort my own consciousness is of the utmost value to me; the opinion of the human race has much weight, for this is one of the cases in which mankind is a good judge.

Now, much of the Pain and Misery in the world of man comes from a violation of the moral laws of Nature, from Error and Sin. Can this evil be reconciled with the Providence of the Infinite God; or is it an Absolute Evil? Let us first look at Error, then at Sin, at each with its consequences.

In treating of the misery which comes therefrom, I will speak of it first, on a large scale — in its Political Form, of the Errors men make in their Civil Government.

The natural moral law, in its political operation, requires that in the State there shall be complete and perfect National Unity of Action, — the nation being as complete a whole as a man's body, — that is necessary for all, that there may be a complete Whole; and a complete and perfect Individual Variety of Action — each man doing just what he is fittest to do and can do best, — that is necessary for each man, that he may be a complete person, with free spiritual individuality, as free and independent in the State, as my hand and feet are in the body, and as much in his proper place and about his proper function. By this means there will be a combination of efforts, but a distribution of functions; national unity of end and design with personal diversity of means thereto. The centripetal power, the Government, and the centrifugal power, the Individual, will be combined into a cosmic harmony like that "which doth preserve the stars from wrong."

This is the ethic ideal of a State, the political tool necessary to the welfare of mankind. Nothing short of that with its industrial and economical contrivances, will allow the individual all his natural and unalienable rights, and enable him to have the normal use, development, and enjoyment of every limb of his body and every faculty of his spirit. It is the political condition to complete human welfare. But there is not a nation in the world which has attained it yet. It is the ethic ideal of a State which the foremost men of the world are striving to set up. It can only be reached by the gradual development of human nature, which can take place only through progression by experiment. Some of the experiments will fail, through Mistakes — a violation of the rule of expediency; through Errors — a violation of the rule of right, will fail in consequence of man's intellectual or moral weakness. If the failure is persisted in misery follows, and at length destruction; the pain warns us of the blunder.

Now I have not heard enough to show in all cases how this suffering proves remedial, and to demonstrate the perfect Providence of God in the history of man. For, to do that it would be necessary to have an amount of knowledge, both of human nature and of human history, which no man possesses as yet; which perhaps it is not possible for mortal man ever to possess. But

I can see the beneficent effect and tendency of this in so many cases, that the general analogy is clearly made out, even without recurring to the Idea of God as Infinite to "vindicate the ways of God to man." Yet without that Idea I confess I should feel little general confidence in such a vindication.

Look at some of the examples of this kind of suffering. Here are nations which eminently lack National Unity of Action. That is the case with all the governments in Spanish America. The Hispano-Americans have not yet made a national harness which will hold all the people. Their political experiments have not succeeded very well. Their civil instrument is a poor tool, which works rather badly and hurts the nation's hand. As a consequence there follows a great deal of suffering; the nations, each taken as a whole, are poor and weak; the individuals, taken separately, are also poor, ill-educated, oppressed, or oppressing, and not enjoying high modes of happiness. Their suffering is the consequence of their economical Mistakes and moral Errors.

But how shall they ever get a better form of government? Only by making the trial. And if they suffered no pain from the present failure they would make no effort for future success. The pain urges them continually to alter and mend. They cannot be rich, happy, well educated, nor even tranquil, until they have this national Unity of Action. Hence they are in a state of continual disturbance and fermentation. Mexico alone has had twenty-seven revolutions in less than thirty years. Would it be a good thing if God were by miracle to remove this power to suffer on account of these causes? Shall he miraculously give them a constitution and frame of government; and miraculously dispose all men to accept it? That would be to treat those creoles like mules and oxen, not like men. A woman wishes to walk cool in the summer's heat; shall God miraculously give her the great shadow of a peculiar cloud, or leave her to make her own umbrella, and walk rejoicing in its shade?

Here are other nations which as eminently lack Individual Variety of Action — Spain, Italy, Austria, Turkey, Russia, not to mention others. A great amount of force must be misdirected by the nation, as a whole, to keep the individuals in their unnatural condition: as a consequence there is a diminution of the productive power of the people as a whole — soldiers and policemen so numerous, mechanics, merchants, farmers, so rare, — and accordingly the nations are poor, and the government unstable and corrupt. Individual men suffer from the unnatural restriction. This twofold misery is the unavoidable consequence of their political Error, it notifies men of the failure of their experiment. But the mischief can only be got rid of by making new political experiments. The national tool works badly, it hurts the hands of the People; they must take it again to the forge, heat and warm it over anew in some other revolution and make a political instrument better suited to the work they wish to accomplish. Shall God alter the nature of man to accommodate the Spaniard, the Neapolitan, and the Turk, making human welfare to come from tyranny and ignorant exploitation of the People as well as from a wise and just frame of government? Shall he miraculously prevent the anxiety of a tyrant, or the misery of his victim? A woodman's axe is dull; shall God alter the constitution of the trees, and increase the toughness of the woodman's arms; or leave him to sharpen his axe, and then hew down the trees with more comfort?

Look at the human race as one person: from the beginning till now man has been devising an instrument to produce welfare. Every experiment has been a partial success, each also a partial failure. So far as the attempt succeeded the result has been delightful; so far as it failed, painful. Suffering follows Error; man abandons the Error, abolishes the mischief, tries again, making out better next time. The pain has only been adequate to sharpen his wits, like hunger and thirst to make him work in other forms. Thus man gets his political education and political enjoyment. He tries despotism — that tool does not please him; then a monarchy, then an aristocracy, then a republic, and improves continually in his constitutions as in his agricultural and military tools. Man in his political development hitherto has not suffered proportionately more than a little girl, under ordinary circumstances, in growing up to womanhood. But no one complains and thinks it an Absolute Evil that the wind sometimes blows off the hat of the little maiden; that she now and then falls down and soils her frock; that her hoop runs off the side-walk; or that she fails to get the right conjunction in her French exercise and cries with chagrin at the recitations. Mankind, like little Miss, suffers from corresponding evils, has the diseases of childhood, in a political form. Anarchy, despotism, revolutions, — these are the measles and whooping-cough of the human race, one day to be outgrown. The present political condition of mankind as much belongs to the present age of mankind and comes as naturally in the process of human development, I take it, as the greenness of apples belongs to the month of June, and the immaturity of boyhood to early years. Shall we complain that the boy is not born a man grown; that the apple is not mature in June instead of October?

Political Oppression in its many forms is one of the worst evils which now afflict the enlightened nations. But it comes unavoidably from the nature of man — finite and progressive in his social as well as his individual condition. For human development it is necessary that men should gather in large masses, in nations; to accomplish that political experiments are necessary; the first attempt of a finite and free creature is not likely to succeed and produce the effect which is ultimately desirable; the experiment may fail, and its failure must bring pain. Besides, man is politically progressive, and outgrows his institutions as the individual his baby-clothes. Those which pleased him once become a source of pain, no longer suiting the altered condition of the race. Here, as elsewhere, the pain is a warning.

Sometimes we can see the particular good results brought about by some special evil. The Boston Port-Bill, the Stamp Act, with the other oppressive legislations of England, hastened the separation of the American child from her mother — to the lasting gain of both and also of the human race. A thinking man sees manifold examples of this sort in all the history of mankind, God

> "From seeming evil still educing good,
> And better thence again, and better still
> In infinite Progression."

Suppose man had been made incapable of suffering from political Errors, when they came in the experiments of the race. The Hebrews would have been content under the taskmasters of Egypt, and so have continued slaves until they were degraded beyond possibility of elevation on earth: till they perished outright. If the Puritan had not smarted from the oppression he suffered, he would have borne it patiently till now; and have become what despots love — a passive tool of tyranny; the world would have lost the brave development of manhood which has come from that hardy stock. The horse and the ass are the servants of man; they do not suffer from that state of subordination; they take it

> "With a patient shrug, —
> For sufferance is the badge of all the tribe," —

and are content. Treat them kindly, give them enough to eat, do not overwork them, and you have done the beast no wrong. The dog is the only animal perhaps, who voluntarily puts himself under the protection of man. He does not suffer by human subordination; it does not necessarily debase him, or prevent his development and his canine welfare. If his pliant nature yields to man's plastic hand, and takes new forms, his happiness has also new forms. "What a generosity and courage he will put on when he finds himself maintained by a man, who is to him instead of a God, or *Melior Natura!*" But man is debased by such subordination; and if he did not suffer and smart when another's will was imposed on him, the degradation would be ruin before he was aware of the peril. If he did not smart with pain under analogous thraldom, when treated well, well fed, well clad, and not overworked, the nations had been slaves this day to a few men with minds full of mastery.

The ruder a nation is, the less developed in the

higher faculties, the more external force is necessary to keep individuals together and in order. But the less is such force debasing or painful to the sufferer. It requires more external force to establish national Unity of Action in Russia than in America; the constraint which a Russian needs and bears without pain, would be intolerable to a New Englander, or a Briton.

Much misery appears in a Social Form, the consequence of Errors made in organizing men into communities. The ethic ideal of society is an organization of men and women so skilfully constructed that each man shall do the normal work which he can do best, with the most advantage to himself and to all his fellows; that he shall develop harmoniously all his faculties with entire natural freedom, and at the same time have the advantage of the aid and companionship of other men, all likewise doing their best thing. Here there will be a perfect Social Unity of Action and at the same time perfect Individual Variety of Action — normal personal freedom. On the one hand, there will appear the Solidarity of Mankind, at least of the special community; on the other the Sacredness of the Individual. Each man will be deemed a Fraction of society and so a factor in its product, but also an Integer; and both the functions, that of the fraction and the integer will be sacredly respected. In this case the social usages, and the public opinion they rest on, will correspond exactly with the faculties of man in their actual state of development; and with the natural moral laws of God. There will be the same blending of the centripetal power of the whole and the centrifugal power of the individual into that cosmic harmony which I spoke of before, whereby "the most ancient

Heavens are fresh and strong." Then the various persons of the community will work together with as little friction as the Planets in their course; with as little waste as the forces which form a rose or a lily. The laws, customs, and habits of society will be just and natural. There will be no crime, — no man sacrificed to another man, or to the mass of men. There will be no pauperism because no laziness, no waste, and no rapacity: a diversity of functions, but concentric unity of purpose and a combination of efforts to achieve it. Every man will be in perfect harmony with himself, with his fellow men, and with Nature, — in perfect circumstances. So he will be in perfect health both of body and spirit. Labor will be as delightful to men as to emmets, beavers, and robins building their nests: birth, life, death, all will be natural, all beautiful. Such is the ethic ideal of a community. Nothing less will correspond to the nature of man and the normal mode of action of the human powers; nothing less to the social moral law of God.

But there is no such community in the world; there never has been. Behold what pain and misery come of our attempts to organize men! A community is at present a jumble of human forces; not a concord, but a discord. How many men are out of their natural sphere! This man was born a hunter, but he sits uneasily on a shoemaker's bench all his life, dyspeptic and ill tempered. How many an idle profligate is cursed by the money which his ancestors gathered together, his riches hindering his manly development! How many are covetous and grasping! Think of the want and the crime; think of the licentiousness and intemperance; of the sickness which cuts off such hosts of men in childhood, while only here and there one dies a natural death. Consider all the ghastly forms of irregular action which you find in a great city, in Boston, New York, London. Think of the indispensable attendants of a great town — hospitals, asylums for the crazy and the old, for orphan babes, almshouses, jails of manifold denominations — the moral sewerage of the town, — of the police, swarming like buzzards in the streets to remove the refuse of mankind. The constable never sleeps. The jail-van is always in motion. Law and crime jostle each other in all the street. Gluttony and beggary meet at every corner. St. James and St. Giles glower at each other in Christian London. The angel of mercy follows the footsteps of the prostitutes, and watches over the bedside of her brother who made them such. What pain and misery in modern society! Boston is one of the most favorable specimens of a modern town, almost equally charitable and rich, but even here a good man can hardly walk the public streets and then repeat his private prayers without a shudder, — his heart making great leaps as he remembers the ignorance and misery about him.

This suffering is an "abomination to the Lord," as much as the older heathen form of making children "pass through the fire unto Moloch;" it is against the ideal of human nature. But if you look a moment you see the cause of the misery and its function. Man is finite, social, gifted with partial freedom, progressive also. Sociality on a large scale is indispensable to his development; great cities are as necessary for mankind as a garment for a boy. They have ever been the fireplaces of human education — intellectual, moral, and religious development. Man's advance in general development must take place by the aid, in part, of large combinations of men. To form them, nay, to group a hundred men together, he must make experiments. They may fail through Errors or Mistakes. All human advance, social or individual, is progression by experiment. If men do not suffer from the failure they will not know it is a failure; will continue it and perish.

Suppose men made a social experiment and it failed in consequence of the intellectual or moral deficiency of the projectors, because it did not fulfil the economical, or moral conditions of social well-being; suppose we did not suffer pain from the consequences of this Mistake and Error, and consequently continued in it and never rectified what was amiss in our experiment; would that be a better scheme than the present one? It is as idle to grumble at Providence because men suffer from social Mistakes and Errors, as to find fault with God because a mill does not grind corn when its wheels are placed on the wrong side of the dam. I wish to write, but have put no ink in my pen. Shall God fill it for me miraculously; or enable me to write with a dry quill? He gave me the head and hand to furnish ink withal; mankind the head and hand to organize communities aright. My disappointment and the world's misery notify us to take heed.

When the social machine is so constructed that it provides shelter, food, raiment, education deficient in quality or in quantity, or distributes these needful things in an unnatural and therefore unsatisfactory manner, is it not a wise and benevolent contrivance that pain should warn us of the Mistake and Error? If the bodies of the neglected poor did not shiver with cold and damp and wet; if they did not ache with hunger, with fear, and the troop of ghastly diseases which invade the rearward ranks of men in all our human march; if ennui and the multiform maladies of body and spirit did not attack and disturb the class of men whose natural social burdens are borne by others; if crime did not rise up and cry with its inarticulate mowings against the social waste and wrong; if the exploitered servant did not take his revenge by unfaithfulness; if the neglected, the poor, the outcast, did not steal and rob, burn houses, and murder men; if the slave did not run away, did not waste his employers' goods, and slay their children; if the spoiled child did not turn out a profligate, and gnaw the bosom which bore him, — men would persevere in their social folly and perish. Animals are unconsciously taught by instinct — gregarious not social. Their organization into packs and flocks and herds is made ready for them like the pattern of their nests, and the garment which grows on their shoulders. Man is consciously teachable, self-instructive; he learns by experiment; not merely gregarious but social, he is to construct his own social organization, as his garments and his house. There is always power enough, intellectual and moral, in each generation of men to construct the social or political organizations which that generations needs, which correspond to its state of development at that time. This is ideally demonstrable — for it follows by unavoidable deduction from the infinite perfection of God; and historically demonstrable from all the past ages of human progress and the present condition of men. But as men have a partial freedom, they may use or neglect this power of social organization. If they neglect the means which God has provided as adequate for his purpose and their social welfare, is it not benevolent in him to make things so that pain shall ring an alarm bell, as it were, and warn us of the Error? If

I will not put my cloak about me when the north air bites, shall God abolish winter to save me the trouble of thought? If I have sense enough, and yet will eat green apples and not ripe ones, is it not well that I suffer?

Suppose that men not only suffered no pain in consequence of their social folly in violating the natural law of the universe, but they did not die in consequence of the error. Then the first experiment would be the last; there would be an end of progress. We should advance no more than the beavers, or the bees. So there would be no continued growth of the faculties of mankind, no consequent increase of happiness, no qualitative advance in mode, no quantitative in degree. Man would have stopped long ago in some low stage of development; perhaps never have advanced beyond the culture of the men who have grown up amongst wolves in Hindostan, — a barking, a ferocious, and a stupid pack.

I know how terrible this suffering is, how much in quantity, of a quality how sad; how many innocent men suffer from the average folly of mankind, through no Mistake or Error of their own. But take the whole world together this pain is not in excess, and its function is plainly benevolent. Before us marches the attractive Idea of better things, a pillar of fire continually advancing towards the promised land which flows with milk and honey; behind us, the Egyptian host of ignorance, and fear, and tyranny, and want, drive us on. Both are ministers of God's Providence.

See what evil comes in the Domestic Form. The ethic ideal of a family demands the marriage of loving men and women to their loving mates, two equivalent and free persons uniting in connubial love, manhood and womanhood combining into humanity. But are such marriages common? Is the wife thought the equal, the equivalent of the husband; is the family always based on love, connubial, parental, filial, friendly love? The masculine element oppresses and enslaves the feminine. Man exploiters woman all the world over. How many live unmarried — against their nature, against their conscious will. Polygamy prevails "over three quarters of the groaning globe." In Christendom the marriage of one to one is the ecclesiastic and legal ideal, the marriage-type. Is it also the fact? How much is there of involuntary singleness — painful and against nature; how much vice of many forms, odious to the thought; what unhappiness from ill-assorted wedlock begun in haste, repented of at leisure, but made permanent by statute and public opinion? What a world of misery comes from the Mistakes and Errors men have made in the domestic organization of mankind and womankind!

Here the same reasoning applies — the proximate cause of the misery is the Mistake; the function thereof is to warn men and stir them to better experiments. All this matter of love might have been settled by laws that could not be broke, and like oaks, with no chance of mistake, men might

> "languidly adjust
> Their vapid, vegetable loves with anthers and with dust,"

or like the free birds of heaven be mated by instinct, Does any one think that would be an improvement? Attracted by the Ideal of a perfect family, driven by pain from the actual, mankind moves on, each generation of Jacobs and Rachels improving over the family of their predecessors, and with a continual increase of domestic bliss. The pain which comes from married and unmarried Error is not excessive for its work. Look the world over, disguising nothing, and you see how nicely this misery is fitted for its function and one day it will end. Only the boy cries over his multiplication table.

See the evil which comes of Mistakes and Errors in Religion — from Errors about Piety its sentimental part, about Theology its theoretical part, and Morality its practical part. Absolute Religion is the service of the Infinite God by the normal use, development, and enjoyment of every limb of the body, every faculty of the spirit, every power which we possess over matter or man. This is a service which is "perfect freedom." This is the Ideal of religion; nothing short of this answers to the spiritual nature of man and the natural law of God. Every thing short of this is an Error, or a Mistake.

But no considerable body of men has yet attained this Form of Religion. It is not consciously made the ideal of any sect of religionists in the world. How much suffering arises from the common notions of religion in the most enlightened nations! I have spoken of this so often in previous sermons that it is needless to say much now. But what fear among "Believers" of the popular theology, what littleness, what absurd singleness of the soul which longs for union with God; what meanness and cowardice is found in men who try to wring and twist themselves into the spiritual contortions demanded by Hebrew, Mahometan, or Christian Priests! What spiritual hunger is there of Unbelievers! The ecclesiastical bodies founded on the popular Mistakes and Errors — how impotent they are to lead the nation to any great good work! What manifold evils come of this cause! Look at the condition of the Christian world: its general Theology scornfully rejected by scientific men; the Roman Church dead; the Greek Church for many centuries without life; the Protestant churches of Europe divided, feeble, ruled like armies by kings; and in many places what is officially called "Religion," exacted of the people by the tax-gatherer and the constable; the churches of America divided, wrangling, and all unable to direct in natural ways the immense energies of this great Commonwealth; — nay, not daring to oppose the colossal Errors and Sins of the nation, or even to rebuke the political atheism which denies the Higher Law of God! See what imbecility comes from a theology which calls on its followers to renounce reason; for the sake of being spiritual, to give up the exercise of their spirit. What pain comes from belief in eternal punishment, the priest tormenting men before their time! What misery comes from fearing a dreadful God! Look at the oppression still practised in the name of religion — in Italy men shut in a Christian jail for reading the Christian Bible; in almost every Christian state laws forbidding freedom of speech on matters relating to Christianity, the gallows reaching its arm over the pulpit. See how many men in America are driven to infidelity, to denial of all conscious religion, by the absurdities taught in its name; how many are annually forced to hospitals for lunatics, incurably crazed by what is called religion. Acquisitiveness is doubtless the disease of America just now; but the lust of money is less powerful than the popular theology in bringing men to public Bedlam.

The theological mistake is incidental to human nature, — finite, free, progressive; the misery is an unavoidable result of the mistake, and has a benevolent function under the Providence of God. As perfect Cause he foreknew the history of mankind, all our Mistakes in religious matters, and wisely put pain as an unavoidable consequence of avoidable Mistakes and Errors. If the mass of men in Northern Europe had not suffered from the false theology, false morality, false piety, and manifold oppression in the name of God imposed on them by the Roman church, the world had been under Leos and Juliuses and Adrians to this day. Had not the unsatisfactory schemes of the Roman, Grecian, Hebrew theologies given pain to mankind, Christianity would have perished with Jesus; nay, if men had not suffered from the mistakes of Egyptian priests, Moses would never have led Israel out of the iron house of bondage and the gross darkness which covered the people. The oxen suffer not from the letters which their master burns upon their horns; the Roman ass is not pained by the image of St. Anthony which his superstitious master puts on him with a priestly blessing; if men suffered no more from false ideas of religion, we should be as oxen and asses, driven by other masters, and that to our ruin.

In religion as elsewhere, God has provided for a continual progress; but it is all progression by experiment; by many experiments which fail we reach the one that succeeds, and through the Red Sea escape from Egypt to the land of Promise. How long it took mankind to invent a machine driven by a river, or a flame of fire, that could spin and weave cotton! And does it appear strange that man should err long and wide before he attains a perfect scheme of religion? Fetichism was once a triumph, and satisfied the aspirations of devout mankind; next man outgrew it, but cautious and conservative still sought to wear the strait, scant girdle which devoured his loins; at length urged by intolerable pain, attracted by a better idea, he threw it away. Polytheism, Hebraism, Classic Deism, Romanism, have the same history, the same fate — once prayed for, then outgrown, and next prayed against and cast away. But the good of each is continually preserved. The Mosaic religion was an advance over the popular service of God in Egypt four thousand years ago; the Jewish form of Christianity rose far above Moses; the Pauline form transcended that; Romanism is a compromise between the Christianity of Paul, the Mosaism of the Hebrews, and the Polytheism of the Greeks and Romans. The human race went forward as they became Catholic Christians. Luther took a step in advance of Rome; Zuingle, Calvin, his fellow reformers, great men all of them, helped us still further on. But, pained by their imperfections, cheered by the Spirit of God in the soul of man which still tells of lands of promise before us, and still sends fire-pillars in every night to show the way over sands that furnish water, and through rivers which dry up to let us pass — the race still journeys on from Thebes to Jerusalem, from that to Rome, thence to Wittenberg, Basle, Geneva, Westminster; and there is no end. Every step in religion is an experiment; if a wrong step it is painful. But the pain is medical. The fires of Moloch in Syria; the harsh mutilations in the name of Astarte, Cybele, Jehovah; the barbarities of imperial pagan tormentors; the still grosser torments which Romano-Gothic Christians in Italy and Spain heaped on their brother men, the fiendish cruelties to which Switzerland, France, the Netherlands, England, Scotland, Ireland, America have been witness, are not too powerful to warn men of the unspeakable evils which follow from Mistakes and Errors in this matter of religion. The present sufferings from belief and unbelief, it is easy to learn the lesson which they read. If we misuse the deepest and most powerful force in man, the pain which comes therefrom must needs be great. To pluck out a hair brings little pain; but to rend off a limb, to tear out an eye — a dreadful misery forbids that sacrilege. Did not pain warn the Christian nations, the Protestant and the Catholic, as it ever has warned all loiterers, all wanderers, we should stray further and further from our God, or else stop in our onward march; and in either case lose the progressive joy of manly development of our religious powers.

There is now intellectual and moral power enough active in the present generation to correct the evils of the popular theology of Christendom, the defects of its ecclesiastical machinery, and so to remove the suffering which comes from that. If we fail to apply these powers to this work, it is surely wise in the great Father to have so made the world that pain shall at length compel us to put off the shoe which pinches, and not suffer the foot to be spoiled.

This fourfold Error in the formation of the State, the Community, the Family, and the Church — has brought a flood of misery upon the world. But it has forced mankind to a fourfold improvement — political, social, domestic, religious; to a fourfold increase of human delight and blessedness. Every age has power to mend its machinery and to devise better. These Mistakes and Errors were foreseen by the Infinite God, at the creation, provided for, and the checks to them all made ready beforehand. Even here there is nothing imperfect, but the motive, material, purpose, and means continually reveal the infinite perfections of God.

You see how a child makes Mistakes in getting command of his body; how he stumbles in learning to walk and hurts his limbs by the fall; but his wise mother cheers and encourages him. How he hurts his hands and feet before he learns the qualities thereof, and their normal relation to the things they touch! What experiments he makes that fail before he learns the economic conditions which hedge him in! See how mankind toils and experiments in getting the entire command of any of our present instruments, living or inanimate. What pain comes of each Mistake! The ox gores his master; the horse throws him; Actæon's hounds devour their lord — it is more than fable; the Pine-bender is snatched up in his own tree. What a useful thing is fire; what a powerful instrument in the world's civilization! It has been domesticated, I doubt not, some twenty or thirty thousand years. But even now what Mistakes we make in its use; what evils it brings! not a venturesome baby in the best ordered family, but puts his finger to the flame and starts when that schoolmaster sharply reminds him of the distinction between the Me and the Not-Me; not a little village, never so dull, but it loses now and then a house, or barn, by this unruly servant; not a city but has its conflagration, its police and engines to quell the element and keep the fire within its limits. Condense a thousand million men to one great consciousness; consider the human race as one man twenty or thirty thousand years old, all his burnings do not make a greater proportionate amount of suffering than what befals our venturesome weanling who puts his disobedient fingers in the candle's flame. Would it be benevolent in God to take from boy or man the possibility of a Mistake in the use of fire, the consciousness of pain from such a Mistake?

Steam will probably work as great a change in the affairs of man, in domestic, social, political relations, as fire has done hitherto. But see what havoc it now makes of human life, with such reckless men in America tumultuating over land and water so heedless of the unchanging laws of God. What pain we suffer in getting command of this instrument! It has been so with all the forces of Nature which man has tamed and domesticated. The entire amount of suffering is always proportionate to our lack of skill to manage the instrument; the more valuable the forces are the longer it takes to learn all their powers and acquire the full mastery over them. It is easy to tame a dove, hard to domesticate thunder and lightning.

In the fifteenth century their were three Magi in Europe, new-comers, looking for One born king of the world, — Mariner's Compass, Gunpowder, Printing-Press, such were their titles. What a world of mischief they wrought, disturbing everybody, — coasters, crossbowmen, scribes! What spread of mischievous falsehoods took place; what slaughter of men; what shipwreck in mid ocean! How grim they looked! But those Magi all three of them came out of the eternal East of human consciousness; following "the star which once stood still over a stable," they now fall down before Democracy, the Desire of all Nations; while Herod seeks the young child's life to destroy him, they open their treasuries and present gifts, their gold, frankincense, and myrrh.

Now to get the full mastery over the spirit of man,

to learn all the complicated powers of mind and conscience, heart and soul, so that mankind shall know all their modes of action, individual and social, as the chemist and the housewife know the powers and modes of action of fire, or as the engineer knows the powers and capabilities of steam; to provide these various complicated and progressive faculties with their proper harness and machinery — political, social, domestic, ecclesiastic, — for all their manifold purposes — that is a task far greater than the taming of cattle, the domestication of fire and steam; far more difficult, requiring far more time for the work, and demanding innumerable experiments, continued for thousands of years, each incidentally subject to failure, and that unavoidably attended by pain and misery which can only be removed by correcting the Error, and mending the Mistake. But the misery is all along remedial, is never excessive for its work and function. God achieves the maximum of effect with the minimum of means; the maximum of welfare with the minimum of misery. The whole amount of pain endured by mankind from political, social, domestic, and religious Mistakes and Errors, in the whole human history, is of a merciful and educational character; comes from the same cause, for the same purpose, as the pain of burning the finger when thrust into a flame, and bears no greater relation to the whole consciousness of mankind than the suffering of an ordinary child in growing up to maturity.

It is true the sufferings are often borne by such as had no part in producing the cause of suffering; nay, who sought to remove it, and on earth their misery is not adequately compensated, — but this life is only a part of the whole human duration, half a hundred years out of eternity. The infinite Justice of God —

foreknowing all, provided for every thing, before the world, or an atom thereof, was embarked on its endless voyage — must have provided a compensation somewhere. This retribution to the parts which suffer from the Errors of the whole must take place somewhere in the world created by the perfect Cause, controlled by the perfect Providence; for it is impossible that the Infinite God should create from an imperfect motive, of imperfect material, for an imperfect purpose, or as imperfect means thereto. When I cannot unriddle the details and see how John the Baptist and Jesus are to be recompensed for their early and violent death, how a recompense is to be afforded to the poor daughter of want, whom the Errors of society force unconscious into degradation, into crime, and an unnatural grave, half immature in body and wholly undeveloped in all the high qualities of womanhood, I am ready to trust the Infinite God. The warrant of ultimate human welfare is indorsed on every person, on each living thing, in the handwriting of the infinite God; and though I could not trust the promise of any of the popular finite deities, I am as sure of the Infinite God as I am that one and one make two, or that I myself exist. The instinctive desire of human nature is God's Promise to pay; Eternity his time.

Then look at the pain and misery which come from the intellectual Mistakes and moral Errors of mankind; leave out nothing, diminish nothing, look St. Giles' in the face; study the sufferings of all the Irelands of the earth; confront all the wars of the world; meet eye to eye that most hideous of living monsters, American Slavery, the lifeblood of three million men dripping from the democratic hand; — examine the political, social, domestic, and religious wretchedness of mankind, does it amount to Absolute Evil? Is there any reason to think so? Surely not. Are present pain and misery excessive for their unavoidable and merciful function? Scrutinize with the nicest analysis of science, and you must confess that so far as the facts are known the benevolence of Providence perpetually appears; and so far as the analogy reaches the same conclusion follows.

Then comes the scientific idea of the Infinite God to fill up the chasms which science leaves unfilled. A church, a family, a community, a State, is each a machine formed of human materials, wherewith to achieve the religious, domestic, social, and political welfare of mankind: if the machine be a poor or ineffective tool, is it plainly wise and merciful, nay, just and loving, that pain should warn us of the insufficiency of the instrument; and repeat the warning till we have abandoned it and made a wiser experiment? As the centripetal and centrifugal forces in the solar system are just sufficient to keep each planet in its orbit, rythmically wheeling about the sun, with no deficiency, and no redundance, so is the pain which follows human Error but just enough to warn us of the ruin and hold us back. The astronomical conclusion is mathematically demonstrable from the facts of observation and the intuitions of consciousness; the human conclusion is not yet inducible from facts of observation, but deducible with most rigorous science from the idea of God as Infinite. The amount of misery is a variable quantity, controlled by the conduct of mankind; we diminish it just as we learn and keep the natural laws of God, the original human means he has provided for his divine purpose.

So much for the Evil which comes from Mistakes and Errors.

Look next at the Evil of Sin — the pain and misery which come thereof. A man knows the moral law of God; he has learned it by experiment, or by intuition which anticipates experience; he knows the true, the moral beautiful, the just, the affectional, the holy. Conscience is powerful enough to say "Thou oughtest!" There it stops and leaves us free to obey, or disobey. It does not say, "Thou must! Thou shalt!" It does not hold us bound. I know the right; I have the power to do, or to refuse to do it. That is my freedom, my most subtle, most dangerous gift; it is the most precious too. Perhaps I shall not do the right I know I ought; I will not make the ideal of my moral nature the actual of my daily work. If the moral or religious faculty compelled me, I should be its slave; not a free man, only a bare tool of the Almighty. If conscience compels me to realize the Ideal it reveals, if the affections force me to live out my ideal love for man, and the soul constrain me to acts of holiness, then I only gravitate to my ideal; I cease to be a free spiritual individuality. It is not I that love, but the force which acts through me, foreign though divine. I obey it voluntarily, then the will of God becomes my personal act, I am a conscious co-worker with the Infinite. I am not a moral fossil, not a moral animal, but a moral man. I feel at one with myself; all my high faculties consent to the Ideal of my conscience and conform in this act of will. I am self-balanced; my own centre of gravity is my centre of motion also; my will accords with the will of God; he and I are at one;

his will my work. I have the delight of my freedom well employed.

If I do not obey my sense of right, straightway there comes remorse; I gnaw upon myself. My wrong disturbs the integrity of the universe. I am not at ease. Conscious of violating my own integrity, I feel ashamed and inwardly tormented because the ideal of my mind and conscience, heart and soul is not the actual of my conduct.

This is the first subjective consequence of Sin; it is a form of pain peculiar, distinct from all other modes of suffering. I suppose every grown man knows what it is. I will not speak from observation of others, but from consciousness and my own inward experience; I know the remorse which comes from conscious violation of my own integrity, from treason to myself and my God, from consciousness of sacrificing my universal Ideal of the true, the just, the moral beautiful, the affectional, the holy, to some private personal caprice. It transcends all bodily pain, all grief at disappointed schemes, all anguish which comes from the sickness; yea, from the death of dear ones prematurely sent away. To these afflictions I can bow with "Thy will, not mine, be done." But remorse, the pain of Sin — that is my work. This comes obviously to warn us of the ruin which lies before us; for as the violation of the natural material conditions of bodily life leads to dissolution of the body, so the wilful, constant violation of the natural conditions of spiritual well-being leads to the destruction thereof. So the pain of remorse comes wisely and mercifully to warn me from my ruin. It anticipates the outward consequence; it comes as the disagreeable smell, or warning look, or repulsive taste of poison. A State with no statute against high-treason, no punishment therefor, would be exceedingly imperfect. Remorse is the subjective consequence, the penal retribution; yea, the medicine and cure for this high-treason against the soul and against its God.

The outward consequences of Sin are the same as those of Error or Mistake, and require no specific description.

Sin is a wrong choice; a preference of the wrong way to the right one. No man loves the wrong for its own sake, as an end, but as a means for some actual good it is thought to lead to. It is one of the incidents of our attempt to get command over all our faculties. In learning to walk, how often we stumble; we stammer in attempts to speak; and babies babble long before they talk. In learning to read, to write, how children mistake the letters, miscall the sounds, miswrite the words! Sin is a corresponding incident — we learn self-command by experiments, experiments which fail.

I think this evil is rather underrated. Consciously to violate the integrity of your spirit is a worse evil than men seem to fancy. Oh! young man, expect Error of yourself, expect Mistakes. Your eye deceives you, so may your mind and conscience, your heart and soul. Expect also analogous wanderings in getting self-command. But do not tolerate any conscious violations of your own integrity; the experience of that will torment you long, till sorrow has washed the maiming brand out of your memory, and long years of goodness have filled up the smarting scar. Men grown see the right, see it plainly; it does not serve their special turn, in trade, in politics, in the pursuit of pleasure or of power. They trample their ideal underfoot. The subjective pain and misery which comes thereof, is a just and merciful contrivance of the eternal Father.

There are men of little excellence but of great conceit, bigoted men, wonted to the machinery of social and ecclesiastical routine, their wheels deep in the ruts of custom, omitting the weighty matters of love to men and God; who tithe mint, anise, and cumin, and thank God continually that they are not like the publican; to such men a sin, a rousing public sin, will do good, and in heaven they may thank God for it. I have known such men, and have thought if they could commit some great Sin, they might become less sinful. Jesus told a rich man,—probably one wedded to wealth,—to sell all he had and give to the poor. There are men so conceited with their own excellence, and besotted with custom, that I have sometimes thought the same Jesus would tell them to do some monstrous thing and get ashamed of themselves, and learn how worthless is their self-conceit. But the Sin-cure, even for such a man, is like healing rheumatism by burning the afflicted member to the bone.

As we get command over the body only by experiment, learning to run, to walk, to swim only by trial; as by experiment we learn the rules of expediency and of right, learning each with many Mistakes and Errors, with many a pain; so by experiments are we to learn the proper uses of the will, to keep the law of God when known. It is only in this way that the individual, the family, the community, the State, the world knows the power of the personal, or the accumulated will, and how to keep the law of God when known. So there are moral experiments in all these forms, and Sins of the Family, the Community, the Nation, and the

World, which come as incidents of human development. The pain thereof is an unavoidable consequence of the transgression, and a warning that the trespass has been wrought. I am glad it cost me efforts to learn to speak, to walk, to know the rule of right, else were I less a man. The pains I have felt from Errors here are joyous pains at last. So too am I glad God gave me power to go astray even when I know the right; glad that it costs me hard efforts to learn the uses of my will, to subject the transient caprice of personal desire to the eternal true, right, moral beautiful, lovely and holy of the Infinite God. And though remorse has been my keenest pain — I know it is my highest birthright which the pain stands over and guards as watchful sentinel. At the creation, the perfect Cause knew all the future wanderings of each man, the Mistakes of the intellect, the Errors of the conscience, the Sins of the will; and as the check thereto he mercifully appointed pain to come to the individual, family, community, the nation, and the world.

Theologians often talk mythologically about Sin, as if there was something mysterious in its origin, its cause, its process, its result, and final end. They tell us that as it is a transgression against the Infinite God, so it is an Infinite Evil, meaning an absolute evil, demanding an eternal punishment. To this scholastic folly it is enough to reply, that if sin be for this reason an Absolute Evil, then, the smallest suffering coming from an Infinite God is an Infinite Suffering, and cancels the Sin.

Sin is said to be a "Fall;" yea, as the child's attempt to walk is a stumble. But the child through stumbling learns to walk erect; every fall is a fall upward. Creeping is an advance over stillness, stumbling over creeping. In the yearling boy the feet are soft and tender, the legs feeble, unable to sustain the pulpy frame. But the instinct of motion stirs the young master of creation to press forward; not content with creeping he tries to walk, he falls, and cries with pain. He dries at length his tears, and tries and falls again, again to weep. But gradually, by trial, the limbs grow strong, the eye steady; he walks erect; he runs down steep places; up and down the snow-clad Alps Hannibal marches through the winter, leading his army of men each a stumbling baby once.

Through weakness of mind and conscience we may err — the Error has its check, and Nature has the cure. No mistake is eternal. At first the little child pricked with a pin only feels pained in his general consciousness, not discriminating the special spot that smarts. By and by, instructed by experience of pain, and so familiar with the geography of his little world of flesh, when hurt he lays his hand on the afflicted spot to localize the grief; at length he learns to scrutinize the cause and to apply the cure. Thus is it with mankind. Weakness of the Affections, of the Soul, of the Will, is not eternal. Sin, with its consequent pain, is transient as Errors and Mistakes. Stumblings of the body, the mind and conscience, heart and soul, belong to babyhood — the early or the late; incidents of our development. If the first step is a fall — the step is still a progress, the fall is forward. In the days of Abraham, Isaac, and Jacob, how poorly women spun and wove. But the bungling craft of Sarah, Rebecca, and Rachel does not retard the mill of Manchester, of Lowell and Lyons. From Sarah to Jacquard what a stride! millions of experiments that failed strew all the way. The mistakes of the first farmers nobody copies now; but the cereal grasses, which, as the story tells, a mythologic queen first brought to Italy, all round the temperate world grow corn for daily bread. What have I to do with the stammering of my fathers ten thousand years ago, when the language had but a hundred words perhaps? Does it bar me from eloquence and all the nice distinctions of scientific speech? Nay my own blunders in babyhood, boyhood, manhood — blunders of the body, of the spirit — do they disturb me now? They are outgrown and half-forgot. I learned something by each one. So is it with Sin, the world's Sin, your Sin and mine. Pain checks all heedless motion; we learn the lesson but forget the pain.

Men start, in these times, with the idea of a dreadful God, who made men badly at first, and then set them a-going; when they stumble he falls on them, brings them to the ground and crushes them down to endless hell; only a few he sends his Son to help and lift up — all the rest lie there and rot in everlasting woe. The pain of this folly will one day drive us from the greatest Error of the human race — from the belief in a devilish God and an eternal Hell. Our successors will forget it as we the follies of our sires who worshipped stocks and stones before they dreamed of Odin and of Thor.

See now the obvious use of Pain and Misery, — they are plainly beneficent. In the State, the Community, the Family, the Church, the Individual Man, it is not hard to see their general function. Evil is partial. There is no Absolute Evil. Man advances forever — the perfect means goes forward to achieve the perfect purpose. Man oscillates in his march as the moon nods in her course. Pain marks the limit of his vibration; the variables of human caprice are perpetually controlled by the constants of divine Providence. Once man, prone and mute, was the slave of Nature, the absolute savage, the wild man of the woods, overmastered by his elementary instincts which so jealously keep watch over the individual and the race; that comrade of the wolf, with many a painful step has journeyed on — his life a progress, his march triumphal. See what the past life of mankind has brought about — fixed habitations, language, letters, arts, science, literature, laws, manners, religion. What a growth from the time when these ten fingers were the only tools of man, and all his mightier faculties lay below the horizon of his consciousness!

Look at the evils of our time — as political oppression, the strong nations ruling the weak with iron rods, the government exploitering the people; look at war, at social oppression, the strong laying their burdens on the weak, in this age of commercial tyranny, at despotism by the dollar which takes the place of the old despotism by the sword; look at slavery — total in Carolina, partial in all Christendom; domestic oppression, woman exploitered by man; ecclesiastical oppression — false Ideas of God, of Man, of the Relation between the two form a three-pronged spear wherewith Superstition goads the race of men in all lands. Look at poverty, ignorance, drunkenness, prostitution, murder, theft, and every vice. What misery comes of all these evils! But they were all foreseen and are provided for in the careful housekeeping of God. The past history shows what checks there always have been; what powers come forth equal to each emergency. If the world were to end to-day — it would seem a failure, man's desires not satisfied, the budding promise of the race not growing into fruit, or even flower. But this is only the beginning of the history of man on earth,

> "A thousand years scarce serve to form a State;"

many a thousand years there must be to form the great Commonwealth of Man where the perfect State, Community, Family, and Church shall have their home.

The pain of Sin is the pain of surgery, nay, the pain of growth. My sin-burnt soul dreads the consuming fire, its pain a partial good. God provided for it all, making all things work together for good. My suffering shames me from conscious wrong, stings me into efforts ever new; and I flee from consuming Sodom with a swifter flight. The loving-kindness of the Infinite Mother has provided also for this evil, for its cure. There is retribution everywhere — for I am conditioned by the moral law of God. In youth Passion tempts me to violate the integrity of my consciousness with its excess, I love the pleasure of the flesh; in manhood Ambition offers the more dangerous temptation, I love the profit of selfishness. If I yield and sacrifice the eternal Beauty of the true, the just, the good, the holy to the riot of debauch, or to the calculated selfishness of that ambition, there comes the subjective consequence, — a sense of falseness, of shame, a loathing of myself, the leprous feeling that I am unclean, the sleepless worm which gnaws the self-condemning heart; then comes the outward evil, the resultant of my wrong, — men band against me, to check my wicked deeds. One wheel is blocked by remorse; and human opposition holds the other fast. So suffering keeps my wrong in check. I am thus pained by every evil thing

I do. In the next life I hope to suffer till I learn the mastery of myself, and keep the conditions of my higher life. Through the Red Sea of pain I will march to the promised land, the divine Ideal guiding from before, the Egyptian Actual urging from behind.

Liability to Mistake, to Error and to Sin, is the indispensable condition of human freedom. That is not absolute but partial, relative. I know the Infinite Father holds the line which tethers me; that He gave to man this human nature in us all, with just the quality and quantity of powers needful as means to execute his perfect purpose and fulfil his perfect motive. I know that he will draw us back and lead us home at last, losing none of his flock, dropping no son of perdition by the way; but a great ways off meeting his prodigals a-coming home, or if they only will to come; yea he has means which move their will without constraint, for he is Infinite God, the perfect Cause, the perfect Providence. The world he makes, from a perfect motive, of a perfect material, for a perfect purpose, and as a perfect means, is the best world which the infinite God could make; the best of all possible Creators must make the best of all possible worlds — with the minimum of pain securing the maximum of bliss.

Men often exaggerate the amount of Sin — its quantitative evil, not its qualitative. Much which passes by this name is Mistake, or Error; many depraved deeds are done with little depravity, perhaps with none. I see the evils which come of conscious or unconscious wrong. Here are men who walk the streets self-mutilated of limb, or feature, by violation of the body's laws; others maimed, still worse, of limb, or feature, of the spirit. Is their Error, their Sin, an Absolute Evil? The Infinity of God forbids. The Man-butcher of New Zealand, the

Man-stealer of New England have not fallen beyond lifting up. One day the better nature of each shall be wakened. Even such transgression is not absolute. The high-priests in Jerusalem who paid Judas his thirty pieces, the price of blood shed by his treachery; the low priests in Boston who paid the latest kidnapper his fee, their praises and their prayers, alike the price of blood shed by his treachery, they are under the Providence of the Infinite Mother who at the beginning provided for all of her children. All these shall one day measure their lives by the golden rule of Love.

I see the enormous mass of human misery which comes of Mistakes, Errors, Sins. I see its cause; I know its prophecy. It tells me of the vast powers of man — of the individual, and the race. The power of wrong is but a mistaken power of right. The wicked Statutes men enact, come as incidents in the nation's moral growth; the wars, the tyrannies, the slaveries of old time and modern days, are wanderings from the path we are to take; local, partial, only for a time. The devastations wrought by misdirection of the religious faculty reveal its power, and foretell its normal triumph in time to come. I lift my eyes from the present to the past. What a triumphal progress has been the march of man! Still is the human face set forward. The Cannibal in New Zealand is far above the wolf-bred child in Hindostan; far before the merely savage man. Even the Kidnapper of New England is in advance of the Cannibal of the Pacific. The increase of crime in all Europe since the revival of letters, marks a step forward. Immortality is for each man. Eternity stretches out before the race. And in the protracted childhood and great Errors of man I foresee his manly and majestic march in days to come. God bound the beasts; it was in mercy to them. Only by change of body can the adult animal advance. For them there is no progress of the family, the tribe, or race. Little is left for their free choice; so as they venture little, they win no more. The God of oxen provides for them as Infinite Providence, by his will, not their own. But the larger venture in man is liable to worse contingencies of ill; destined also to produce a higher resultant of bliss.

Tell me of war, of slavery, of want, of political, social, domestic oppression; tell me of the grim terrors of the Popular theology — its religion a torment, its immortality a curse, its deity a devil; tell me of Atheism, its doubt, its denial, its despair, — its here and no Hereafter, its body without a Soul, its world without a God; — tell me what pain and misery come of all these, and by the greatness of the aberration I measure the greatness of the orbit and the orb; for in the centre of the universe, its ever present Cause, its ever active Providence, I see the Infinite God, I feel him immanent in every particle of matter, in each atom of Spirit; and how can I fear? The nodding of a school-boy's top is not the measure for the oscillations of a world.

The greatest present evil is small compared to what man has already lived through and so far overpowered, that most men deem it blasphemy to say they ever were. Absolute Evil is not in Error, its misery is its check, points to its cure, helps to its end. Is it in Sin? Yea, if Sin were endless; to act wrong, think wrong, feel wrong, be wrong, — at variance with self, with Nature and with God — that is misery, absolute evil were it endless. Not only is all the analogy of the universe against the monstrous thought, each drop of Science drained off from the world of space and time corroding and eating away this ugly thing; but the Idea of God's Infinite Perfection annihilates the boyish dream. Suppose I am the blackest of sinners, that as Cain I slew my brother, as Iscariot I betrayed him — and such a brother — or as a New England kidnapper I sold him to be a slave — and blackened with such a sin I come to die — still I am the child of God, of the Infinite God; he foresaw the consequences of my faculties, of the freedom he gave me, of the circumstances which girt me round, and do you think he knows not how to bring me back, that he has not other circumstances in store to waken other faculties and lead me home, compensating my variable hate with his own Constant Love!

"Come, then, expressive silence, muse his praise."

THE END

www.ingramcontent.com/pod-product-compliance
Lightning Source LLC
LaVergne TN
LVHW021135110826
845150LV00005B/1032

* 9 7 8 1 4 2 5 5 4 9 5 2 7 *